POSTCARD HISTORY SERIES

Around Chamberlain

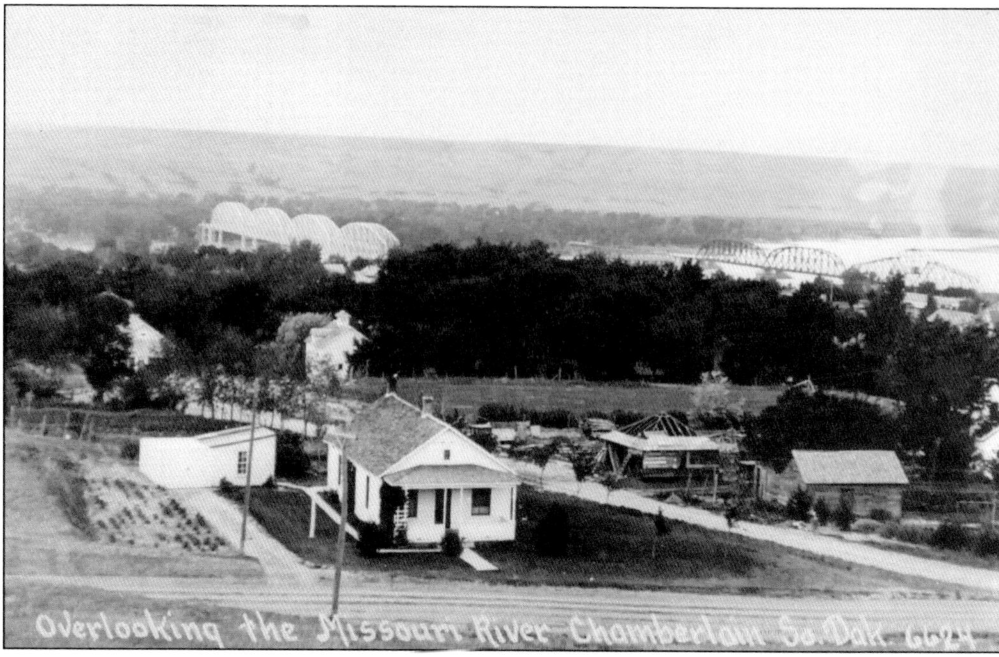

American Island and the auto and railroad bridges appear in the background of this view overlooking the Missouri River at Chamberlain, South Dakota. The streets are yet unpaved. The quaint, well-kept house in the foreground boasts a garden which is seen in the left of the photograph. (Courtesy Gene and Alice Olson collection.)

On the Front Cover: The steel truss bridge over the Missouri River at Chamberlain has long been a landmark for travelers on their way across the state of South Dakota. The bridge is a vital link between the cities of Chamberlain and Oacoma. It was listed in the National Register of Historic Places in 2001. (Courtesy Gene and Alice Olson collection.)

On the Back Cover: This very early photograph is of Main Street in Chamberlain, South Dakota. On the dirt street is a surrey being pulled by a pair of horses, with some distinguished-looking men riding. On the right side of the street are Berry's Dry Goods and Shoes, Chamberlain Steam Laundry, a drugstore, and other buildings. On the left side are a billiards room, land office, and another store. (Courtesy Gene and Alice Olson collection.)

POSTCARD HISTORY SERIES

Around Chamberlain

Gene and Alice Olson with Jan Cerney

ARCADIA PUBLISHING

ISBN 978-0-7385-9385-2

Published by Arcadia Publishing
Charleston, South Carolina

Printed in the United States of America

Library of Congress Control Number: 2012939682

For all general information contact Arcadia Publishing at:
Telephone 843-853-2070
Fax 843-853-0044
E-mail sales@arcadiapublishing.com
For customer service and orders:
Toll-Free 1-888-313-2665

Visit us on the Internet at www.arcadiapublishing.com

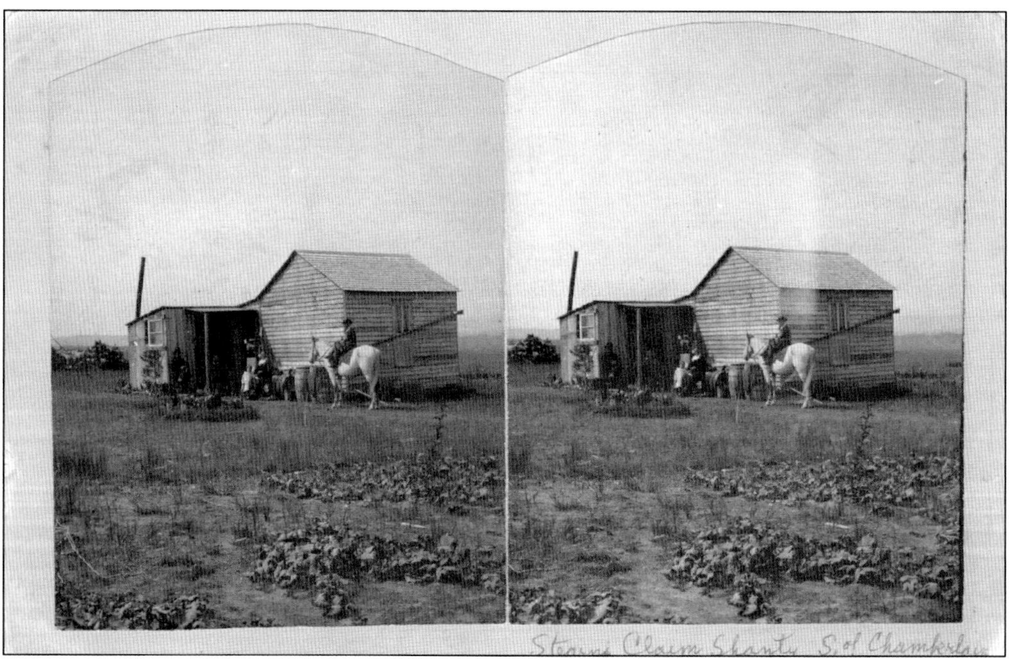

J.T. Stearns was one of the founding fathers of Chamberlain. This Dakota Territory–era stereoscope shows his claim shanty, which was located south of Chamberlain. Stearns Street in Chamberlain was named after Stearns. (Photograph by W.H. Troth.)

Contents

ACKNOWLEDGMENTS

Back in 1969, we never thought we would be helping to write a book. We were living on a ranch in Brule County, South Dakota. Gene did the farming and ranching, and I—Alice—was a registered nurse in surgery at Community Bailey Hospital in Chamberlain. Gene did most of the antique collecting starting in 1954. He had a good eye for what he should buy and keep. We collected a lot of things, some of which were postcards. We always thought it would be nice to have a book of the cards we collected and the history behind them to share with others. Unless otherwise stated, all of the images in this book are from our personal collection.

We dedicate this book to all the people throughout the years who have told us the stories of the early days in Brule County and the surrounding area. We are so happy that our son Greg and his wife, Melanie, also enjoy history and antiques. We thank them for the help they gave us in writing this book.

INTRODUCTION

A gateway to the West, the Chamberlain area has witnessed a panorama of westward expansion unfold, beginning with early native inhabitants occupying its banks and the surrounding plains. Eventually, the fur trappers and traders followed the waterways to trap and trade even before the Lewis and Clark Expedition arrived. In 1804, when the famous expedition navigated the Missouri River, it passed by the present site of Chamberlain on its way to explore the continent's interior. At that time, the river flowed in two channels near present-day Chamberlain and was divided by American Island, which was mentioned in a September 17, 1804, Lewis and Clark journal entry.

The advance of civilization followed the Lewis and Clark Expedition on the heels of the fur trade and the establishment of trading and military posts. When the fur-trading era ended and the native population was placed on reservations, cattle empires and settlers began to populate the western regions.

The surrounding community and town of Chamberlain evolved as the nation expanded west. At first, boats navigating the Missouri River provided the major transportation source and delivered supplies to these newly settled lands. The site of Chamberlain as a river port was chosen for its deep and solid landing, enabling steamboats to dock. The steamer *Milwaukee*, owned by the Chicago, Milwaukee, and St. Paul Railroad Company, came upriver from St. Louis in 1880 and unloaded cargo for the railroad company. It was the first steamboat to land and discharge cargo at the dock. Many boats since that time have pulled up to Chamberlain's shore.

When the railroad decided to build along American Creek to the Missouri River, the location of the town of Chamberlain was solidified, and surveying began in 1880. It did not take long for lots to sell, and Chamberlain quickly advanced from a tent city to one with a growing number of substantial buildings that provided services, such as lodging and meals, for early settlers.

As a result of its proximity to the railroad, Chamberlain became the Brule County seat. Eventually, the railroad would cross the Missouri River and bring more settlement with it. Homesteaders came, and Chamberlain became a home base for many of them. Smaller settlements around Chamberlain benefited as more and more people chose to come out to the West for a new start.

When South Dakota west of the river opened up for settlement in 1890, cattle were driven from the grass-covered plains towards Chamberlain, where they were loaded onto cattle cars for shipment to markets. The advent of the railroad was the beginning of the end for steamboat traffic. Other gas-powered boats would still be in use as ferries until permanent bridges crossed the river for railroad and auto traffic. The age of the automobile brought many temporary visitors through Chamberlain via US Highway 16 and eventually Interstate 90.

Throughout the years, Chamberlain has grown steadily, and its leaders have worked diligently to provide for the inhabitants. Businesses of all kinds graced the streets of Chamberlain. There were grocers, barbers, millers, clothiers, milliners, artists, and photographers, plant nurseries, saloons, cafés, bankers, lawyers, journalists, authors, wheelwrights, wagon masters, and livery stables, and the list goes on and on. There were also sources of entertainment, such as American Island, the opera house, traveling shows, sporting events, horse racing, and dances. Churches of several denominations were established in order to provide for the townspeople's spiritual needs. Doctors arrived, and eventually hospitals were built to take care of physical needs. Education was very important, and schools were established early on and expanded until the best possible educational opportunities were available.

Life has not always been easy. The Missouri River, although an important asset to the community, has also been a struggle to conquer. Even after bridges and dams were built, the river would flood, reminding the town that it was not ever going to be completely under control. Conversely, there were hard times during years of drought. There have been health scares. Wars have altered progress, brought shortages, and taken members of the community away to serve, sometimes never to return. Throughout all of this, however, Chamberlain and the rural areas and small towns surrounding it have bounced back and shown that they have what it takes to survive.

Today, Chamberlain and the surrounding area have become a popular place to visit. Tourists traveling across the state on Interstate 90 stop to take advantage of the river for camping, fishing, boating, and water sports. Hunting is also a big draw for the area, especially during pheasant season. Native American cultural experiences are available at Akta Lakota Museum on the campus of St. Joseph's Indian School as well as on the Crow Creek and Lower Brule Reservations just north of Chamberlain. A variety of nice local establishments provide unique opportunities for shopping. Comfortable hotels and motels are available, as are numerous restaurants and cafés.

Many of the citizens of Chamberlain have lived in the area their entire lives. There are, however, new people arriving at a steady rate who choose to make the Chamberlain area home. Many come for job opportunities at the Big Bend Dam, one of the schools, or at the hospital. Others choose to retire here, drawn by the picturesque river valley and the recreation the Missouri River provides.

This book gives a glimpse into the rich history of Chamberlain and some of the area surrounding it. When Gene Olson began collecting postcards, his interest was centered on the western and ranching culture and the places in which he grew up and spent his life. He was born at Bijou Hills, but grew up around Pukwana and attended high school there. Following their marriage, Gene and Alice ranched south of Chamberlain and eventually established Old West Museum at Oacoma on the west side of the river. Those areas are the heart of this book. When reading and looking through the photographs in *Around Chamberlain*, allow yourself to be transported back in time. Enjoy!

One

Crossing the River

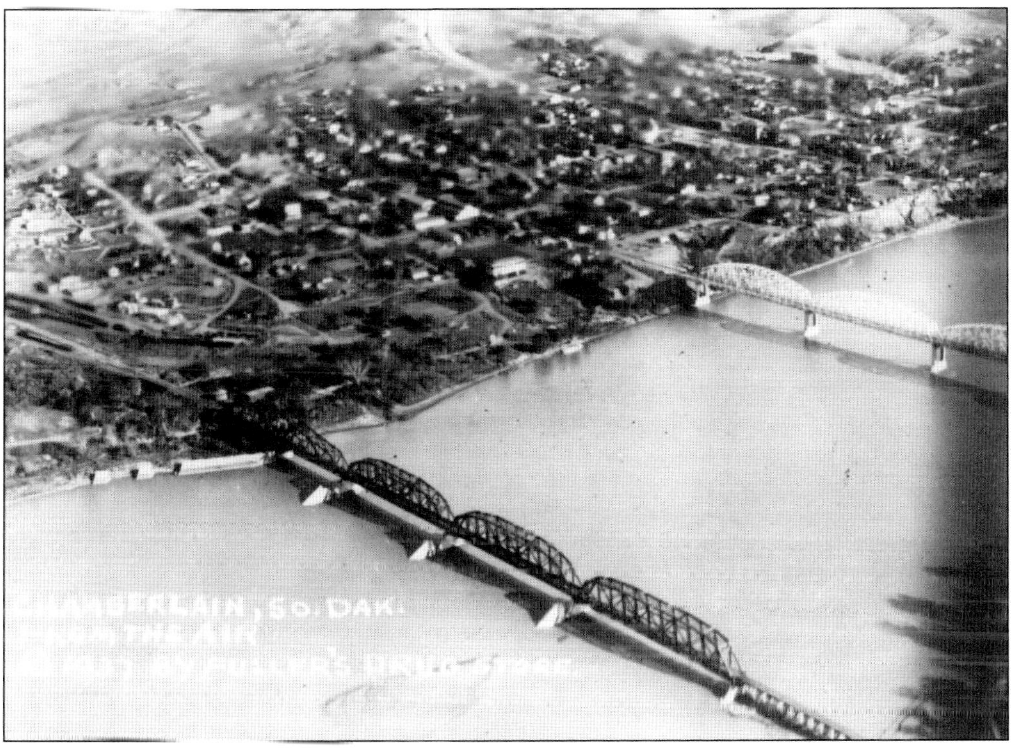

This 1937 postcard shows an aerial view of the Missouri River, the railroad bridge, and the highway auto bridge in Chamberlain, South Dakota. These bridges were the main links for passage to and from eastern and western South Dakota. Thousands of people each year would cross the auto bridge on their way to the Badlands and Black Hills.

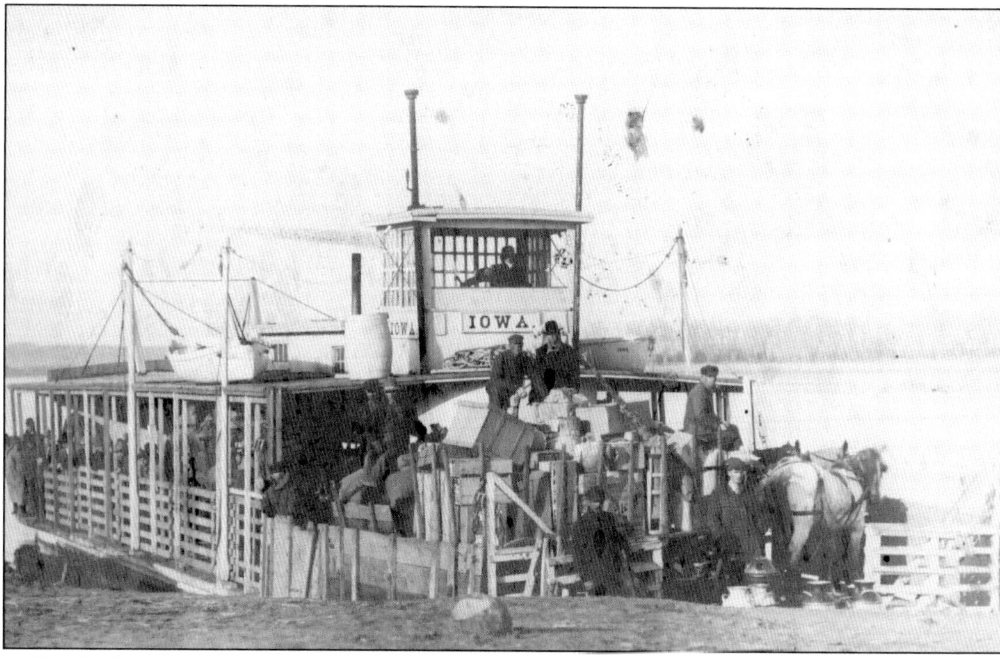

Before bridges, steamboats and gas-powered ferryboats were the main transportation across the Missouri River during the months when the river was not frozen. Besides people, the ferries carried supplies to military units, livestock, lumber for the railroad, and furs from trappers in the area, among other things. The gas boat *Iowa* is seen here being loaded with cargo. The railroad bridge and American Island can be seen in the background. Some other ships known to navigate in the Chamberlain area were the *Last Chance*, *Genoa*, *Viola Belle*, *Far West*, *Milwaukee*, *Rosebud*, and the *Molly Moore*. Some of the early captains included Wait, Ayers, and King. (Both, photograph by Judge, Chamberlain, South Dakota.)

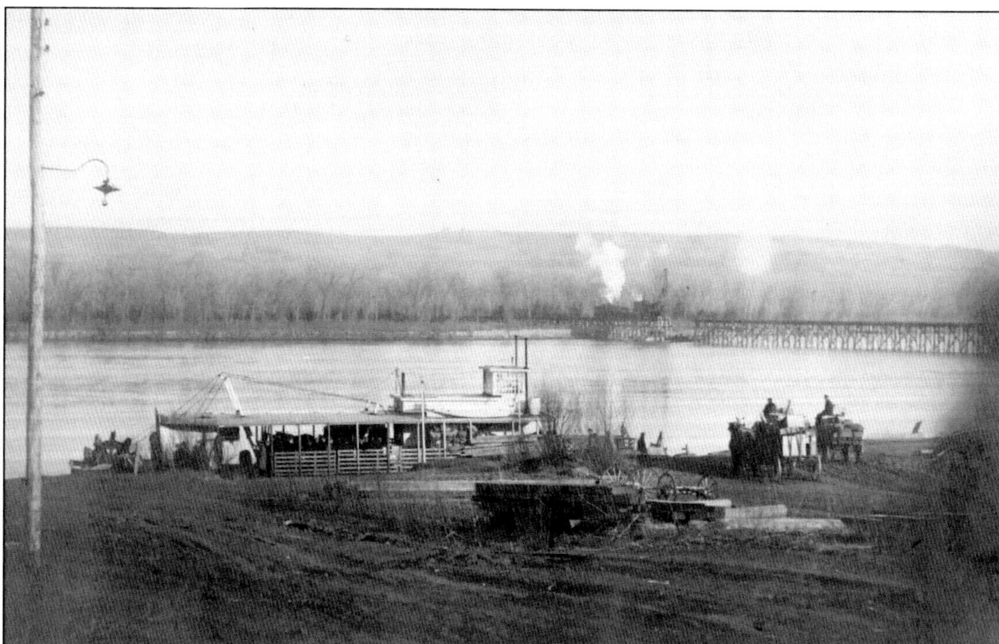

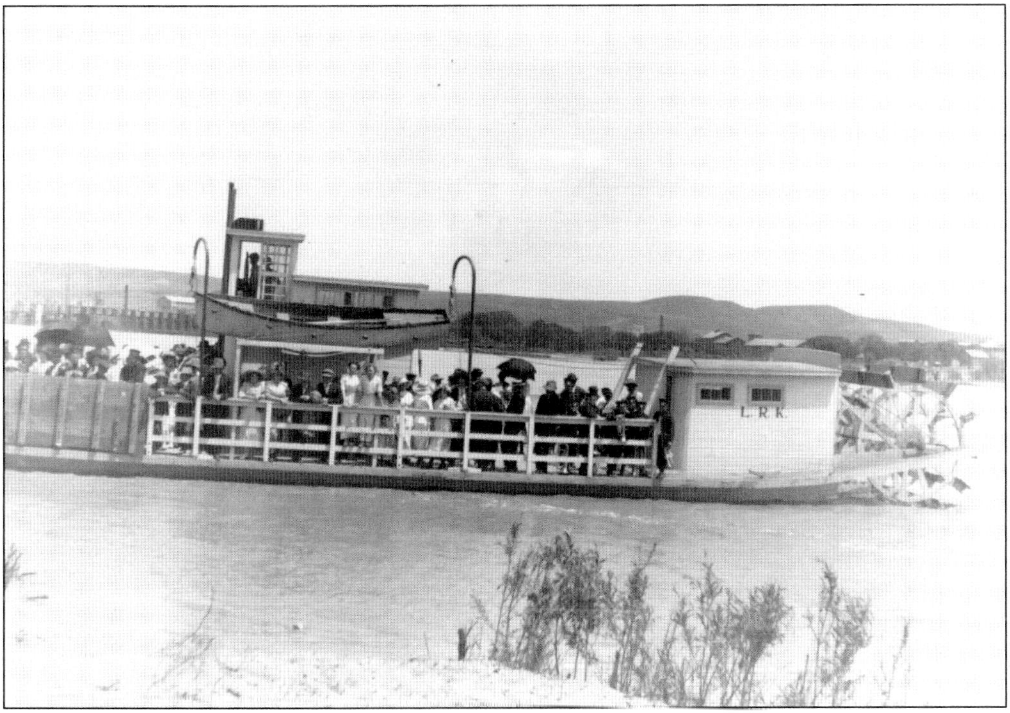

The photograph above is of a ferryboat just taking off on a short trip across the Missouri River. It has a full load of passengers, with most of them wearing their Sunday clothes. It was a sunny day, and many of them have umbrellas open to screen themselves. The initials on the side of the boat, *LRK*, were in honor of Capt. Henry Jasper King's daughter. He was a well-known local ferryboat operator. The photograph below is of a ferryboat crossing the Missouri River. It was one of the ferries in the area that delivered passengers and animals across the river. The railroad bridge is partially pictured on the right side.

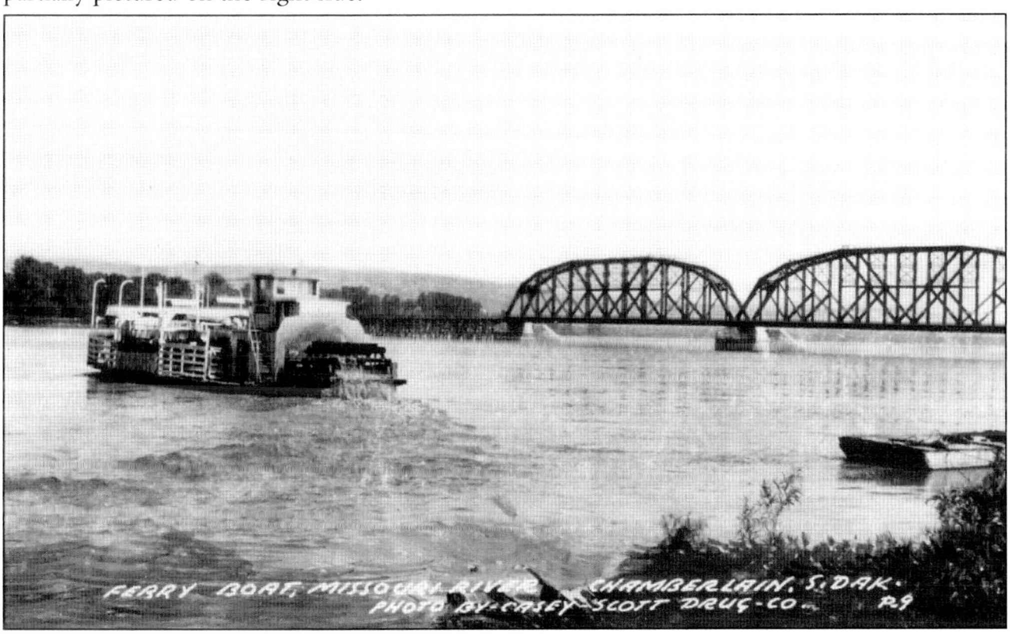

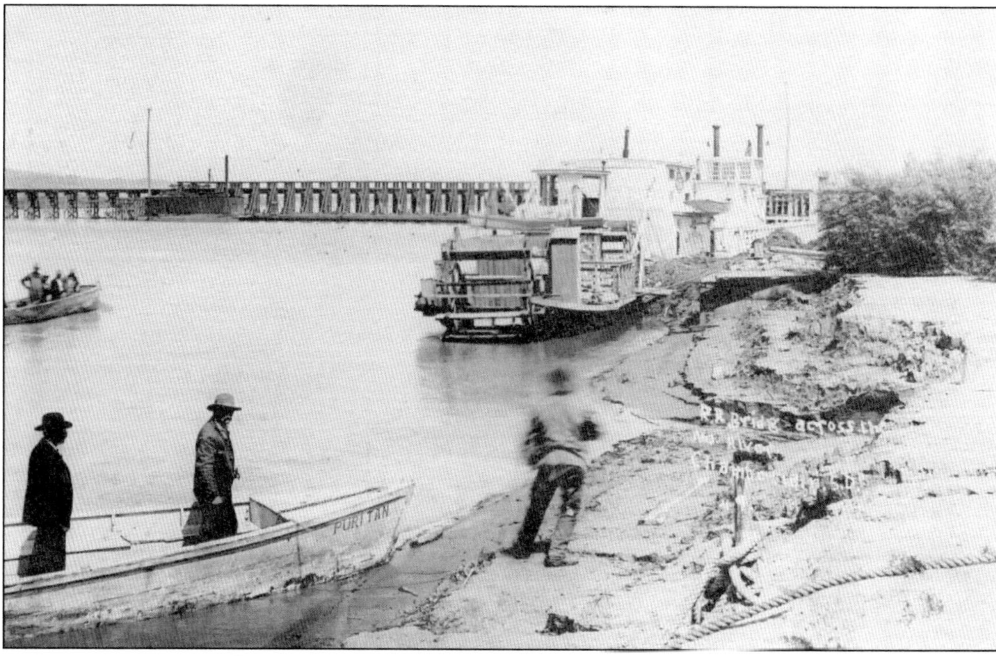

The early railroad bridge is in the background, with a ferryboat docked along the river. There is also a boat called the *Puritan* in the foreground, which was probably used to carry supplies. Another vessel with five men is going downstream on the Missouri River. Notice the heavy ropes along the bank to hold the boats to wooden posts.

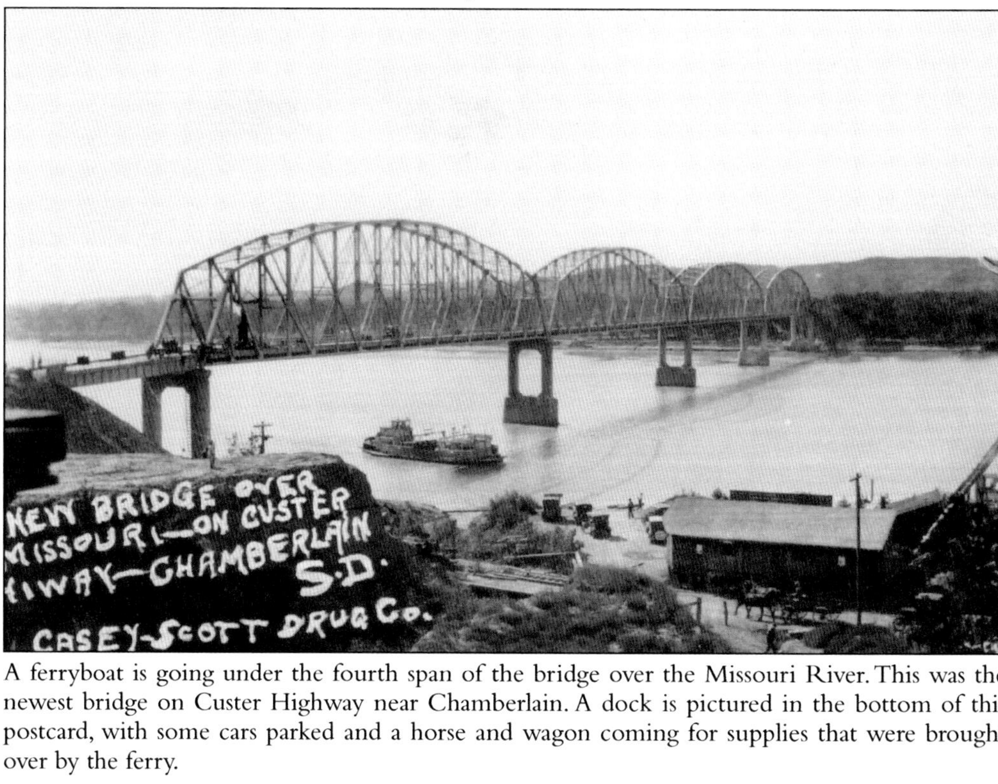

A ferryboat is going under the fourth span of the bridge over the Missouri River. This was the newest bridge on Custer Highway near Chamberlain. A dock is pictured in the bottom of this postcard, with some cars parked and a horse and wagon coming for supplies that were brought over by the ferry.

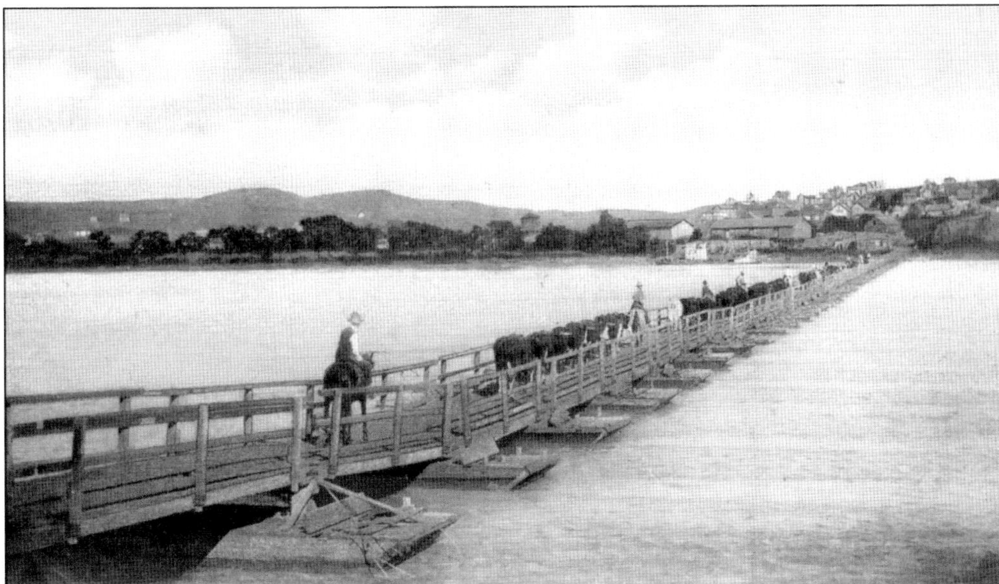

Pontoon Bridge, Missouri River, Chamberlain, S. D.

Before 1905, the railroad had only reached as far as Chamberlain on its way west. The Chamberlain Pontoon Bridge Company formed in 1892 as an alternative to crossing the river on a ferry. The pontoon bridge could not be used in the winter because ice would damage it, so it was necessary to completely remove the bridge from the river during the winter months. These postcards show cattle being driven across the river from the west and cattle ranchers returning to the west after delivering their cattle to market. Driving cattle across the pontoon bridge was a delicate maneuver. The bridge would sink with weight, so cattle would enter the bridge in small groups with cowboys leading and following.

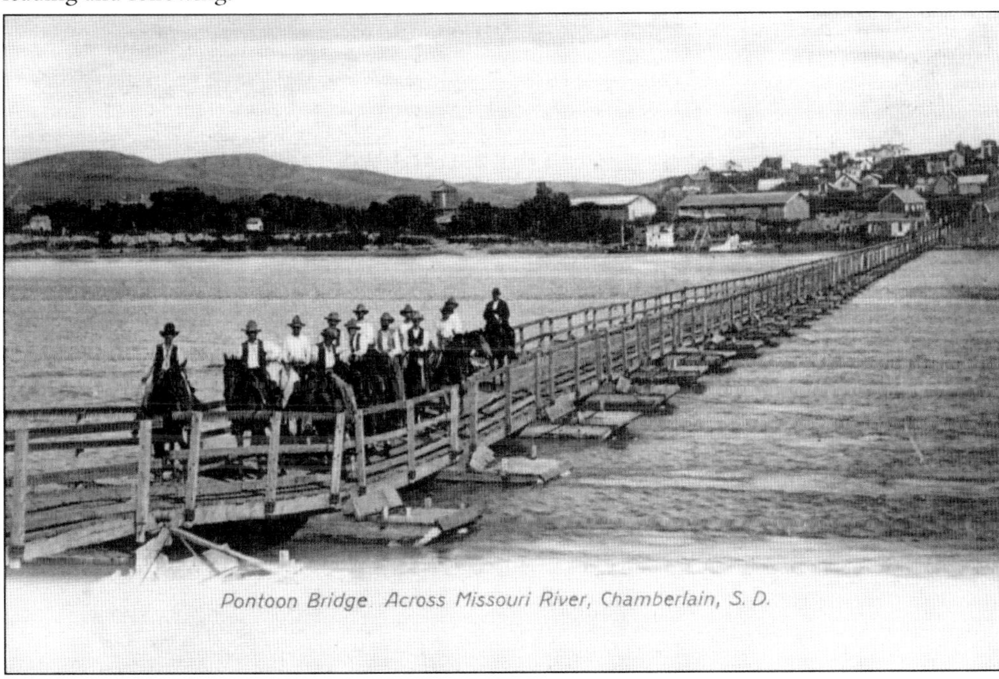

Pontoon Bridge Across Missouri River, Chamberlain, S. D.

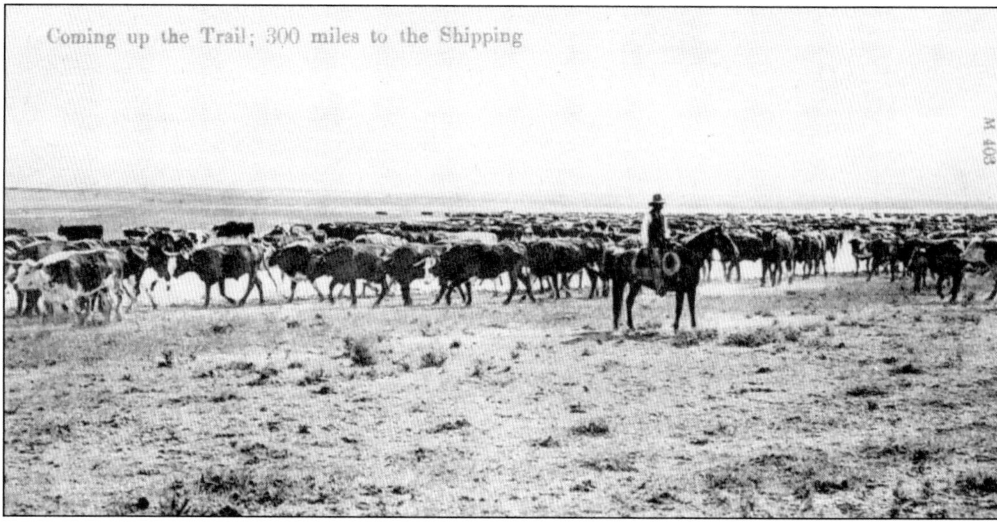

The postcard above shows a typical cattle drive, and the one below depicts another early view of cattle being driven westward across the pontoon bridge from American Island. The steamboat shown was most likely used to ship the cattle back east. Notice the corrals on the boat. There was another pontoon bridge up the river at Pierre, which got more business because the Bad River to the west provided the cattle with water. Pierre also provided more entertainment for cowboys once their jobs were done. In order to entice more business, the railroad had watering holes built along the trails west of the river. The town of Chamberlain also helped by expanding the number of saloons and dance halls.

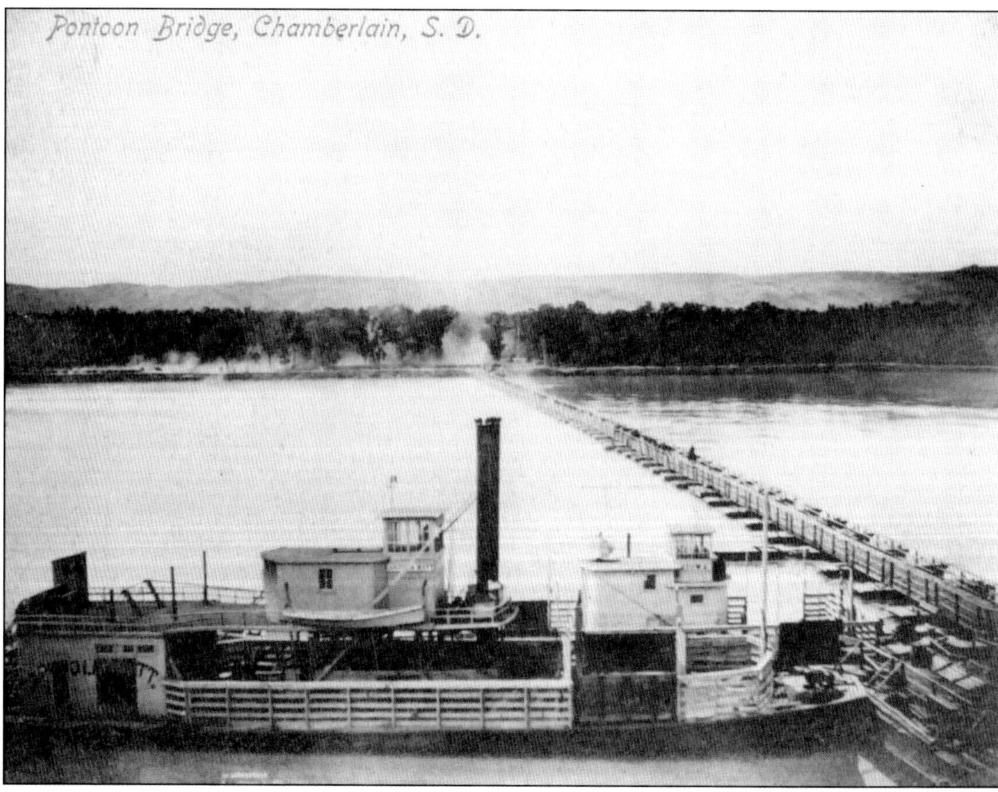

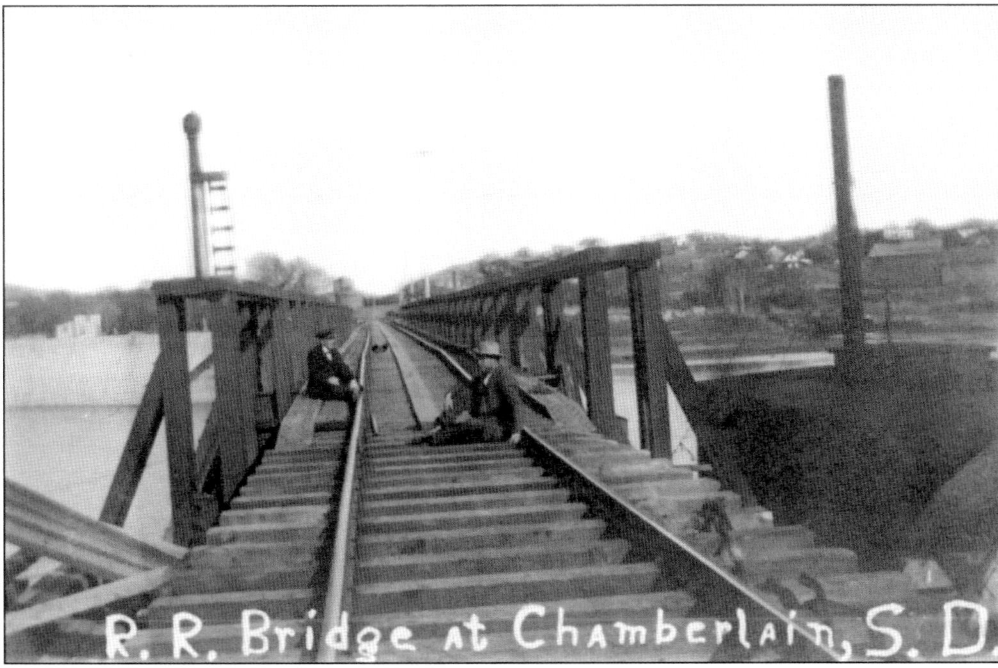

The Chicago, Milwaukee, and St. Paul Railroad, also known as the Milwaukee Road, reached the east bank of the Missouri River at Chamberlain in the fall of 1881. At that time, the land west of the Missouri River was part of the Sioux reservation, and the railroad went no farther. Cargo was taken across the river by ferry and then by freight wagons to points farther west. These two cards show the first railroad bridge being constructed around 1905. It was to be a pontoon bridge with approaches of fixed pilings and decks. This bridge, when completed, would speed up the delivery of much needed goods going west.

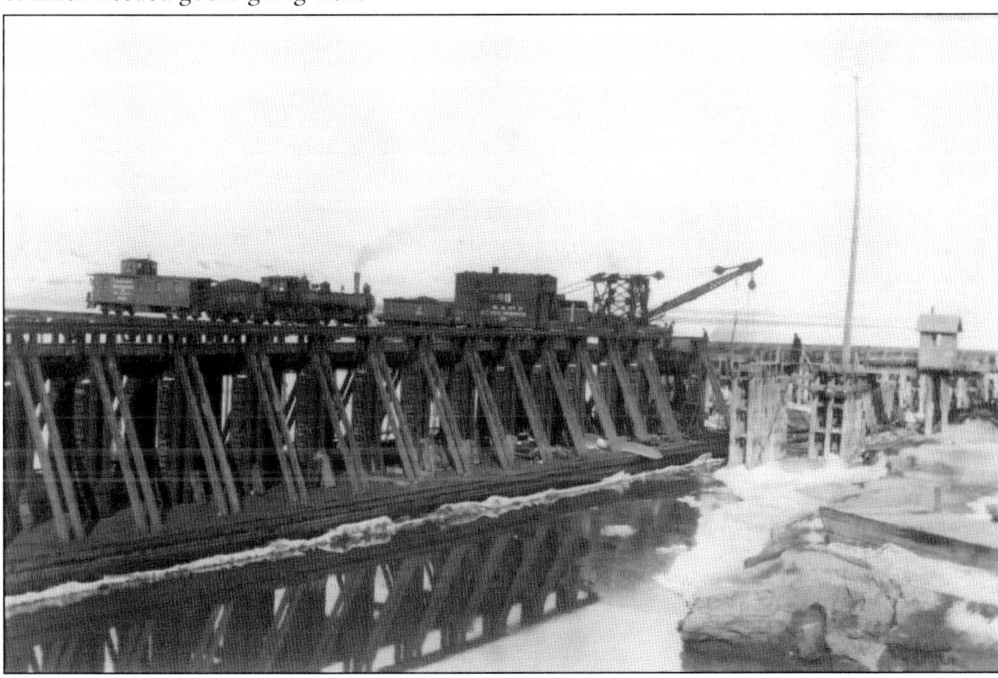

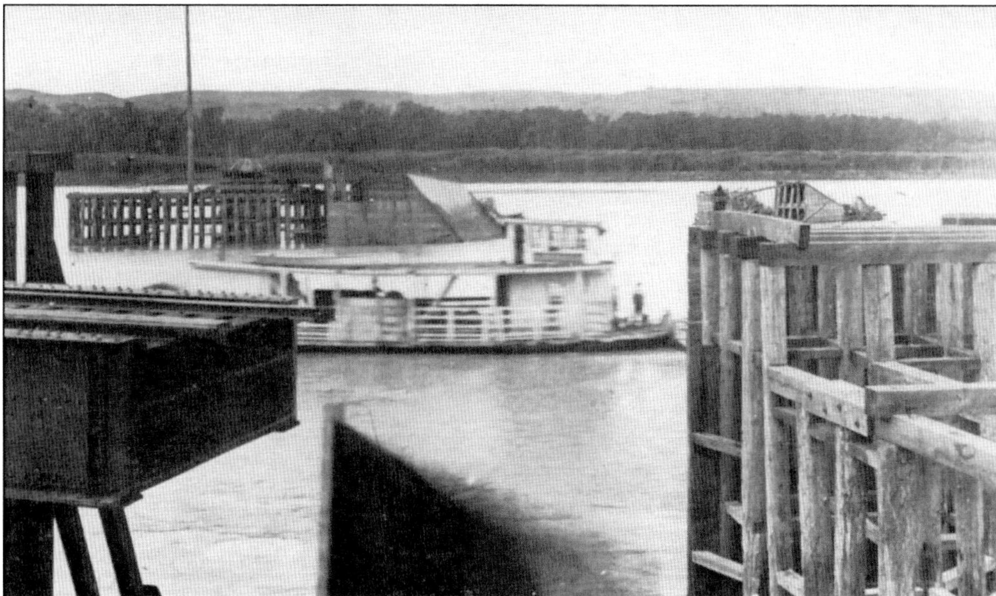

R. R. Bridge, opened, Chamberlain, S. D.

In order to allow boats to travel upstream and downstream along the Missouri River, the railroad bridge was made with an opening at the channel to let the big boats pass through. When needed, a hinge of sorts would open, and the deck would split to allow two sections of the bridge on pontoons to be moved away. The image above shows the railroad bridge opened and a boat ready to go through. In the image below, the opening can be seen in the distance by the east shore. Chamberlain, already a large, bustling city, lies in the background.

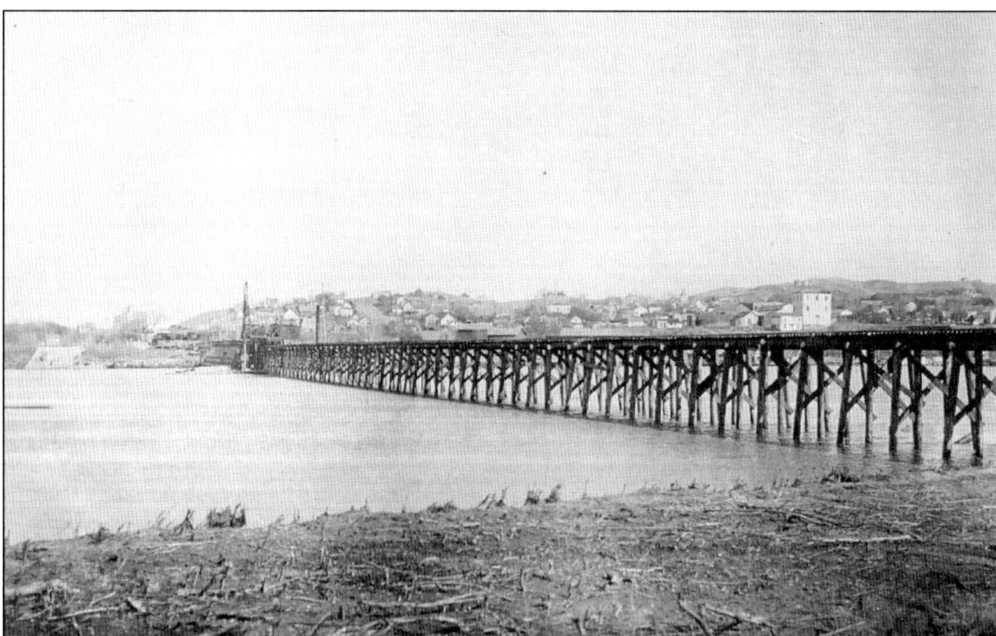

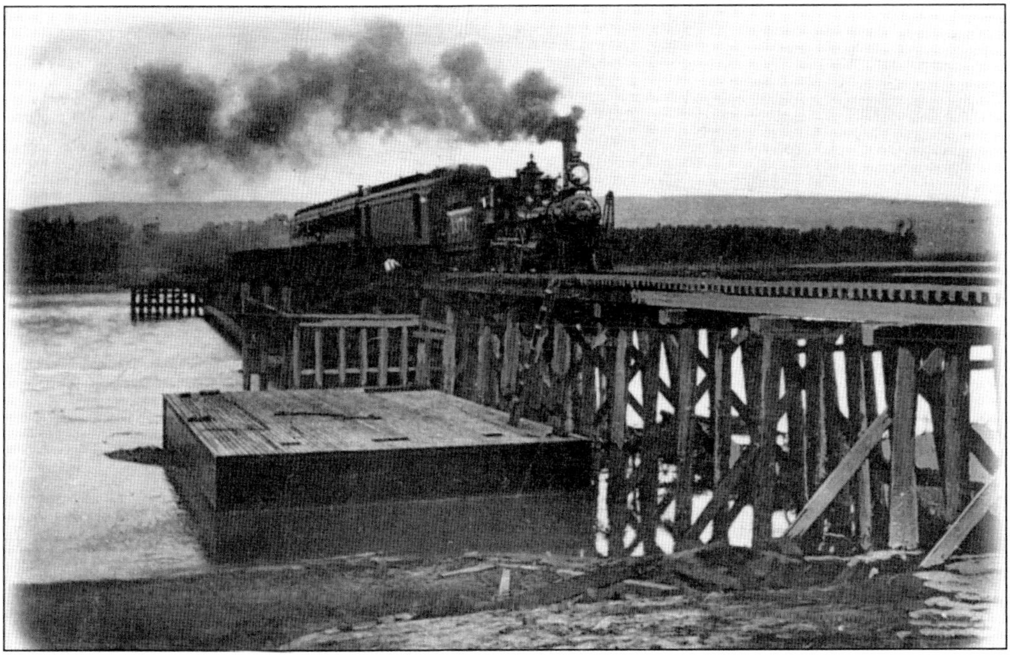

The first Chicago, Milwaukee, and St. Paul train, engine No. 1371, crossed the river in 1905. Transportation of livestock from the west was now much easier, as was the migration of people moving west to new lives in the new territory. The railroad would become an important part of life in Chamberlain, with arrivals from the west transporting cattle and arrivals from the east off to adventure in the west.

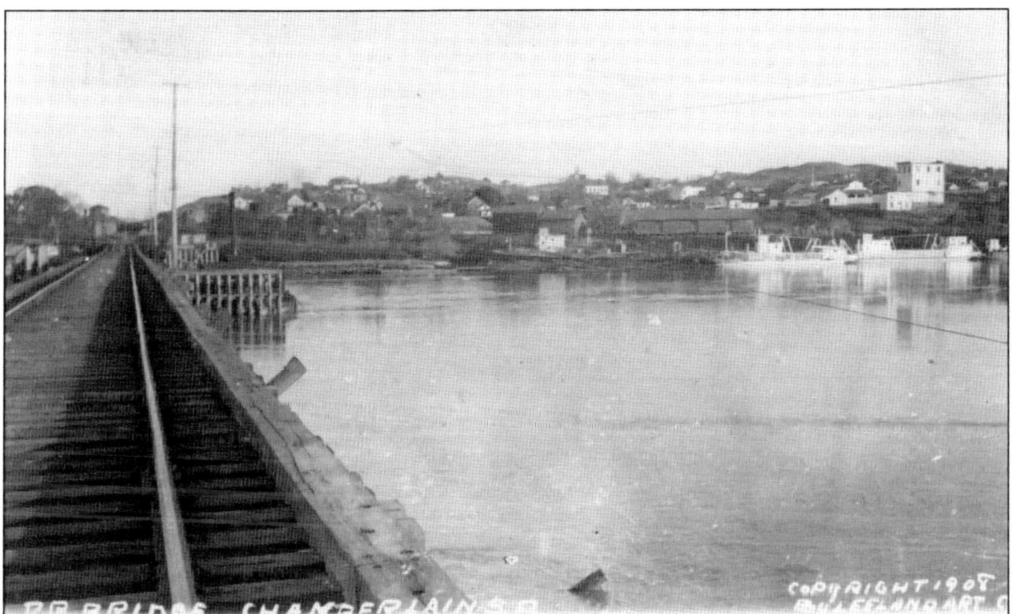

This 1908 view from the railroad bridge is of Chamberlain from the west. The boat landing can be seen to the right, or south, of the bridge. The large white building is the flour mill. Travelers on the train viewing the small city of Chamberlain must have been impressed by the activity and opportunity evident in this photograph. (Photograph by O.S. Leeland.)

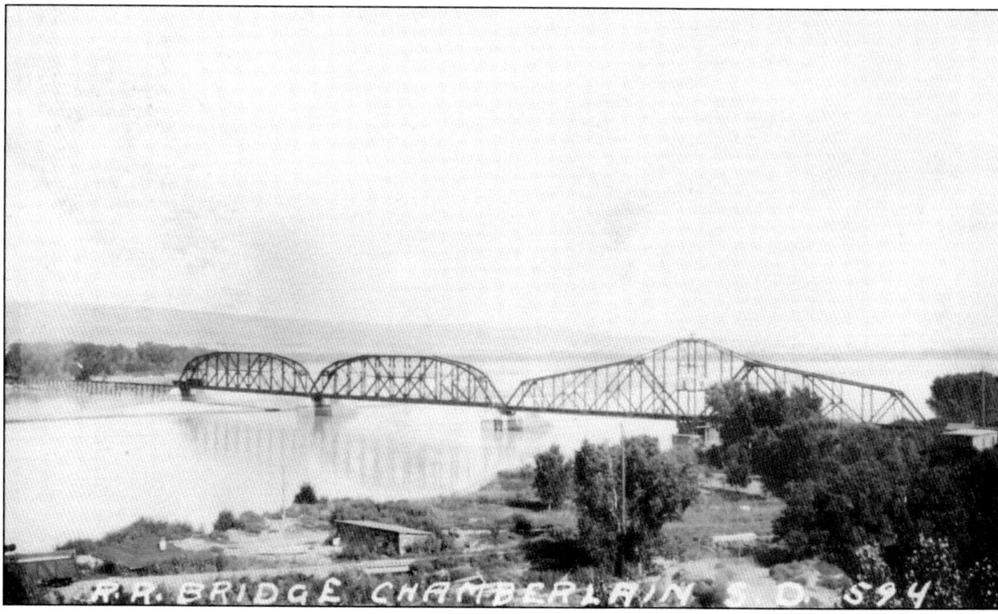

The pontoon railroad bridge was replaced in 1923 by a steel structure in the same area. The bridge was obviously stronger and could handle the trains more efficiently. The longer span was able to turn so as to let the boats through. Young people were known to go out on the bridge for fun. This could actually be a scary activity when the ice was breaking up, hitting the icebreakers on the end of each span. This would cause the ice to fly into the air above the heads of the onlookers and crash into the water again. During this time, the water was very close to the rails. Most were happy to make it off the bridge after such an experience.

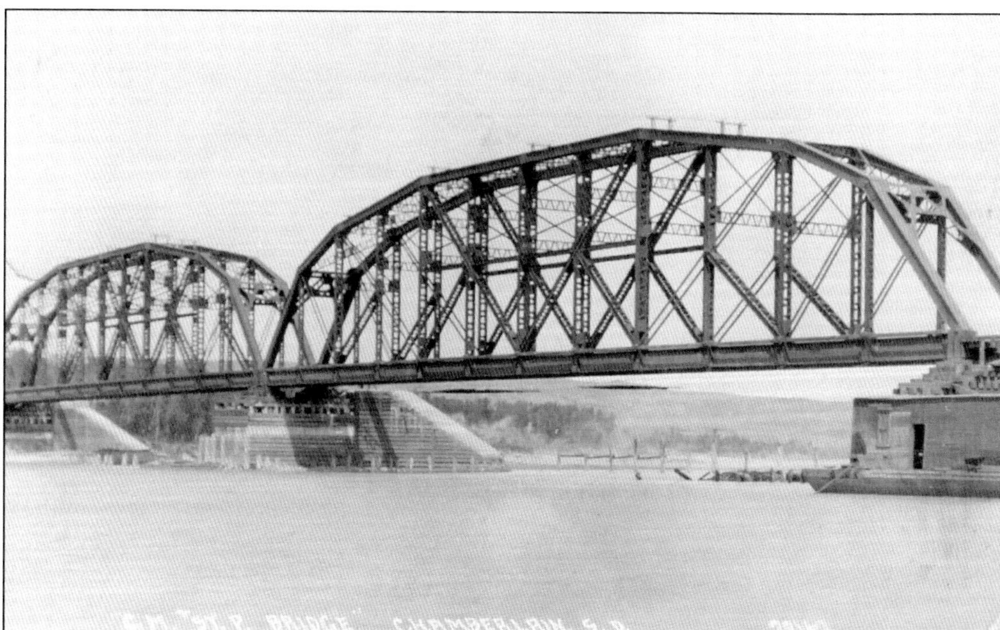

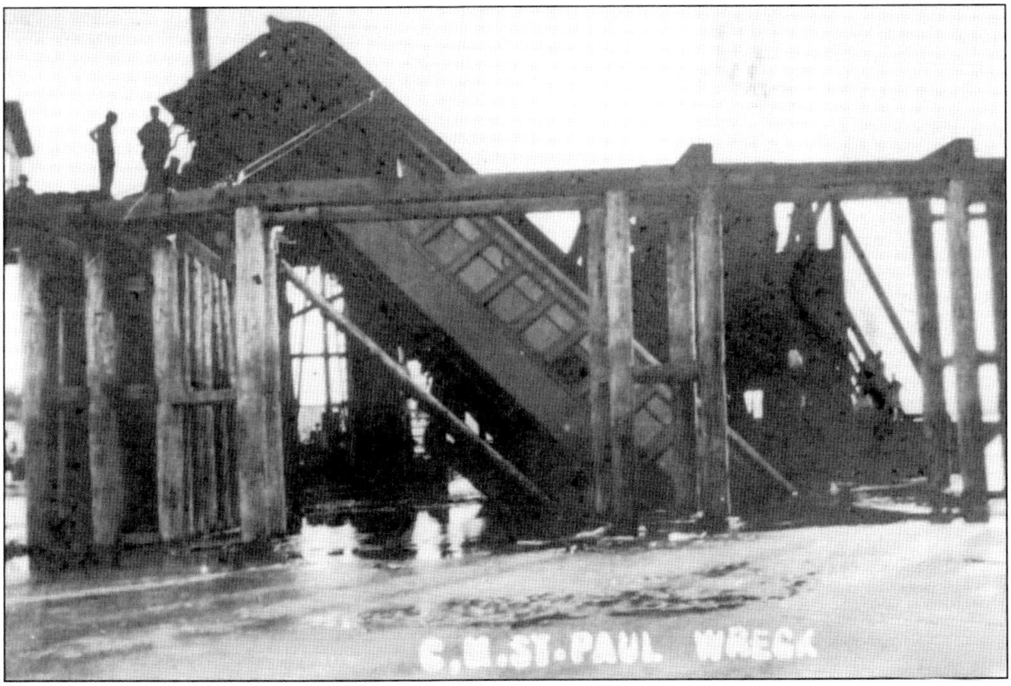

These two cards show some of the troubles the Chicago, Milwaukee, and St. Paul Railroad bridge faced during the early years. The train wreck pictured happened in 1907. As ice broke up, huge chunks of ice, sometimes two and three feet thick, would cause problems nearly every year. The one shown here from 1910 has taken out some of the piling on the west side of the river. The poles and timbers would float downstream and end up on private property. Landowners would use this wood and even construct log cabins with it. At one time, there was a short railroad on the west side that would turn the ice jams away from the piling. This spur line had railcars on it to try and hold it from losing more of the piling.

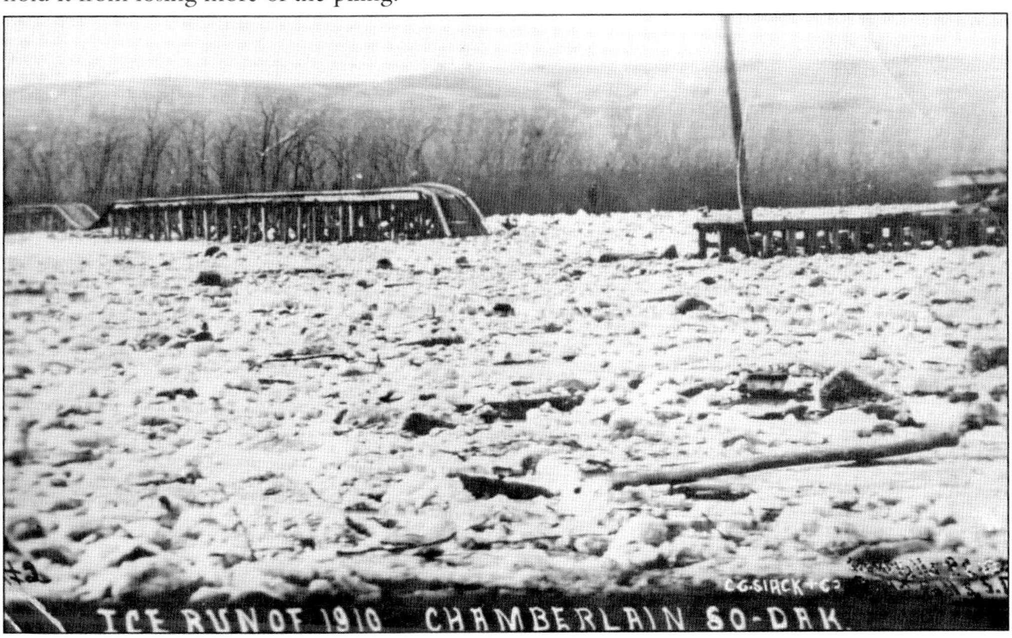

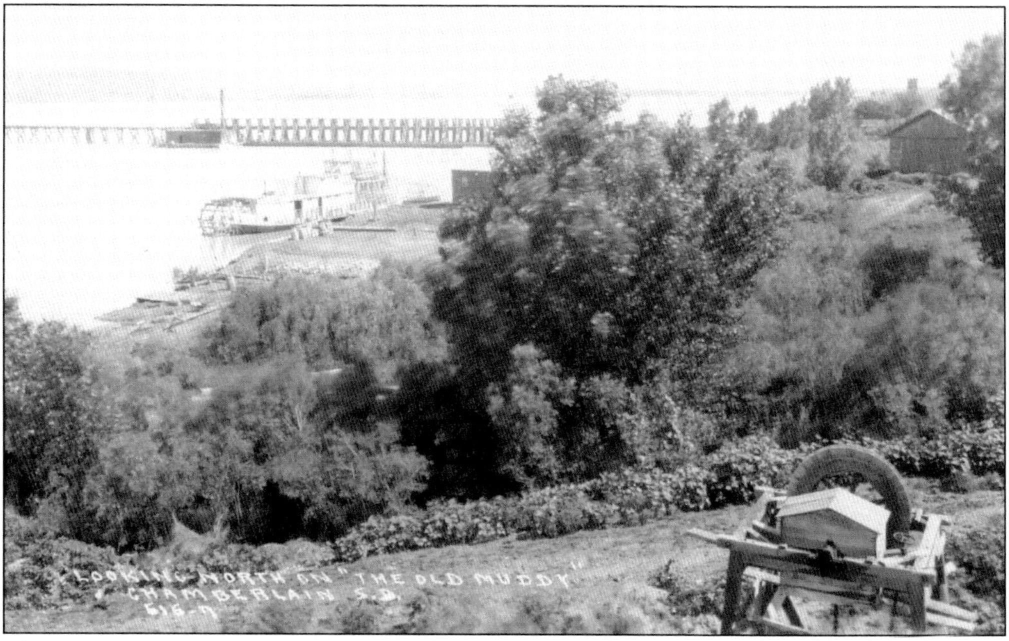

This 1916 postcard view is northward on the "Old Muddy," in Chamberlain. The original railroad bridge is in the background. The area of the bridge to the left is part of what opened to allow boats to travel along the channel. A paddle-wheel ferry is docked at the landing.

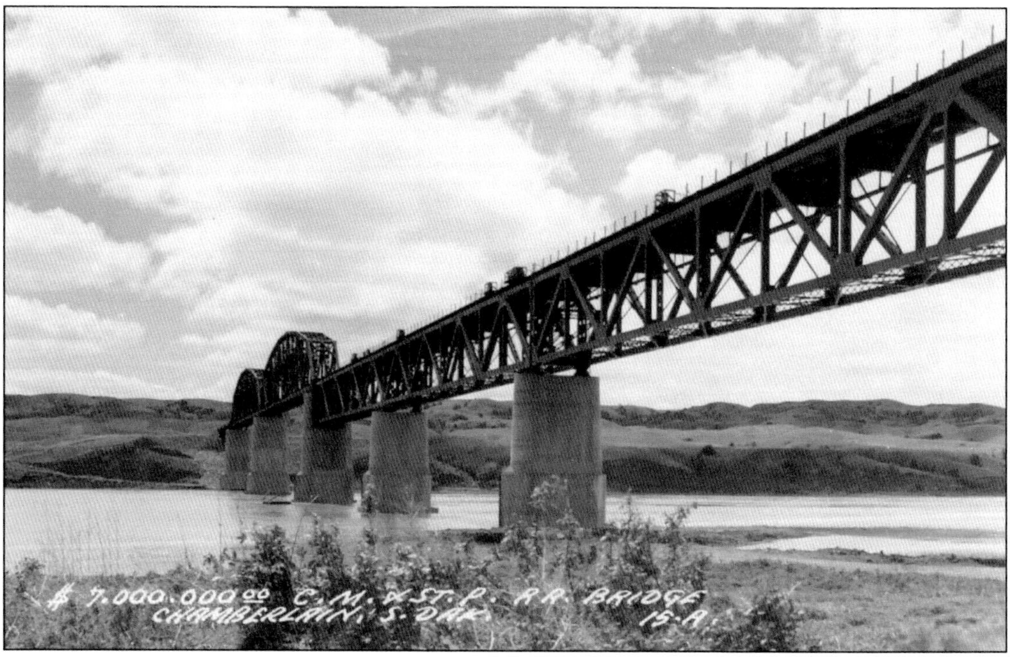

When the Fort Randall Dam at Pickstown was built and the water on the Missouri River rose to form Lake Francis Case, the 1923 steel railroad bridge was flooded out. On January 3, 1953, construction on a new bridge began just downstream. It would be seven eighths of a mile long upon completion, which would make it the longest bridge on the Milwaukee Road system. The bridge was dedicated on December 7, 1953.

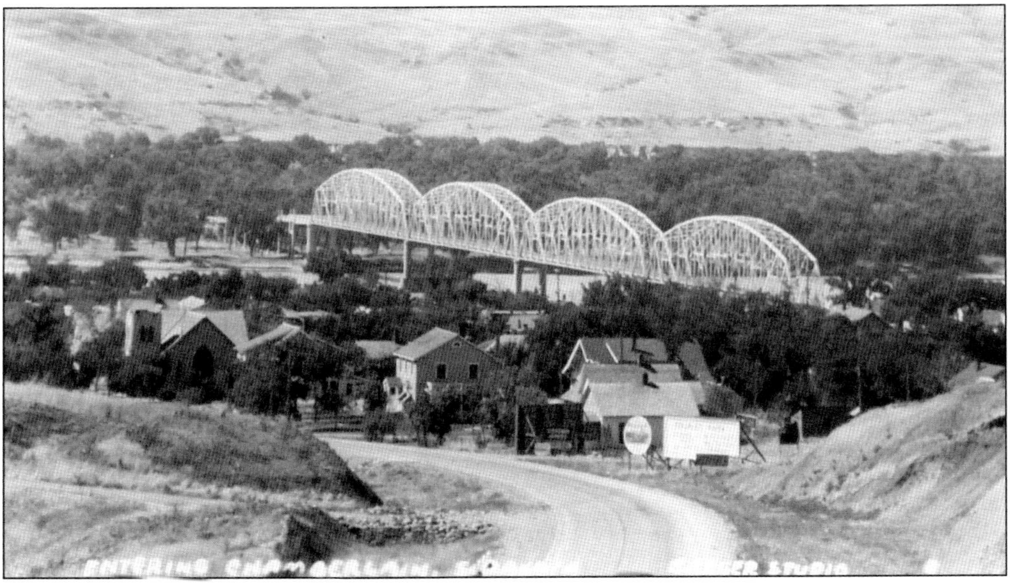

It is hard to imagine what it must have been like to cross the Missouri River at Chamberlain before the bridge was built. Using the ferry, pontoon bridge, and crossing on the ice in winter were all unpredictable options. In 1920, a husband and wife drowned while crossing the ice, leaving nine children behind. Following this tragedy, the desire for a permanent bridge became even more fervent. The people of Chamberlain and the surrounding area were so dedicated to the project that when they found they were to be third to have their bridge built according to the construction schedule drawn up by the South Dakota Legislature, they worked to issue bonds covering 58 percent of the cost to move the bridge construction up in the order. The finished product, as shown in these two postcards, was one of the community's proudest achievements. (Above, photograph by Orrion Barger.)

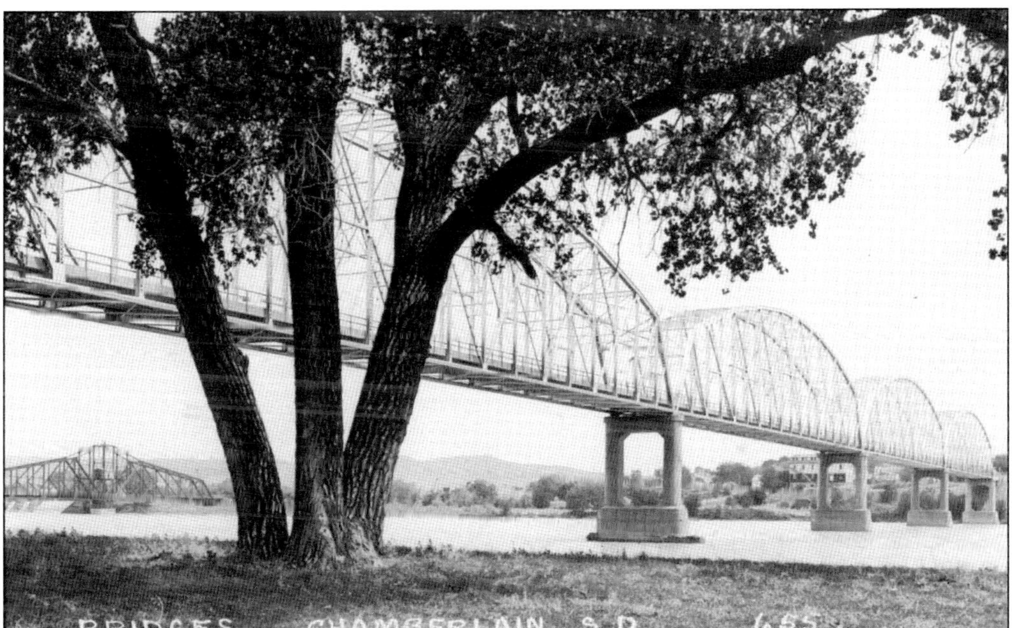

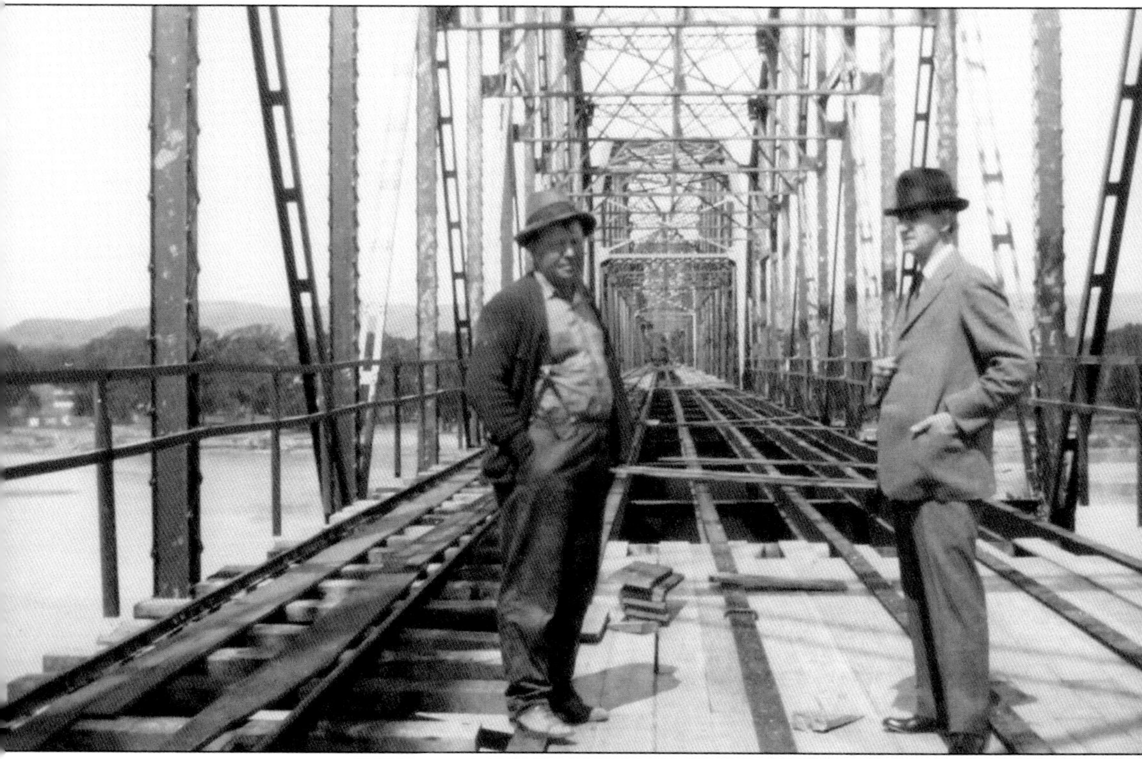

On the right is John Kirkham, state engineer for South Dakota, standing with one of the foremen during construction of the Missouri River bridge at Chamberlain. Kirkham stunned the state highway commission when he stated that he could erect five bridges across the Missouri for close to the same amount spent on the bridge at Bismarck, North Dakota, which was approximately $2 million. Finally convinced, the legislature, in 1921, passed House Bill 327, levying a tax of 1/10 of a mill on all taxable property for the construction of the five bridges. Construction on the bridges could not start until the money was there for all of them, and the legislature thought it would take at least 12 years to get the money. It underestimated the determination of the people of South Dakota, however, and construction began just a few years later.

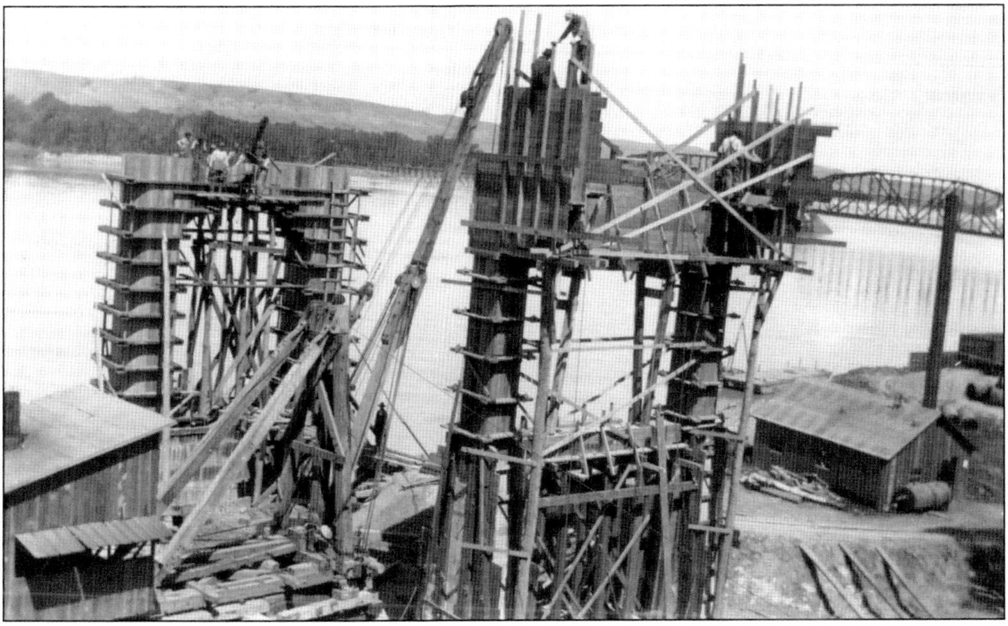

Many real-photo postcards were made to depict the progress of bridge construction. These two cards show work being done on the Chamberlain bridge in the spring of 1924. The photograph above shows the very early days of bridge construction. American Island and the Milwaukee Road railroad bridge can be seen in the background. In the photograph below, concrete is carried up so it can be poured onto the deck of the bridge. Building bridges was a hard and tedious job as laborers had to be very careful of where they stepped while working at all times. The men who worked to build this bridge could be very proud of their accomplishment.

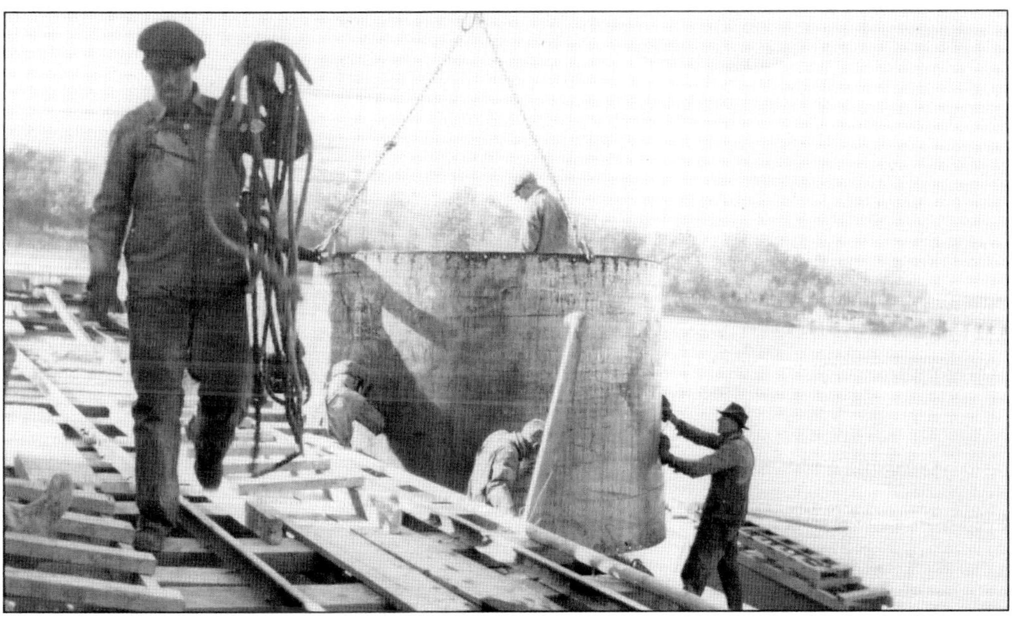

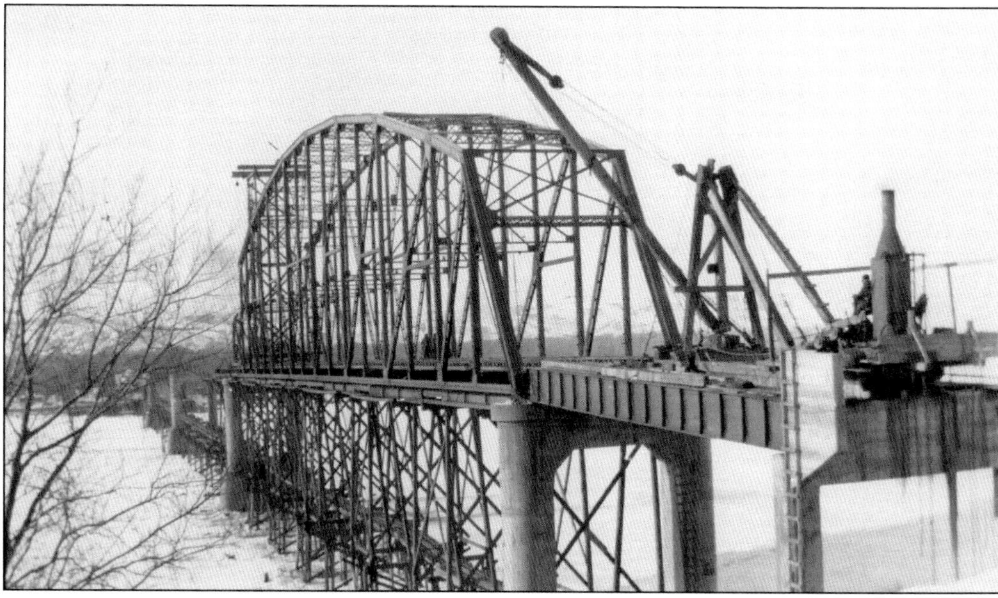

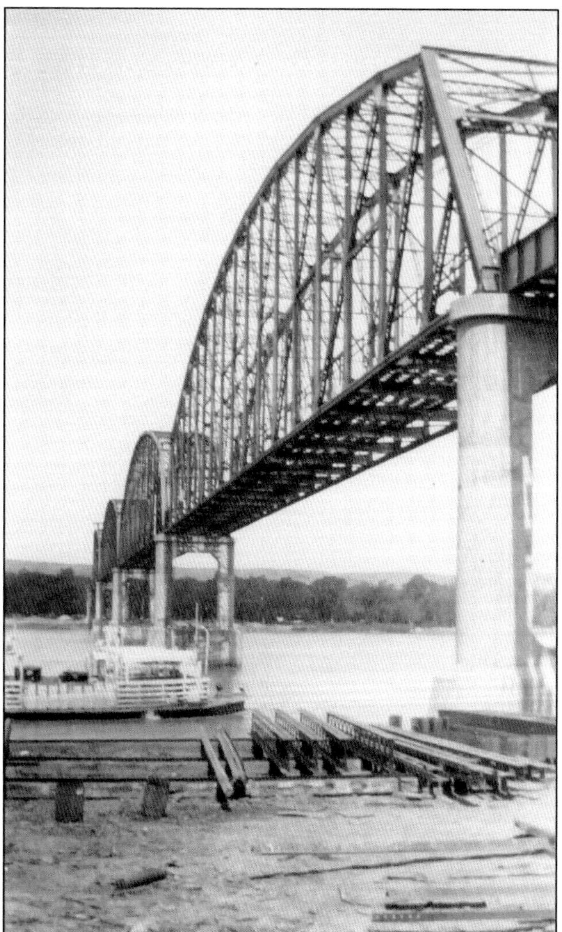

All five bridges in Kirkham's plan would sport through truss spans that would be 250 to 350 feet long. The Chamberlain bridge would have four spans riveted together, each being 336 feet in length. A contract of $345,000 was awarded to the Missouri Valley Bridge and Iron Works Company of Leavenworth, Kansas. The above photograph shows construction of the first span, almost complete, with work on the second span soon to commence. In the left photograph, the bridge is nearing completion, with the ramp yet to be done. A barge and some construction beams are seen under the bridge.

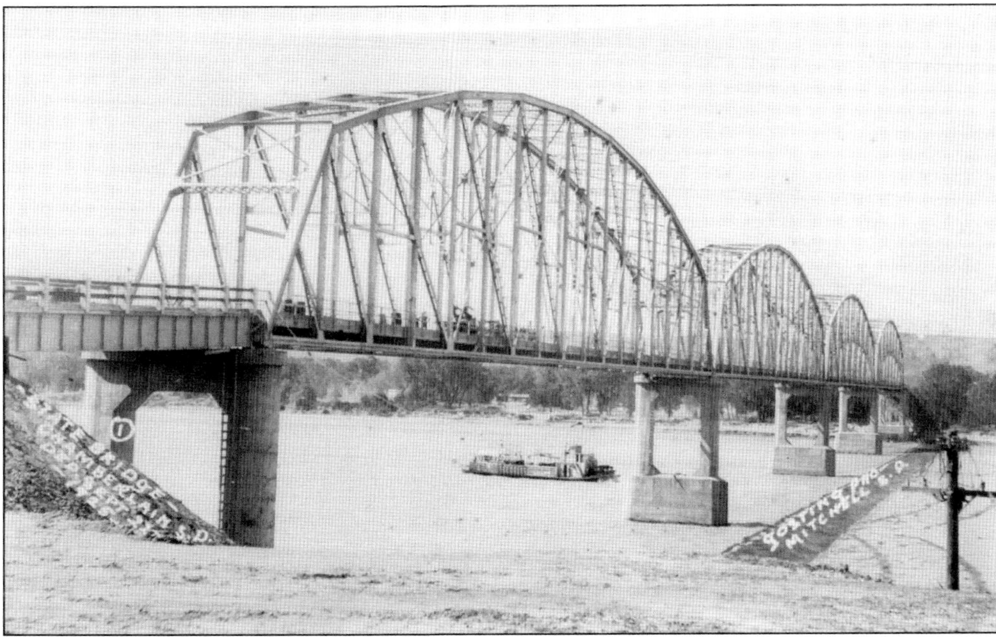

The Chamberlain Highway Bridge was dedicated amongst great celebration and ceremony on September 25, 1925. There were four days of parades, parties, historical reenactments, and visits by dignitaries. This photograph, taken from the east bank of the Missouri River looking west to American Island, shows the bridge on the day of its dedication. A paddle wheeler, no longer a necessary means of transportation, passes beneath.

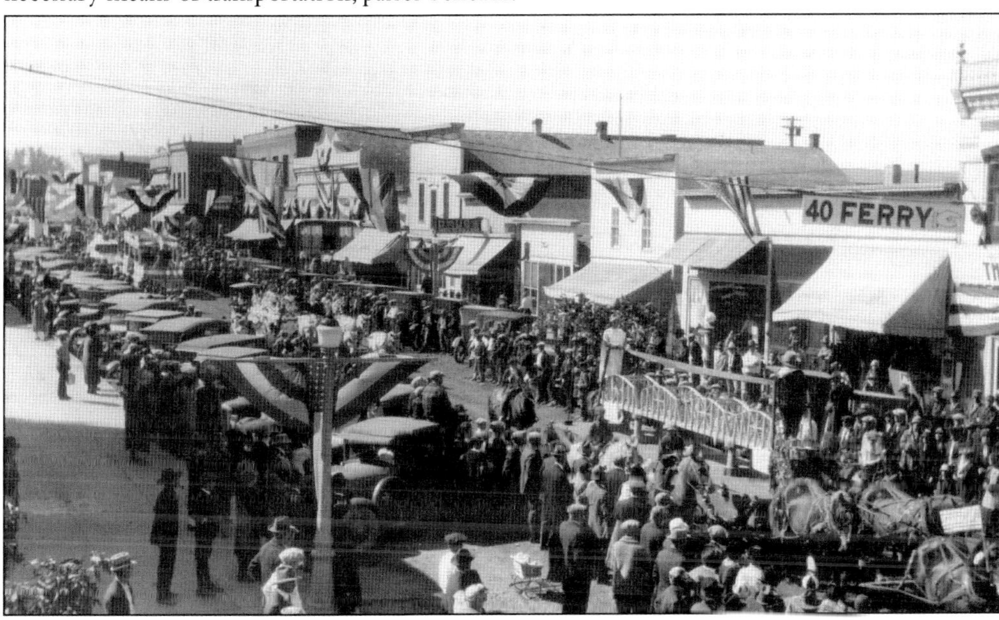

This photograph is from the 1925 dedication of the Missouri River bridge. There was a four-day celebration in September with a parade each day. This photograph shows part of the parade including a nice float with a replica of the bridge. The parade was in four sections, starting out with Indian life, pioneering, homesteading, military, visiting dignitaries, the bridge float, bands, Indian dancers, cowboys, and numerous other floats. There were rodeos with fireworks at night.

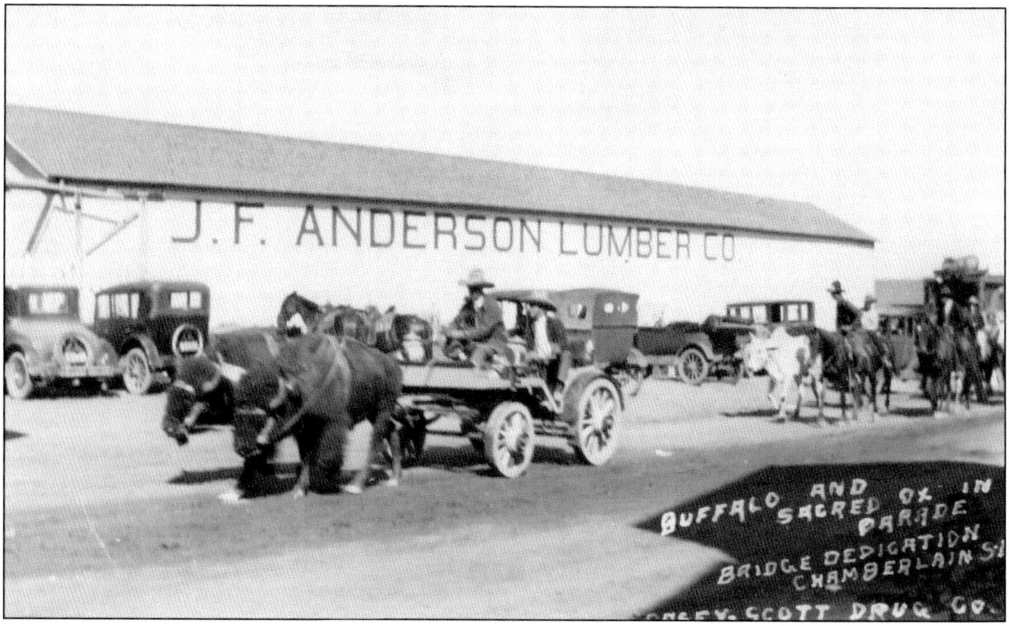

The above photograph shows the parade passing the J.F. Anderson Lumber Company. A team of buffalo is pulling a wagon followed by an albino ox. Older cars, such as a Ford Model A and T, are parked alongside the building. The Anderson Company was along what is now known as the truck route through Chamberlain. The photograph below from the celebration parade shows Main Street Chamberlain decked out in festive flags and banners. Some of the buildings and signs along the way include the Pony Express announcing a show by James Cruze, 40 Ferry, a shoe and boot shop, and the Neil E. Fuller drugstore. A soda fountain is on the corner. In the parade, covered wagons representing homesteading and cowboy life pass by the onlookers.

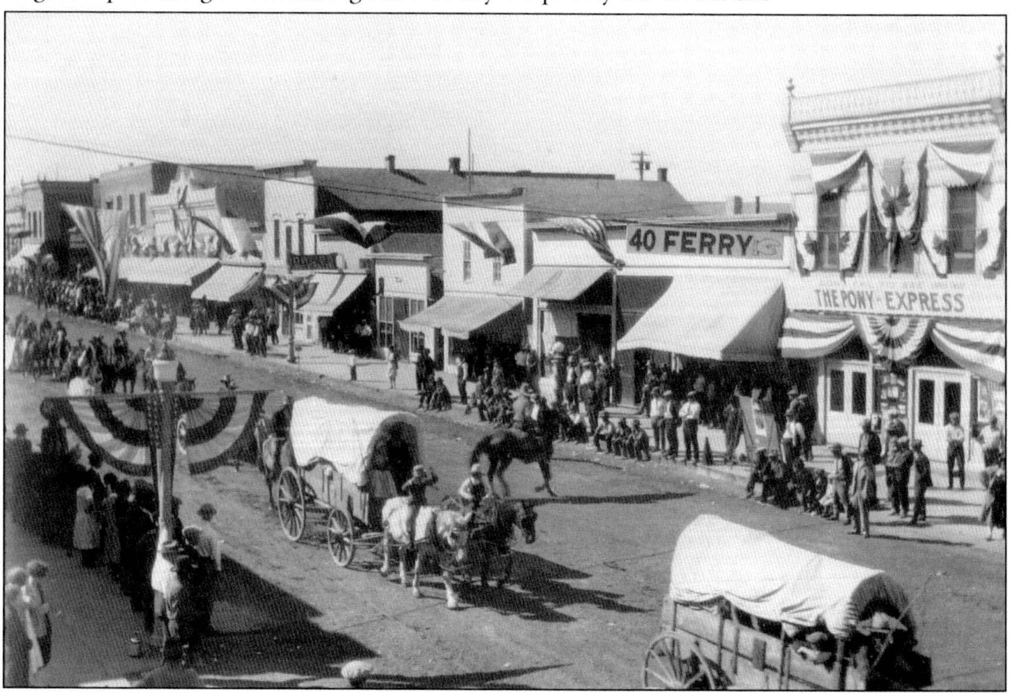

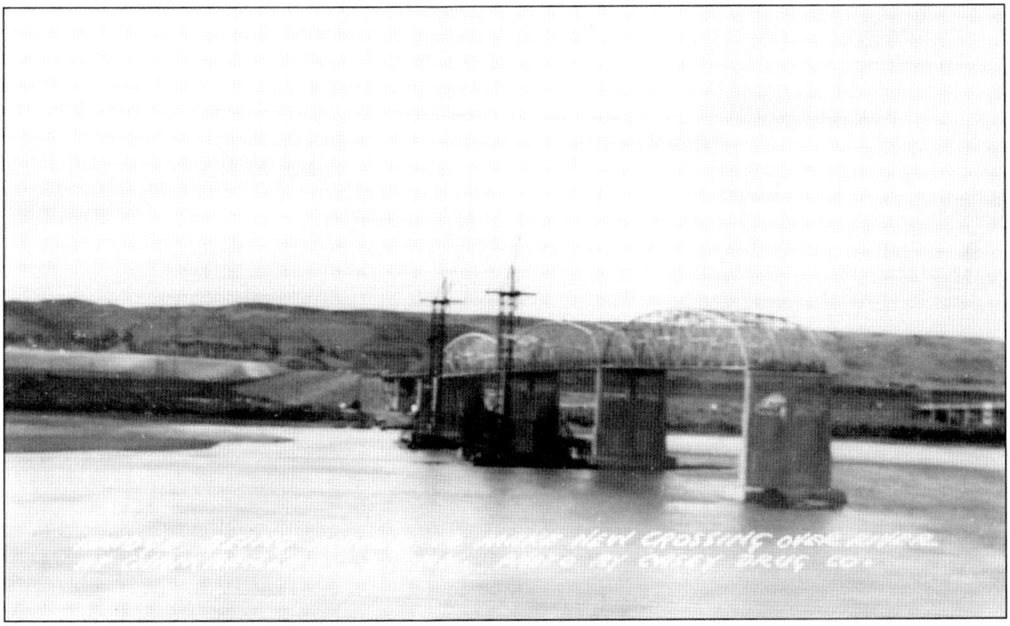

When the dams were built on the Missouri River, the 1925 bridge was no longer adequate. Since there was not enough money to construct a completely new bridge, a plan was hatched to salvage the trusses of the Wheeler bridge, which would be flooded out, and reuse them as part of the new Chamberlain bridge. The Wheeler trusses were floated up the river, but time was lost when the trusses caught on a sandbar near the Carl Olson ranch. There was no choice but to wait for the river to rise and dislodge them. The above photograph shows the spans being moved in place on the new bridge.

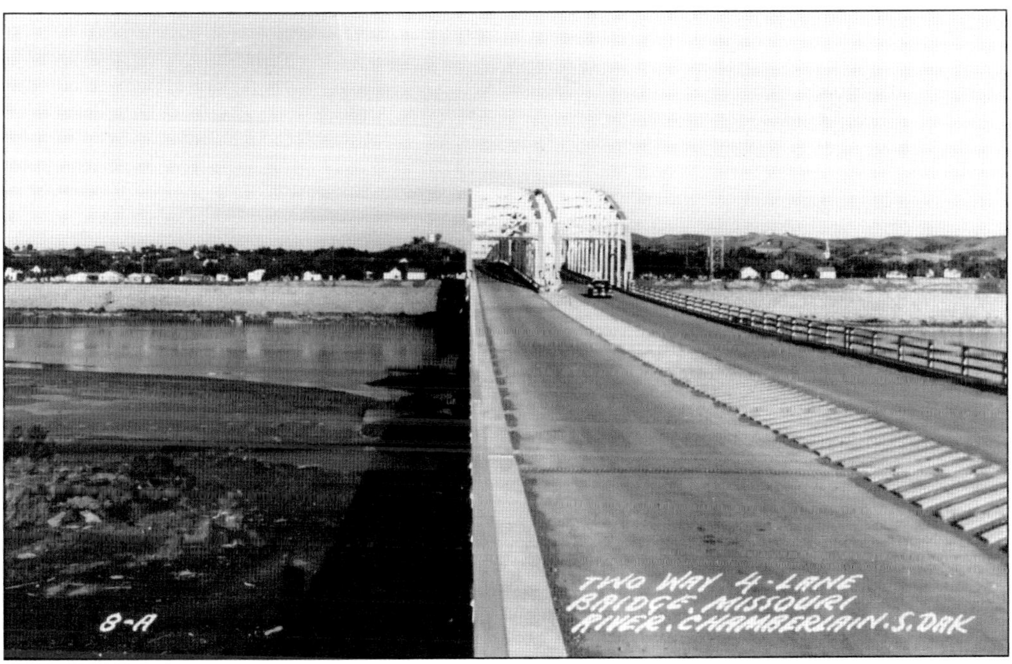

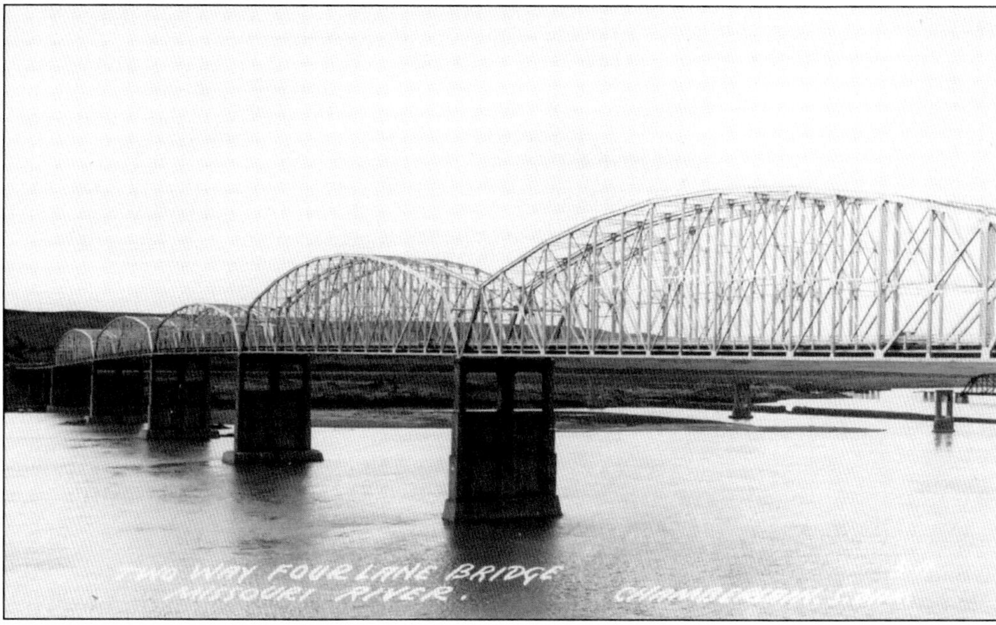

The new two-way, four-lane bridge over the Missouri River at Chamberlain was dedicated on December 7, 1953. It was located just downstream from the 1925 bridge. The four sections on the east end were from the 1925 bridge. The five 256-foot trusses from the Wheeler bridge were used on the west end. Only one new 256-foot span had to be made to complete the bridge.

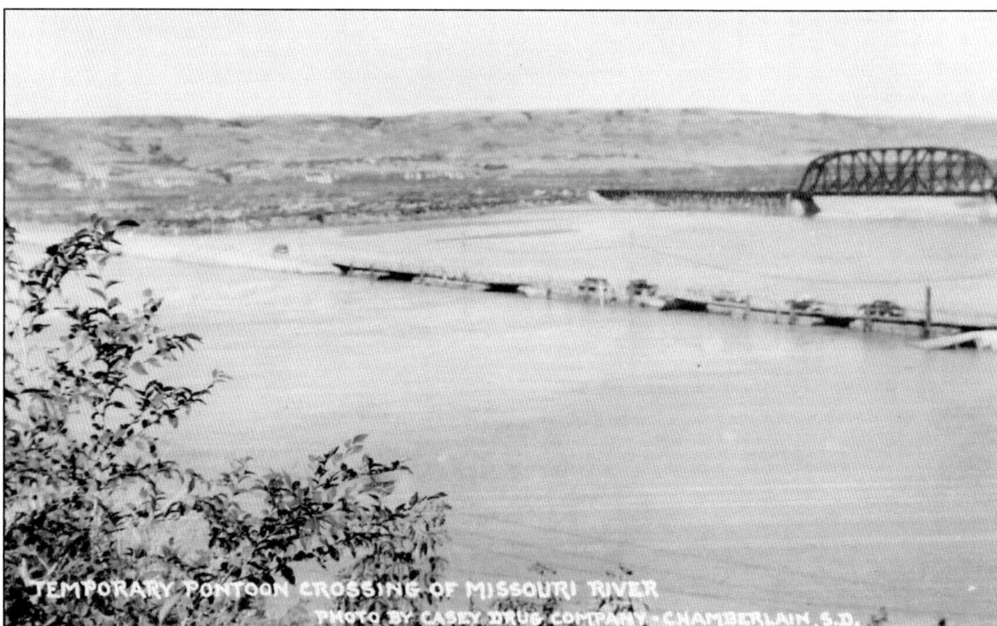

During the construction of the double-lane span, a truss-and-pontoon bridge called a Bailey bridge was set up for crossing the river. There was a stoplight at each end because it was only wide enough for one-way traffic. Cars would sink into the water a little as they crossed. The Bailey bridge washed out in a flood, conveniently on the same day the new bridge was opened.

Two

American Island

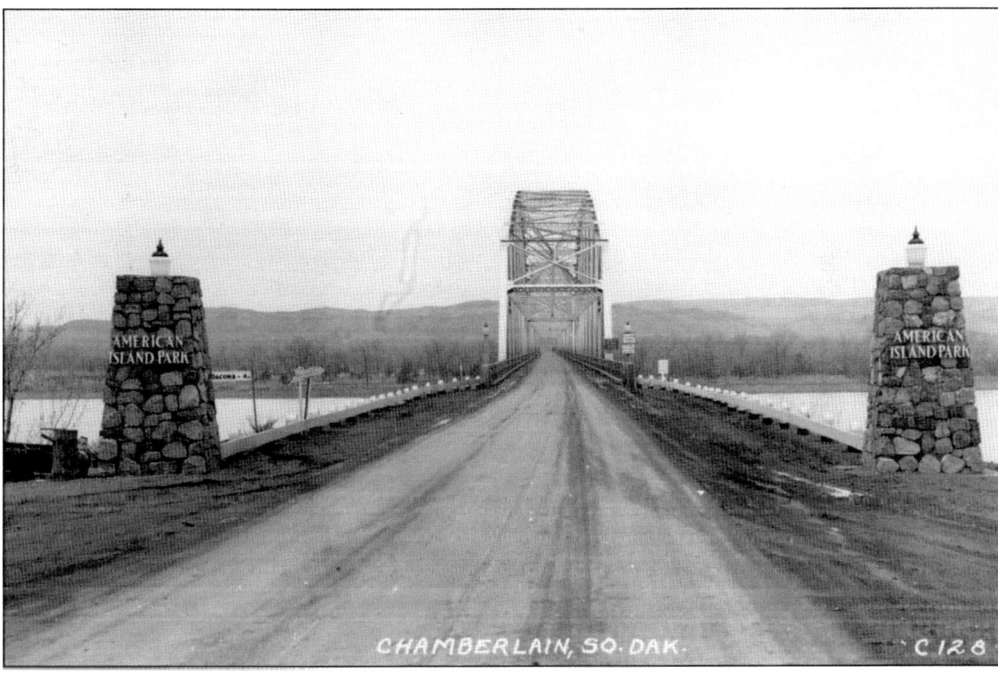

Lewis and Clark recorded that they reached American Island on September 17, 1804. They stayed there several days and also stopped there on the return trip. American Island continued to be a favorite place for rest and recreation in the Chamberlain area. The stone pillars here welcomed motorists as they crossed the bridge over the Missouri River. The small signs announced that there was no toll to cross and that Oacoma was just four miles ahead.

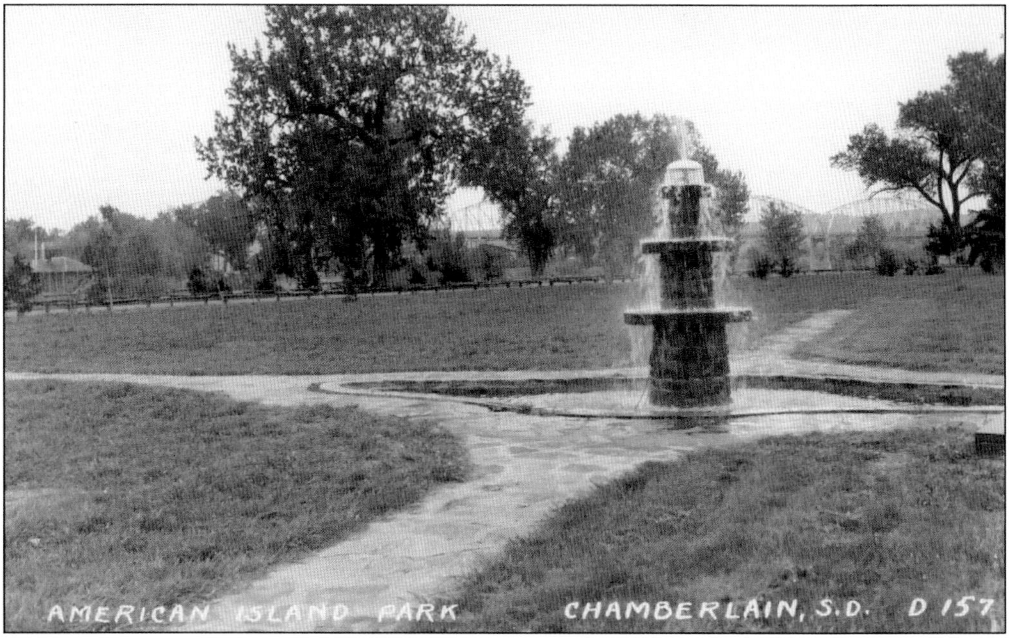

American Island has had many names, including Little Cedar in 1811, Great Cedar Island, and Second Cedar Island. It was first called American Island in the 1884 edition of *Andrea's Atlas*. It was a natural park that was thickly populated by cedar and cottonwood trees, wild berries, and turkeys and other wildlife. Early on, it was the location of trading posts that provided supplies to Native Americans, explorers, trappers, and passing steamboats. The above photograph shows the fountain on the island, with the Missouri River bridge just visible through the trees.

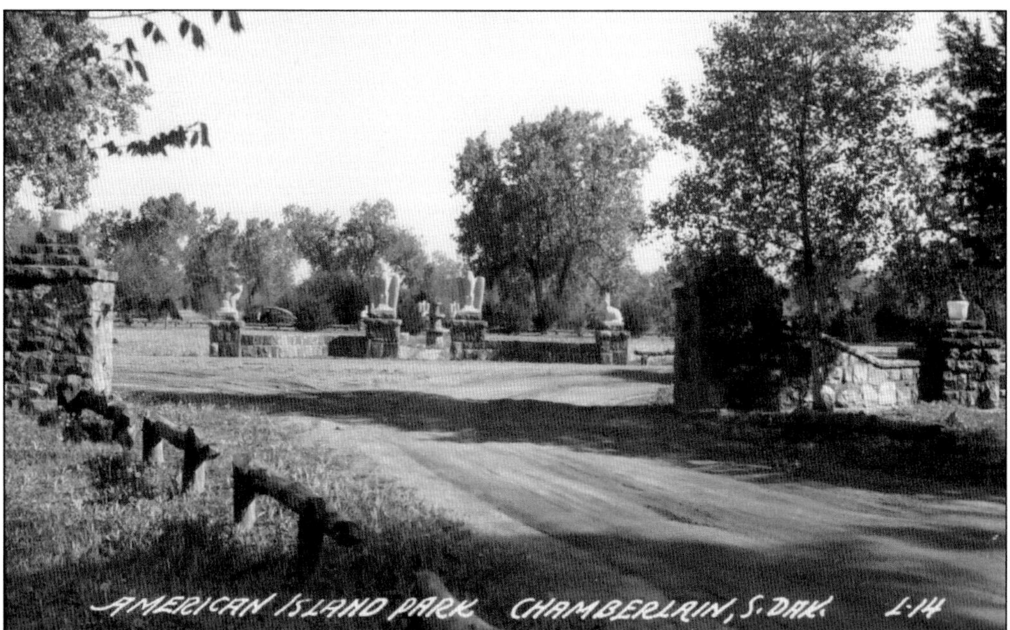

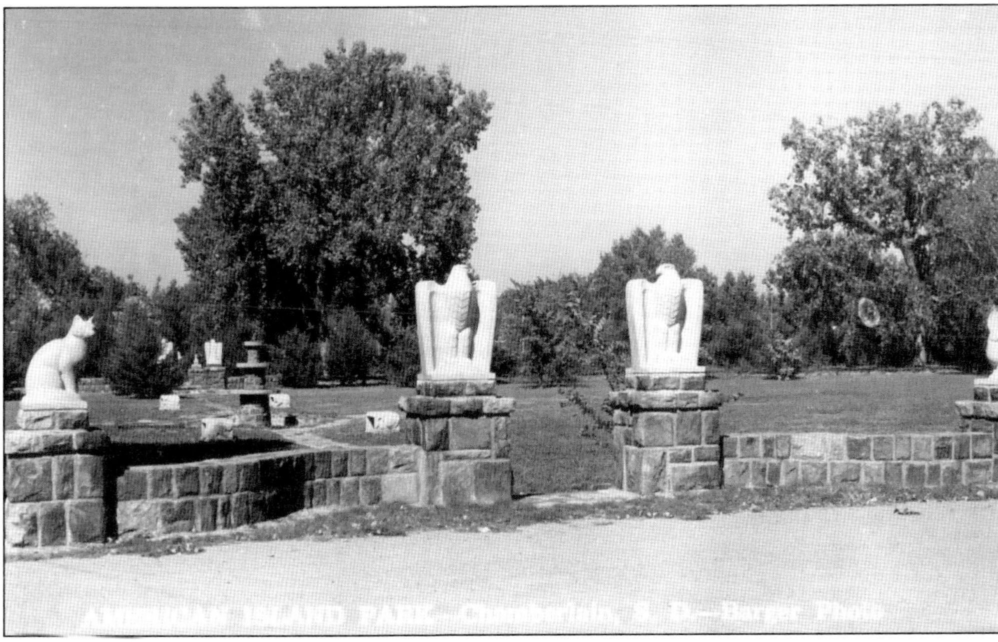

There was a Civilian Conservation Corps (CCC) camp located on American Island. The camp workers were responsible for many of the improvements on the island and around Chamberlain in the 1930s and 1940s. The sculptures seen in the postcards were located at the entrance to the park and along walking paths. They were made by Andre Boratko and supported by a special Works Project Administration (WPA) artist fund. There were eagles, a coyote, a rabbit, a squirrel, and a fawn. Some of these sculptures can still be seen today at public parks in Chamberlain. (Above, photograph by Orrion Barger.)

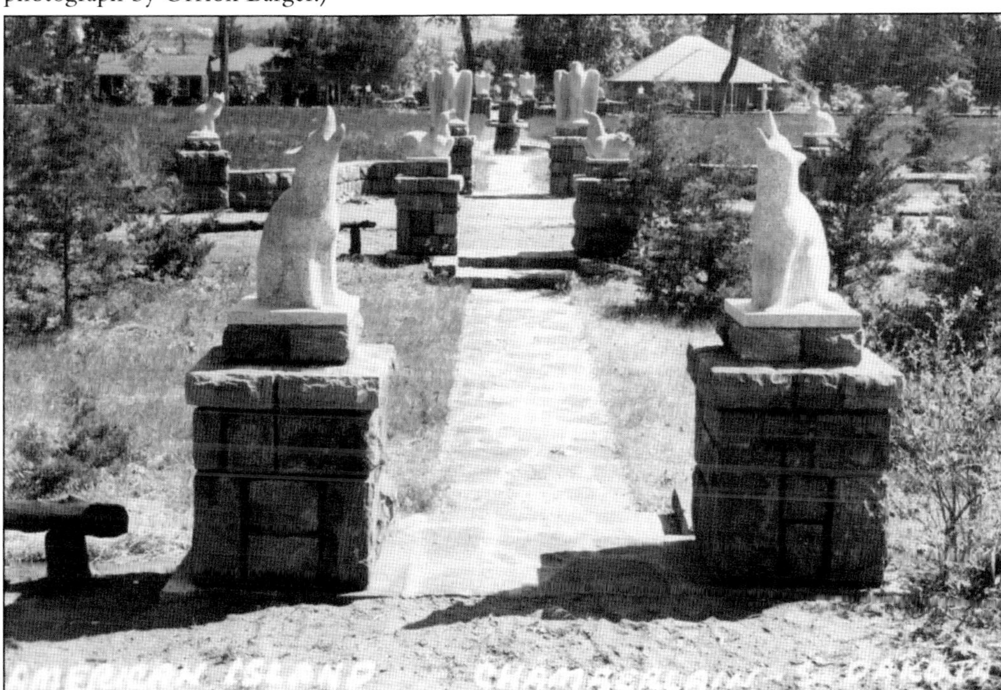

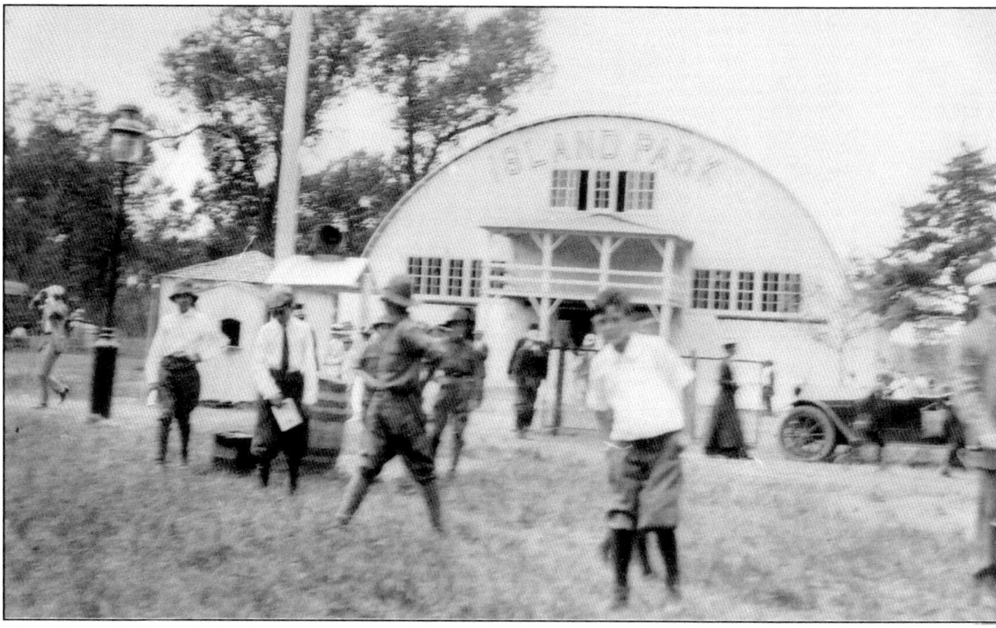

This barrel-shaped building was the auditorium, or Chautauqua building. The first local Chautauqua was held for an entire week in 1913. During Chautauqua, there would be numerous special speakers, soloists, musicians, and plays. One of the most famous individuals to speak here was William Jennings Bryan. Ferries were very busy taking people over to the island for the event. Many others would camp there for the week.

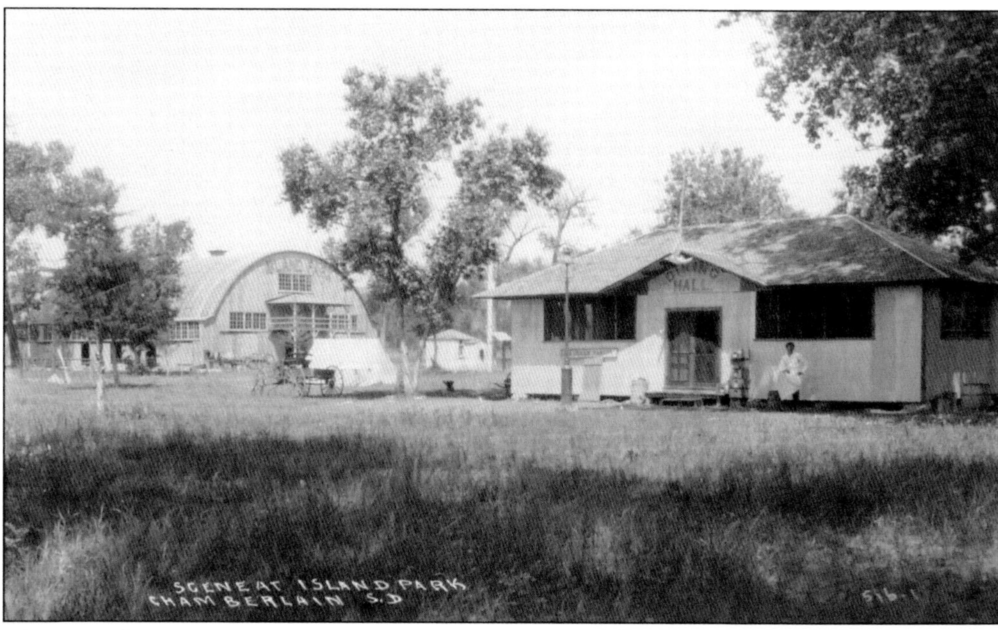

This scene from American Island shows the dining hall in the foreground and the auditorium and dray barn in the background. The dining hall had an ice cream parlor in it. Crates of milk can be seen near the door of the dining hall.

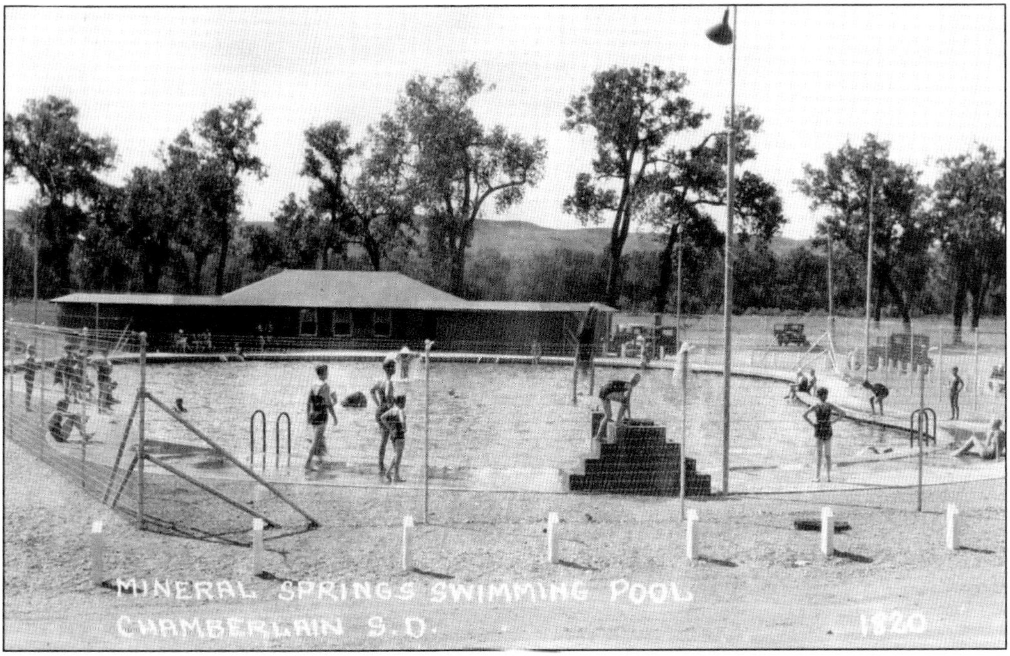

The mineral springs swimming pool on American Island was a popular spot during the summer months. It was a pear-shaped pool, 150 feet long and 100 feet wide. The bathhouse was furnished with dressing rooms, showers, and restrooms. The pool was deep enough for diving, as can be seen in the photograph above. The photograph below shows the fountain at the center of the pool and the Missouri River auto bridge in the background. Some of the other popular outdoor activities available at American Island were golf, baseball, picnicking, rodeo, and horse racing.

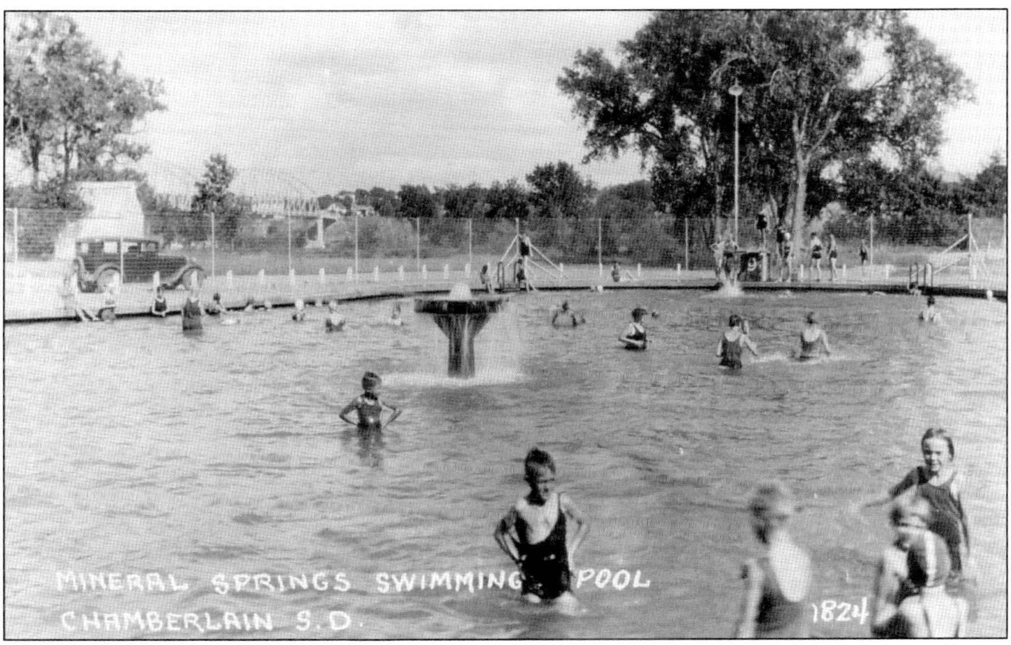

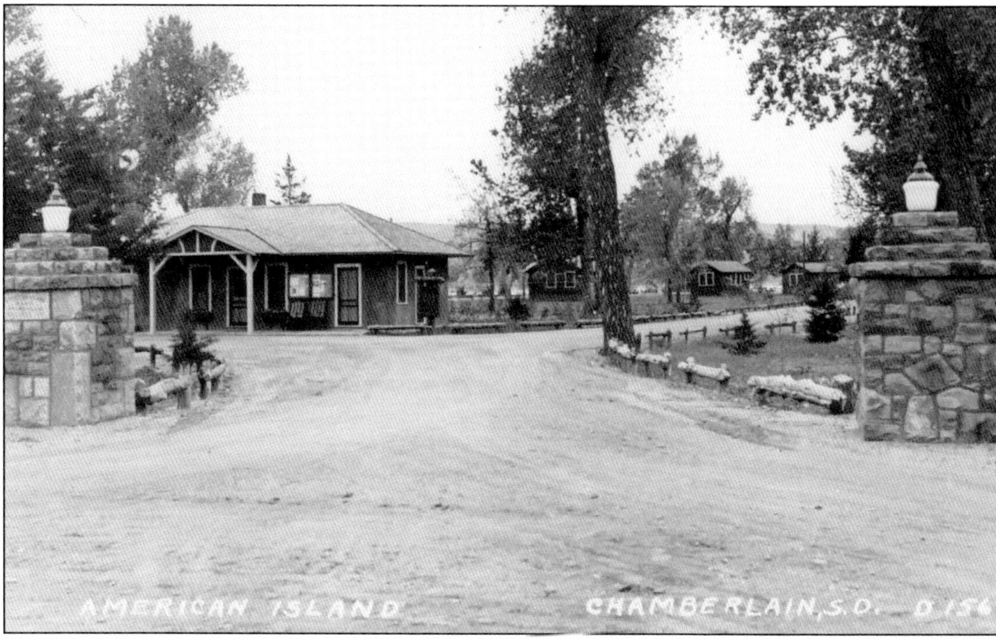

The caretakers' quarters near the entrance are shown in the photograph above. The stone pillars marked the entrance as visitors arrived at the park. Behind are the cottages, which were for rent to campers. The building shown in the postcard below is the Boy Scout building that was constructed using wood donated by J.Q. Anderson. Many farmers hauled the wood to the island, and the building was completed in 1933. It was a popular spot for both Boy and Girl Scout troops from all over the state. The structure was also equipped with showers for use during sporting events.

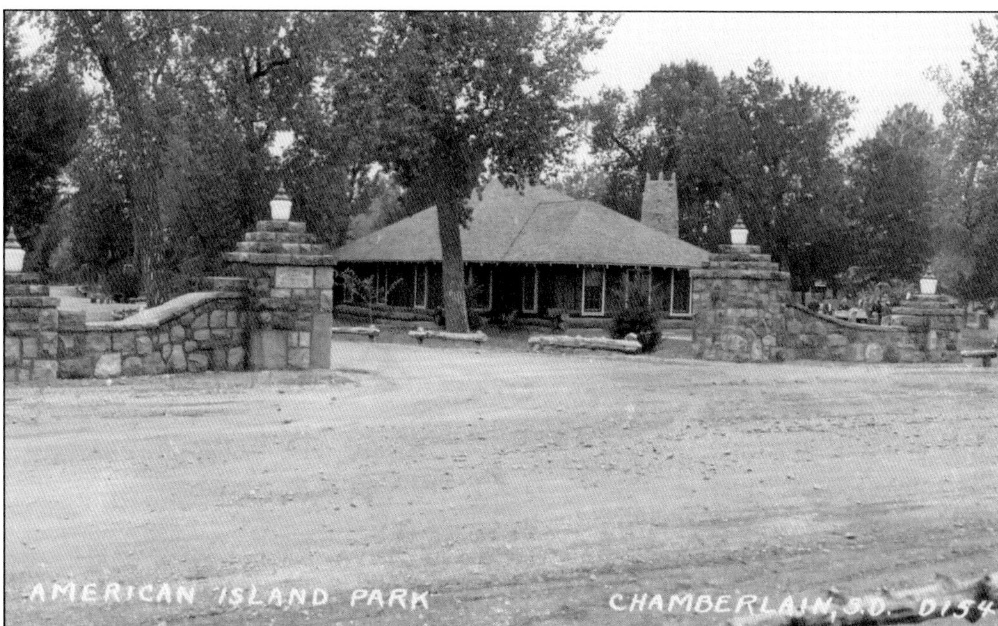

Three

Chamberlain Businesses

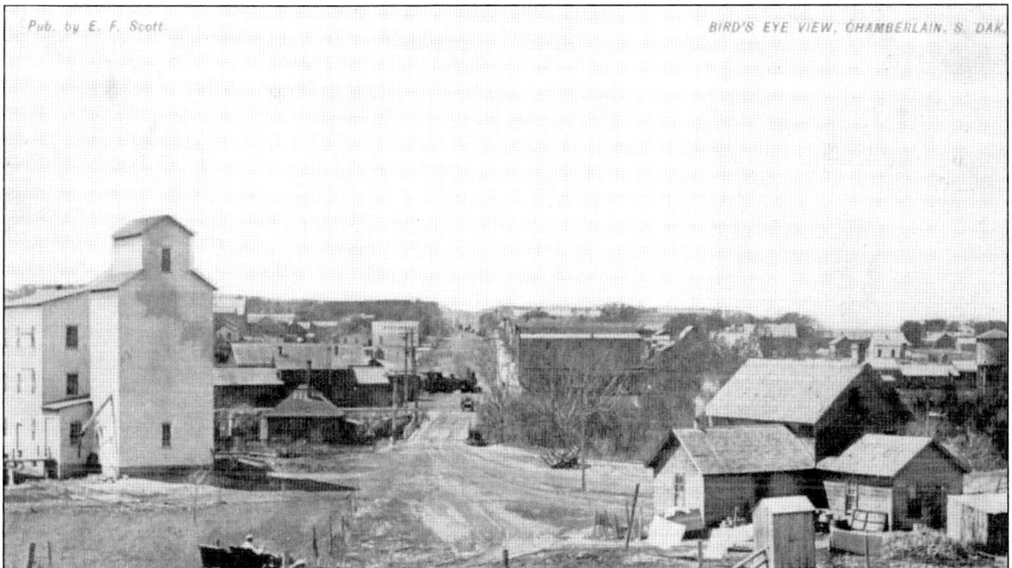

This bird's-eye view is of the Chamberlain flour mill and depot on north Main Street, with the water tower on the far right side. If viewed closely, in the foreground to the right is a privy being held up by two planks leaning into the side.

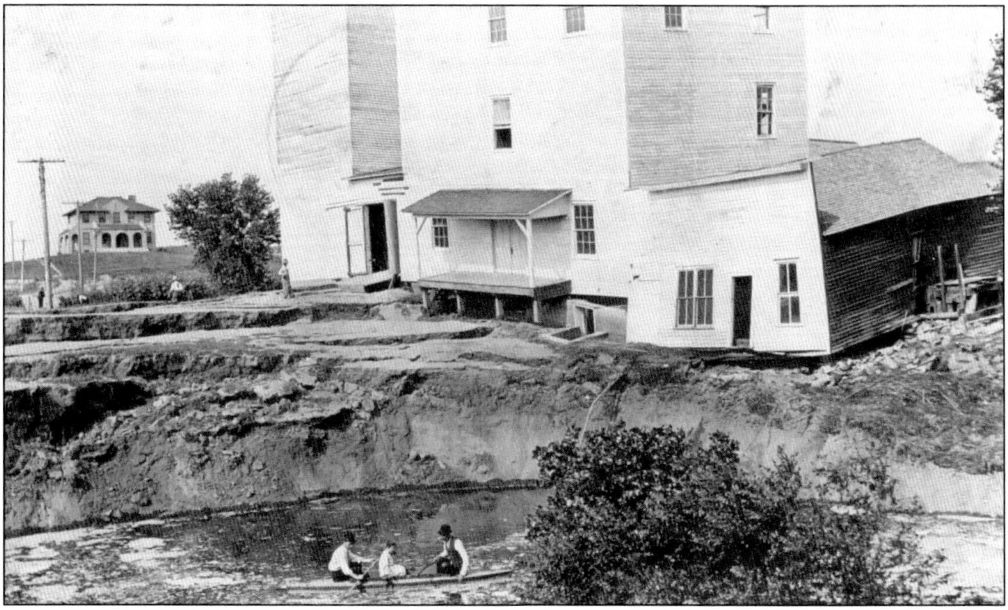

These views show a collapse near the flour mill caused when a well had "gone wild" and was eating away under the structure. The card above was mailed in August 1915 and has the following message written on the back: "Your letter received. Will send you a picture of Chamberlains submerine lake [*sic*]. See if you can tell who is in the boat. Some say there is no bottom in the lake. I think they fished out a Chinaman Sunday." An E.S. Svok signed the card. In the background to the left is a Spanish Mission–style house that was the office for the flour mill and cement plant and is now privately owned. The view below shows some of the collapse near the bridge across American Creek.

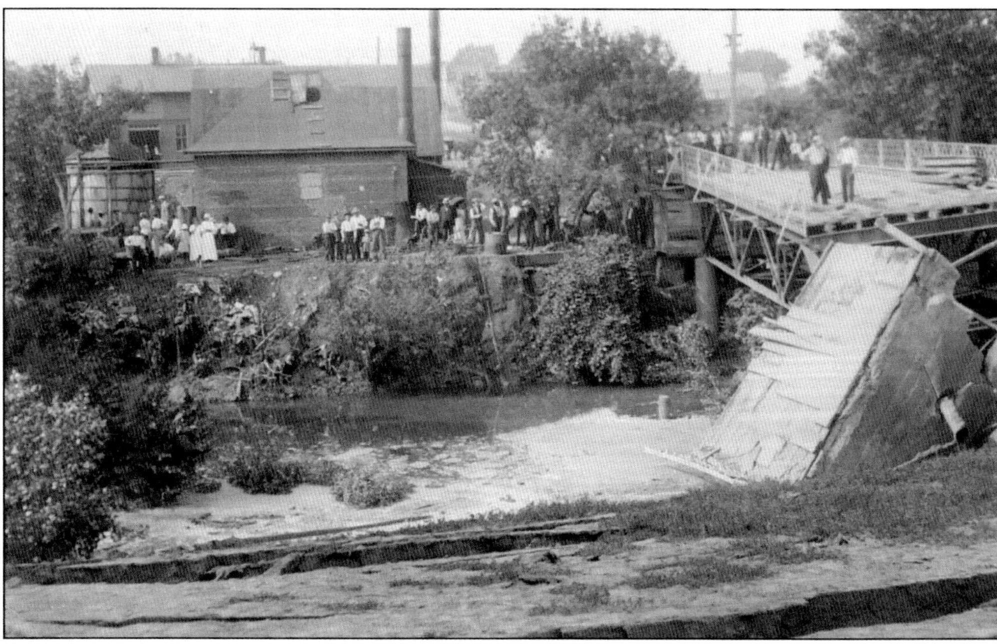

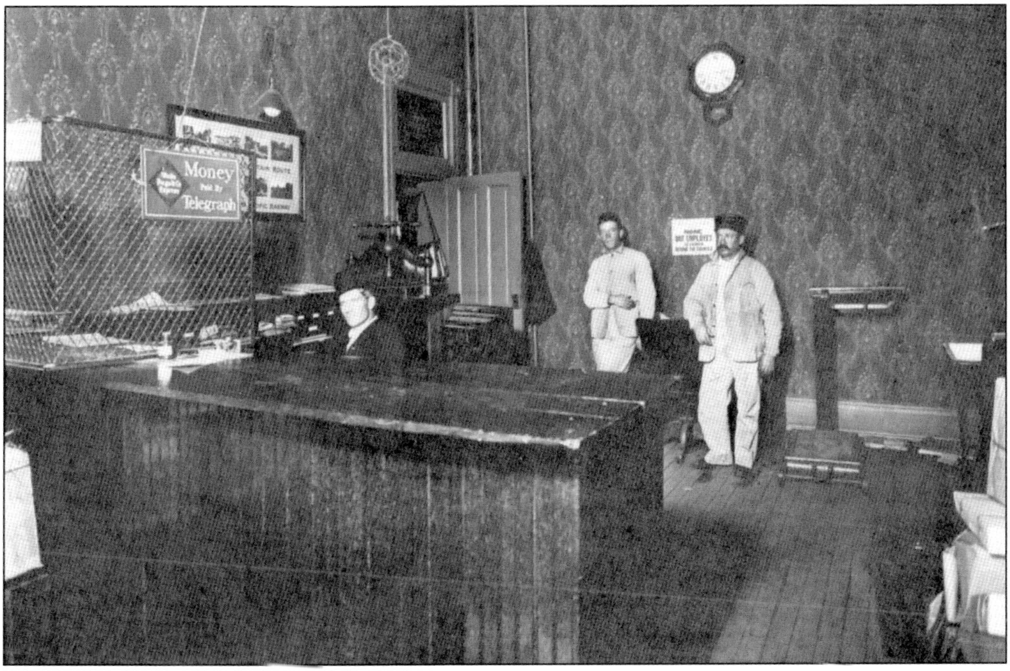

This is the first office of the Wells Fargo & Co. Express in Chamberlain, South Dakota. It featured a large scale behind the counter to weigh items to be shipped. There is a sign that states, "Money paid by Telegraph," along with the Wells Fargo logo. There is also a large press on the back counter. W.G. Cozard is the young man pictured in the center. He was in charge of the office for many years. When he first came to Chamberlain, he was on his way to the Black Hills to run an office there, but stayed in Chamberlain because he fell in love with the area. The photograph below shows the office from the front, with Cozard in the window.

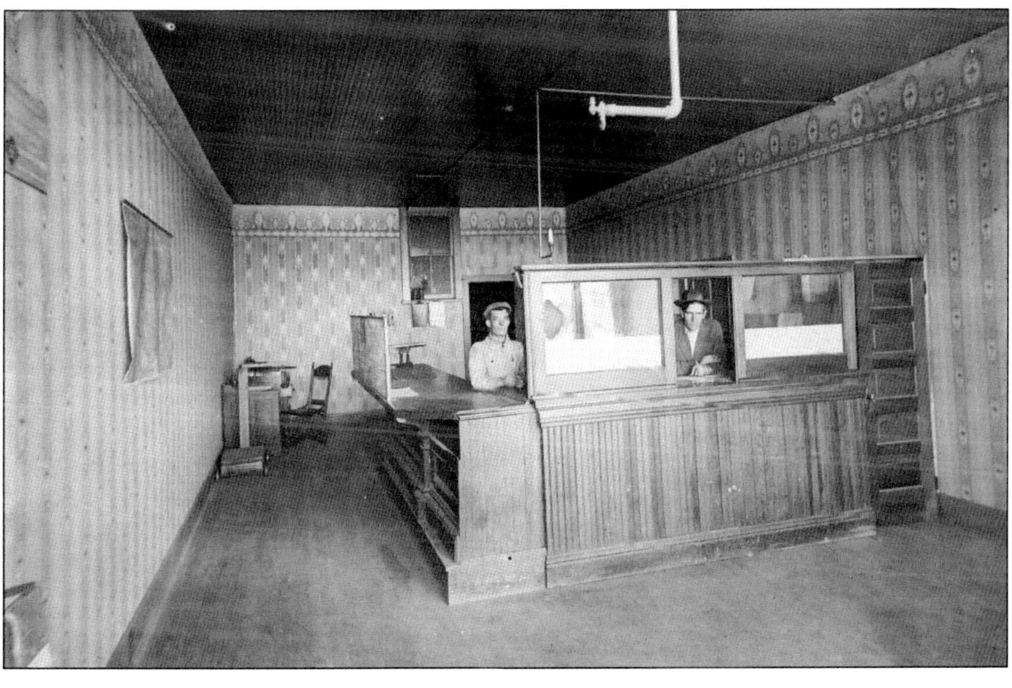

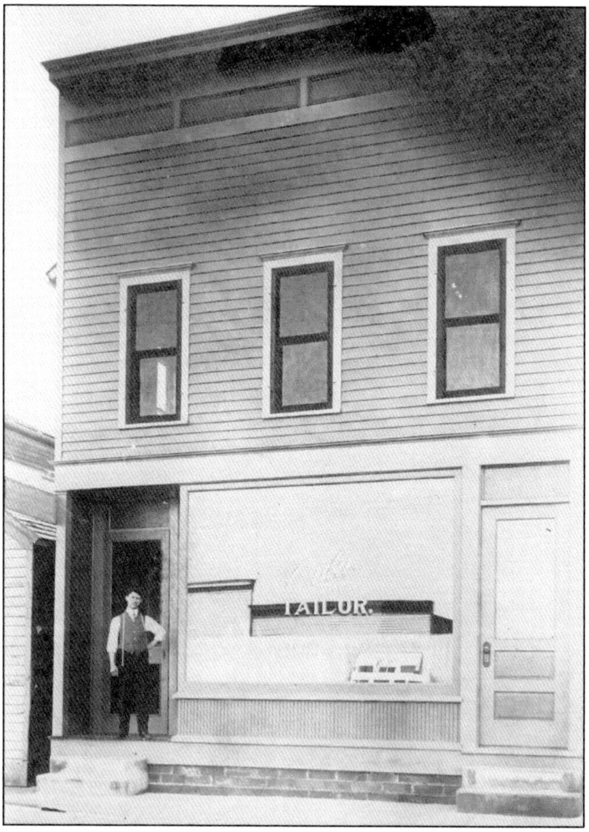

Tailor Frank Duba is pictured standing in the doorway of his shop. This building is still standing on Main Street in Chamberlain and is used by Ameriprise Financial. An expert tailor who could make anything one needed to wear, he was known far and wide for his ready-to-wear suits. In the photograph below, Duba (left) is standing by a display he used for showing how different material would look as a suit with a shirt and tie. The large showcase just behind him is still being used at Old West Trading Post in Oacoma, South Dakota.

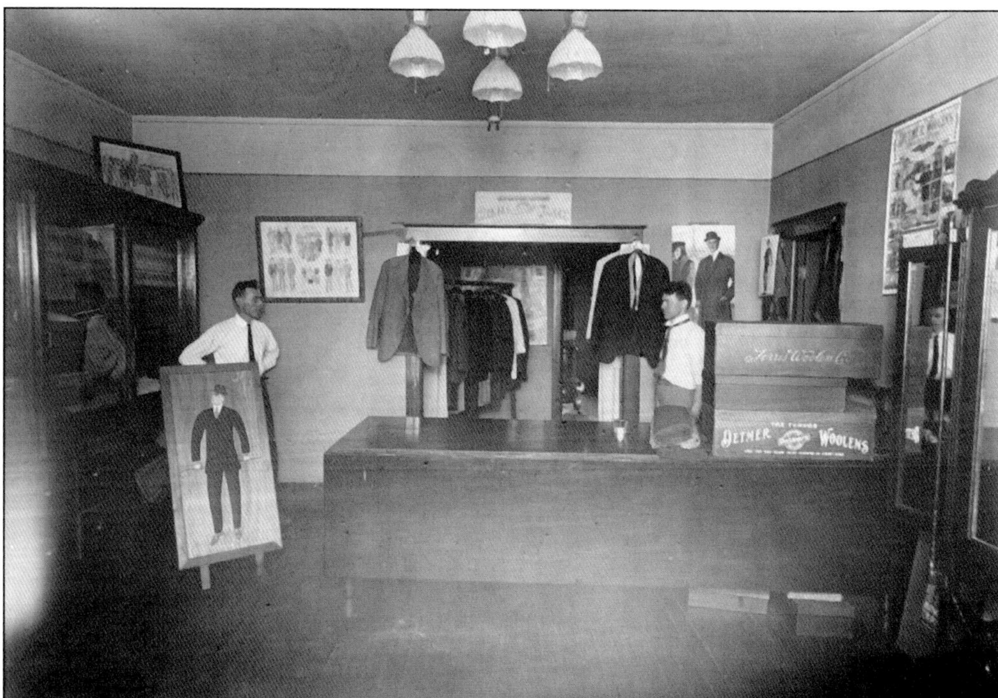

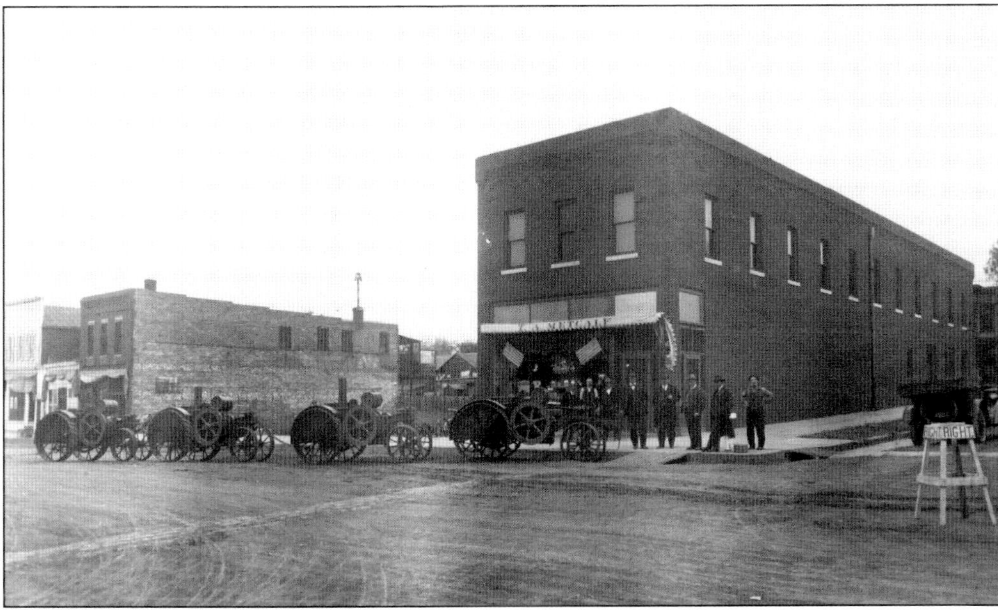

Four new Titan tractors are being displayed in front of the T.A. Metcalf building, which would later become Fuller Drug. This was apparently an important shipment because representatives from the International Harvester Company (IHC) are present in the photograph. Pictured from left to right are H.A. Cuthbertson, Frank Cruisenberry (IHC), T.A. Metcalf, W.E. Howie (IHC), E.A. Jones (IHC), E.H. Henniger (clerk of courts), H.H. Vosburg (harness maker), and J.E. Jamik (salesman for IHC). (Photograph by Judge, Chamberlain, South Dakota.)

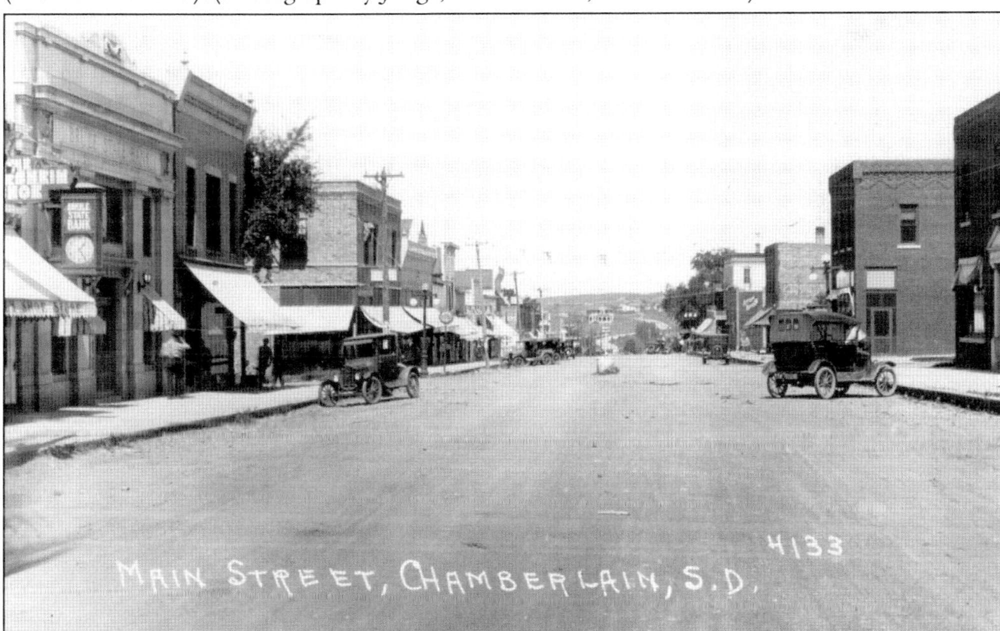

The T.A. Metcalf building can also be seen on the right-hand side in this view of Main Street in Chamberlain. The Brule State Bank is on the left, next to a shoe store. The clock hanging from the bank states that it is 1:25 p.m. Notice that there are no street markings, so one car is parked diagonally and one is parallel.

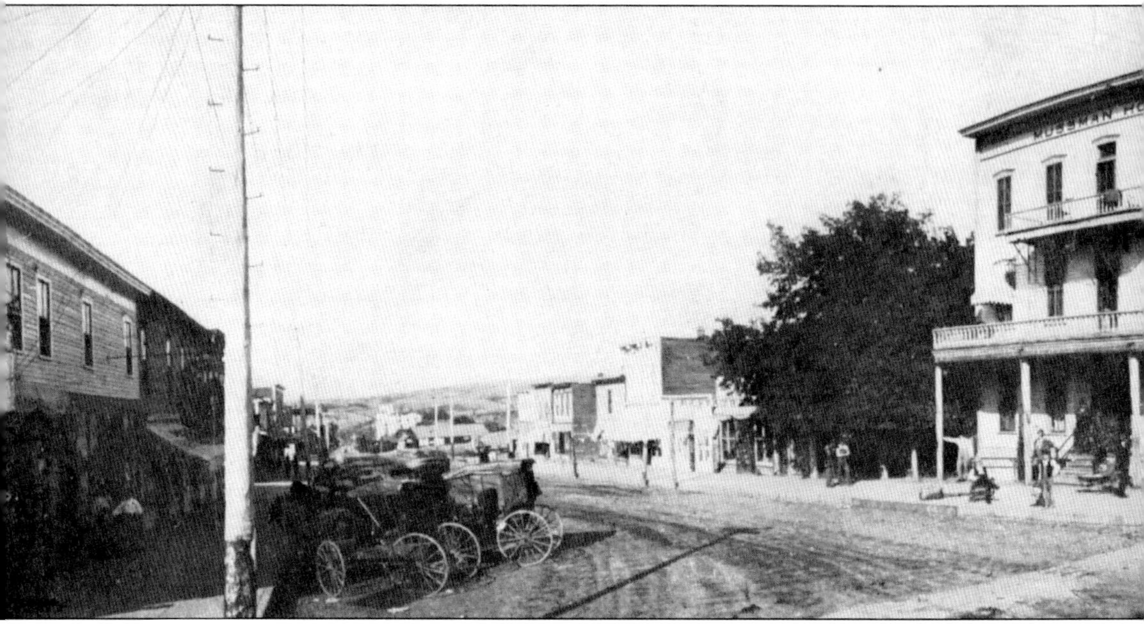

This panoramic view of the corner of Clemmer Avenue and Main Street in Chamberlain was postmarked in 1908. In the center is the Mussman House, and to the right is Banner Groceries. Steamboat captain W.B. Wait owned Banner Groceries, which sold groceries, feed and seed and

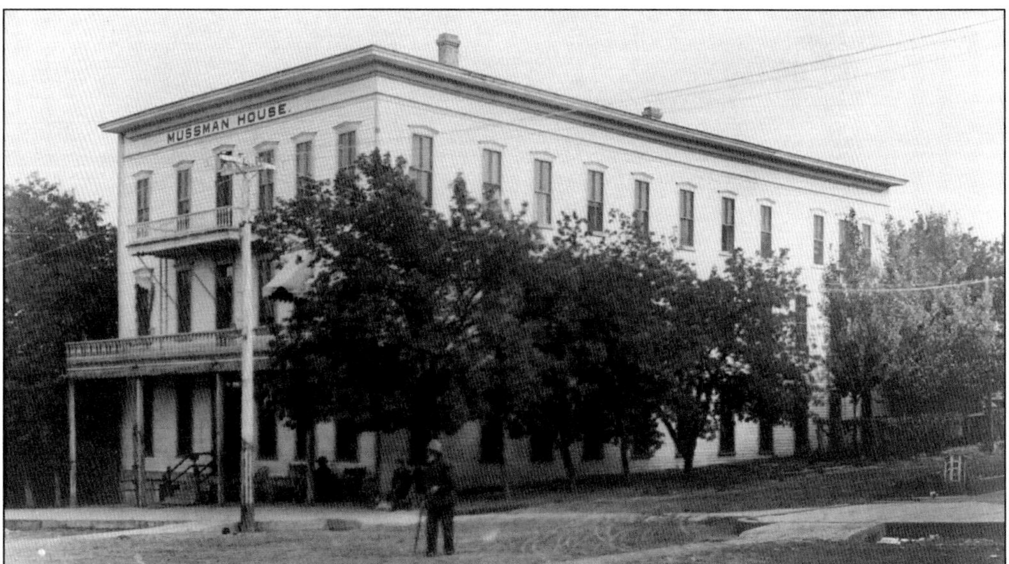

The Mussman House was originally known in the 1880s as the Wright House. It was only a short distance from the depot and was many times called "The Traveling Men's Headquarters" because many salesmen stayed there. Besides offering lodging, the hotel featured a traveling dentist. Henry Mussman took over in 1898, first renting and later purchasing the hotel. It was operated as the Mussman House until 1949. The building was sold in 1975 and torn down soon after to make room for Thiel's Collision Center. Some of the fixtures from the Mussman House were on display at the Old West Museum for many years.

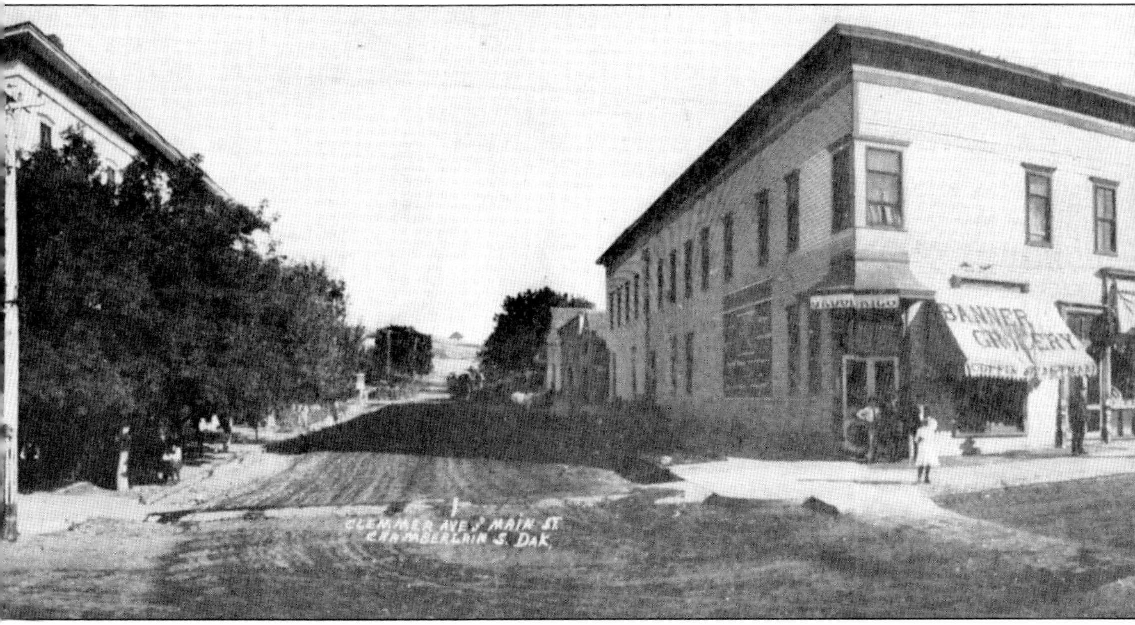

maintained a slaughterhouse in the back. This building would be destroyed by fire in the 1920s and replaced by a new brick structure. Three generations of Waits ran a grocery business at this location before selling out in 1979. A grocery store would be operated in the same spot until 2010.

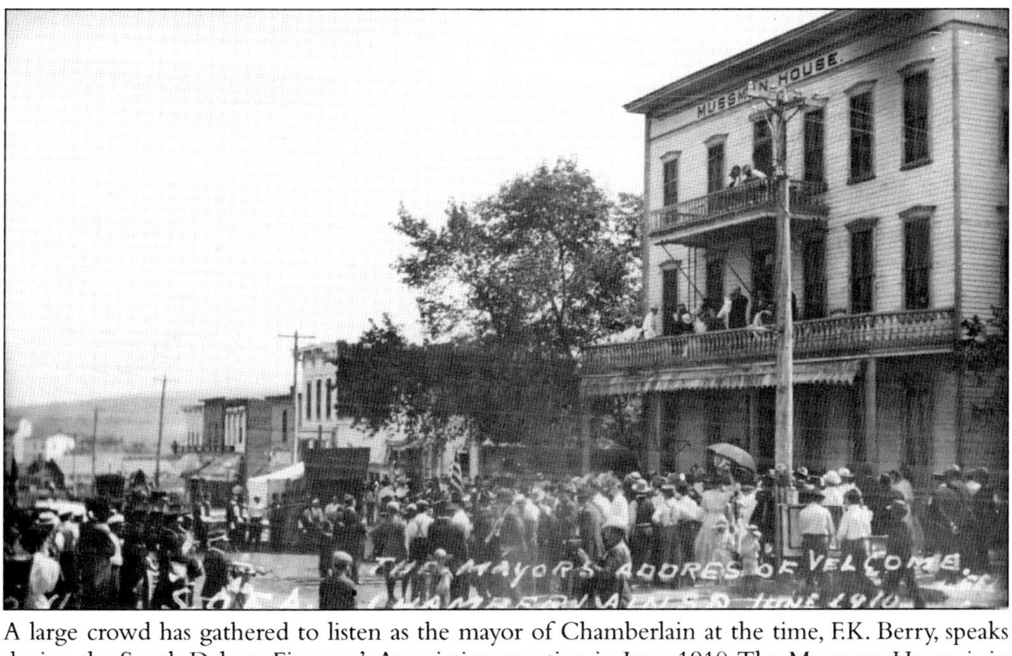

A large crowd has gathered to listen as the mayor of Chamberlain at the time, F.K. Berry, speaks during the South Dakota Firemen's Association meeting in June 1910. The Mussman House is in the background. Notice the people on the balconies on the second and third floors.

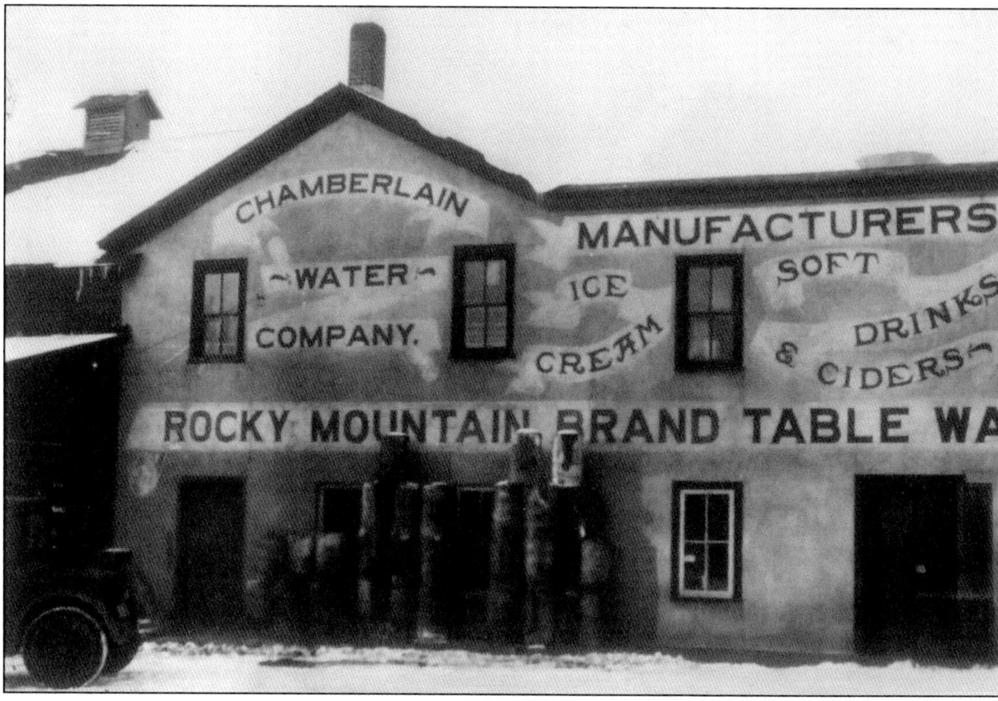

The Chamberlain Water Company building was located just north and west of American Creek. It sold bottled water, soda, cider, and ice cream. Local boys could find a job filling bottles, and many of those bottles, clearly marked with "Chamberlain Water Company," can be found today. Later, the most popular product bottled here would be Pepsi. Notice the containers in front of the building that were used to keep ice cream frozen while it was being delivered to different towns.

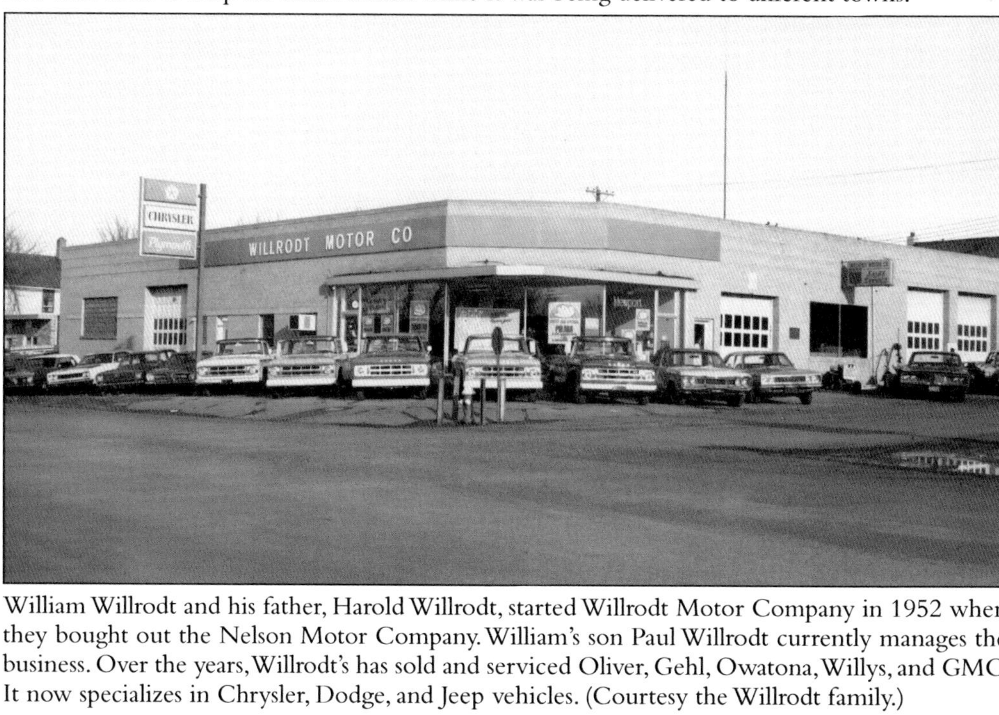

William Willrodt and his father, Harold Willrodt, started Willrodt Motor Company in 1952 when they bought out the Nelson Motor Company. William's son Paul Willrodt currently manages the business. Over the years, Willrodt's has sold and serviced Oliver, Gehl, Owatona, Willys, and GMC. It now specializes in Chrysler, Dodge, and Jeep vehicles. (Courtesy the Willrodt family.)

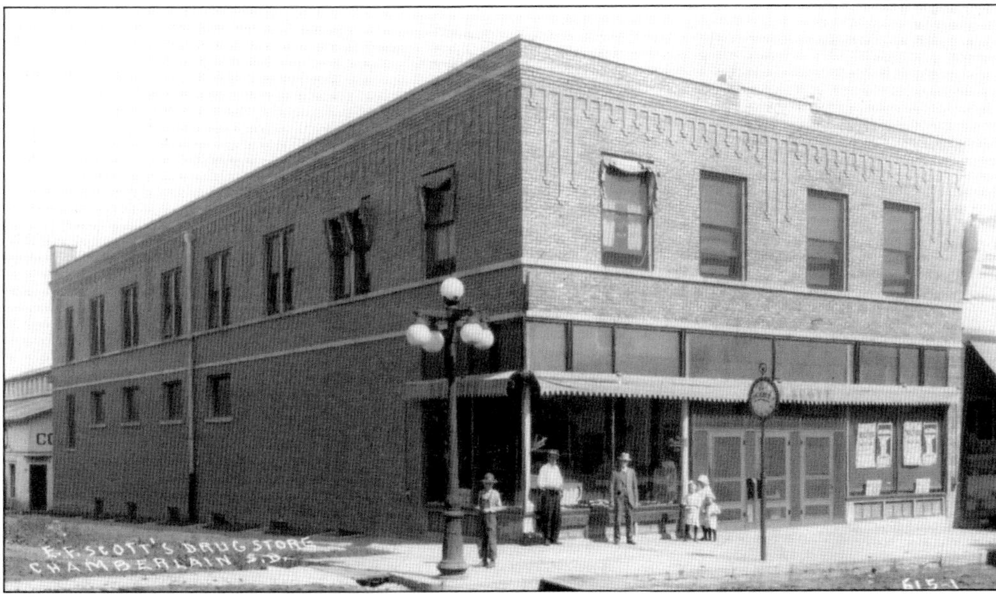

The E.F. Scott drugstore was a tall, two-story building with a basement. Scott sponsored a clock in front of the building, which reads 3:35 p.m. in this photograph. In the windows, there are advertisements for Kodak and Rexall drugs. E.F. Scott's business was later combined with that of the Casey family. This building is still the home of Casey Drug.

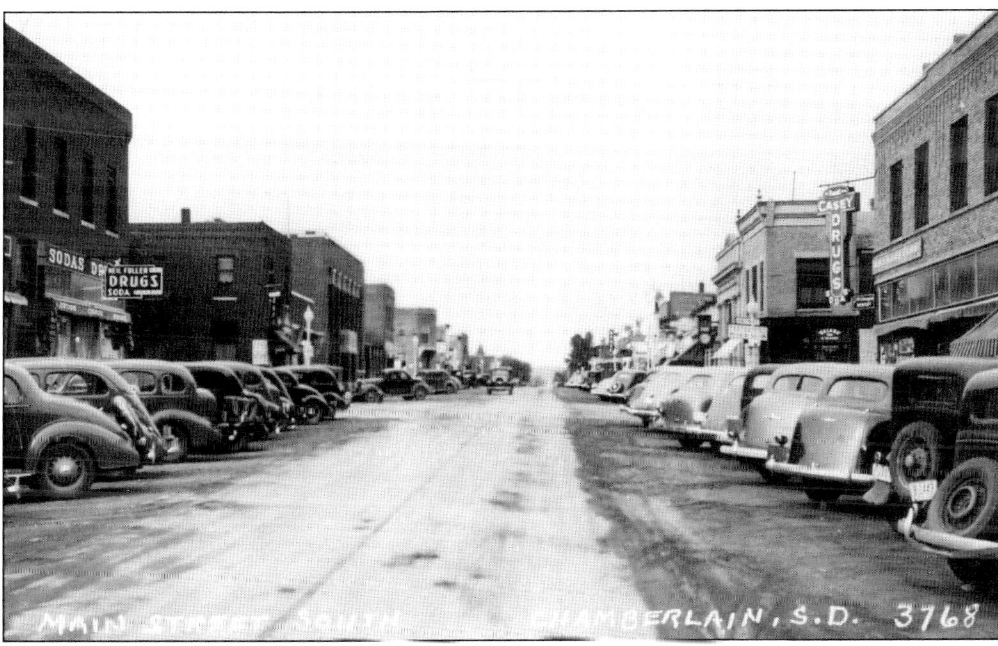

Main Street looking south in Chamberlain is very busy, with almost all the parking places taken. On the left is the Neil E. Fuller drugstore. His awning advertises drugs, cigars, and sodas. On the right is Casey Drug, featuring sodas, drugs, and Kodak products. Further down the street is the Brule State Bank, which later became Northwestern National Bank.

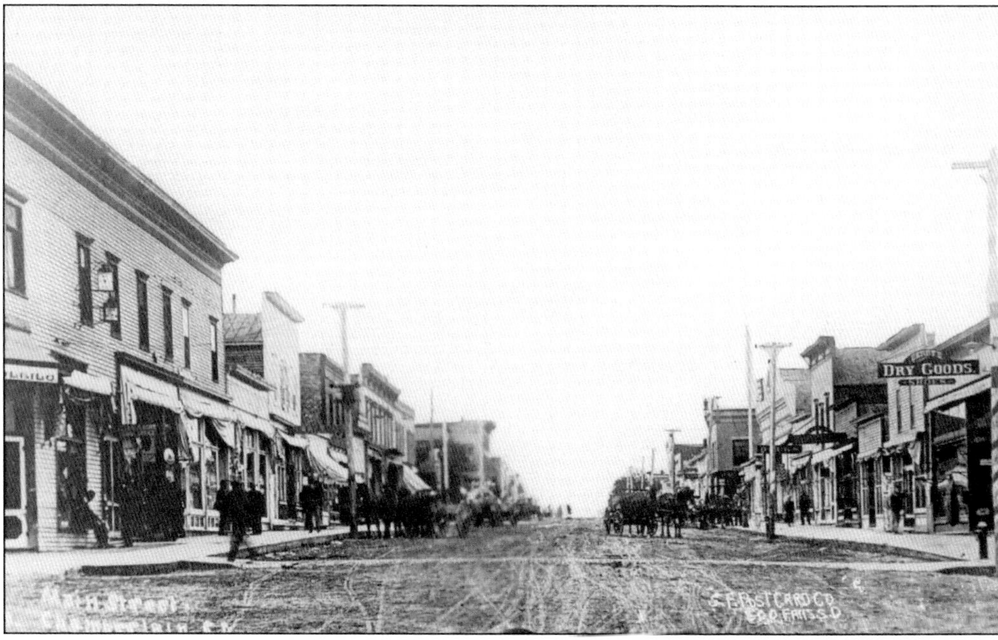

Here is an early view of Chamberlain's Main Street, with not an automobile in sight. A number of businesses are shown, including a government land office on the left. On the right side is Berry's Dry Goods and Shoes. Below is another, closer view of Berry's Dry Goods and Shoes, with a date of August 13, 1919, written on the front. Besides Berry's, N.M. Kramer's Dry Goods and Groceries can be seen down the street on the right. Both views show the dirt-surfaced Main Street of that time.

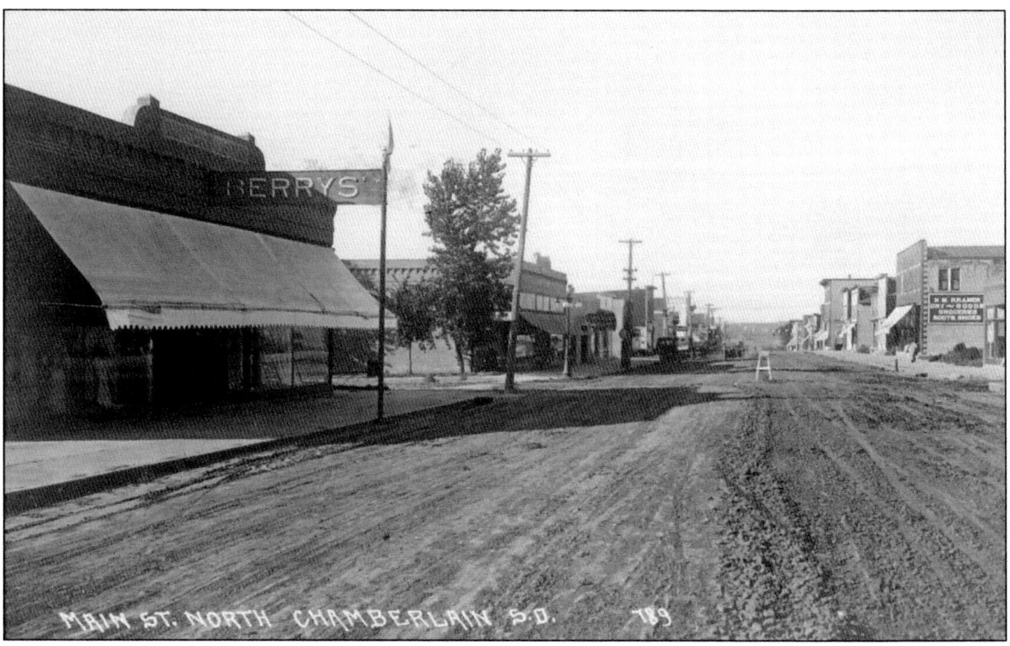

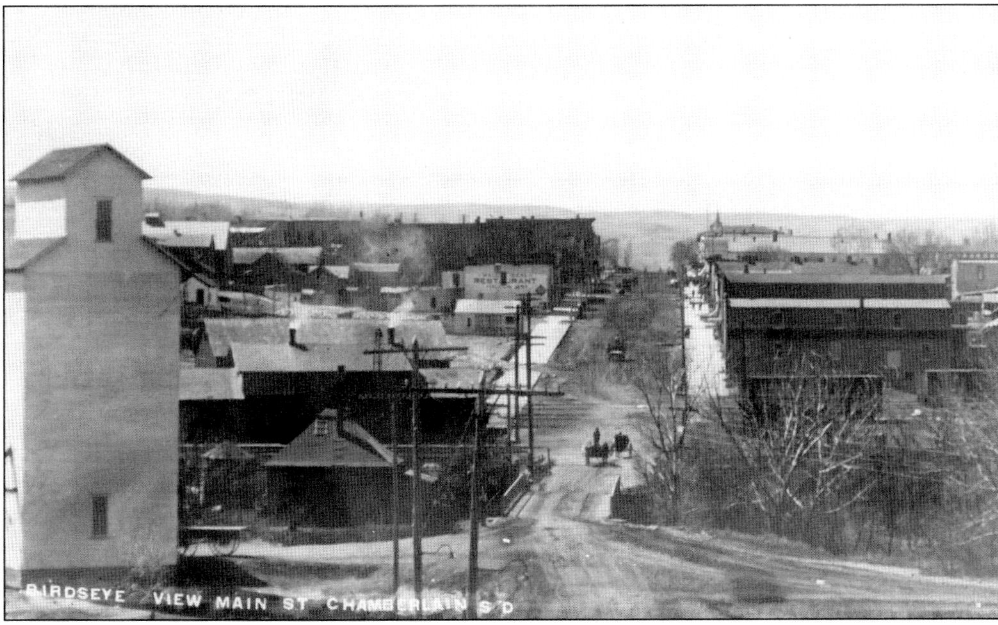

In this bird's-eye view of Main Street, the flour mill is on the left, with the depot behind it. Down the street, there is a sign for a restaurant with meals costing only 25¢. Horse-drawn wagons are rolling down the packed dirt on Main Street. Most likely, these are farmers bringing produce to town and picking up needed supplies.

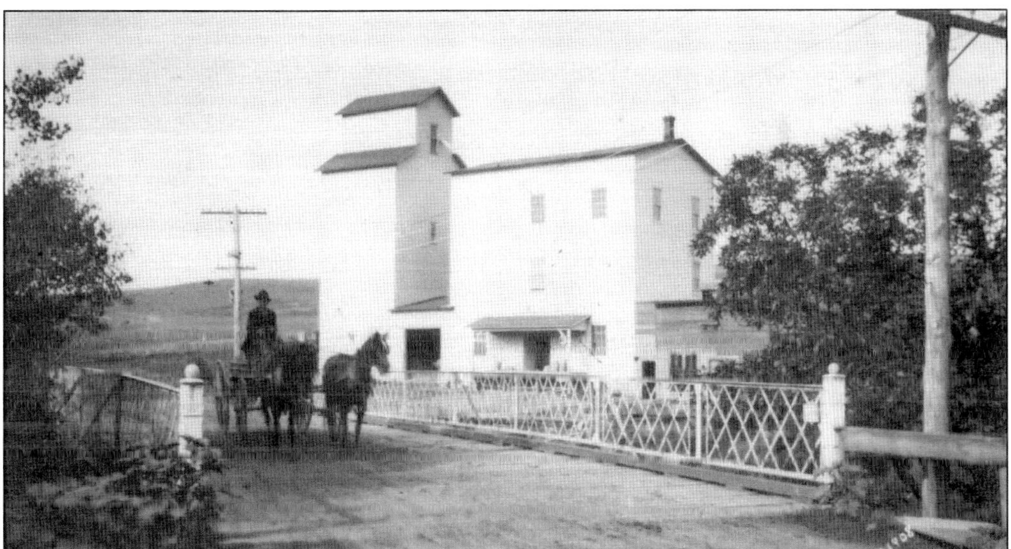

Pictured in 1908 are the rolling river hills in the background of the flour mill and the American Creek Bridge. One might imagine that the man sitting so upright while crossing the bridge is also seen approaching the mill and bridge in the view above. (Photograph by O.S. Leeland.)

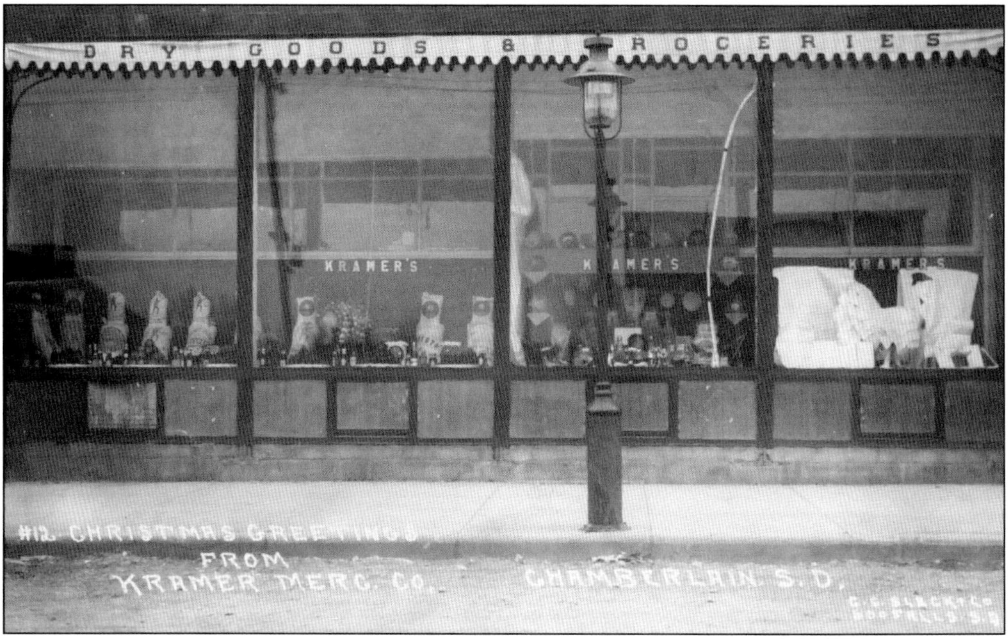

This card was given to customers with Christmas greetings from Kramer Mercantile Company. On back, the following offer is written in longhand: "Send us your orders to be sent by parcel post." N.M. Kramer got his business off the ground in the late 1880s by going to customers in the rural areas around Chamberlain, oftentimes trading for farm produce. N.M. Kramer and Frank Kramer also started Chamberlain Wholesale Grocery in 1903.

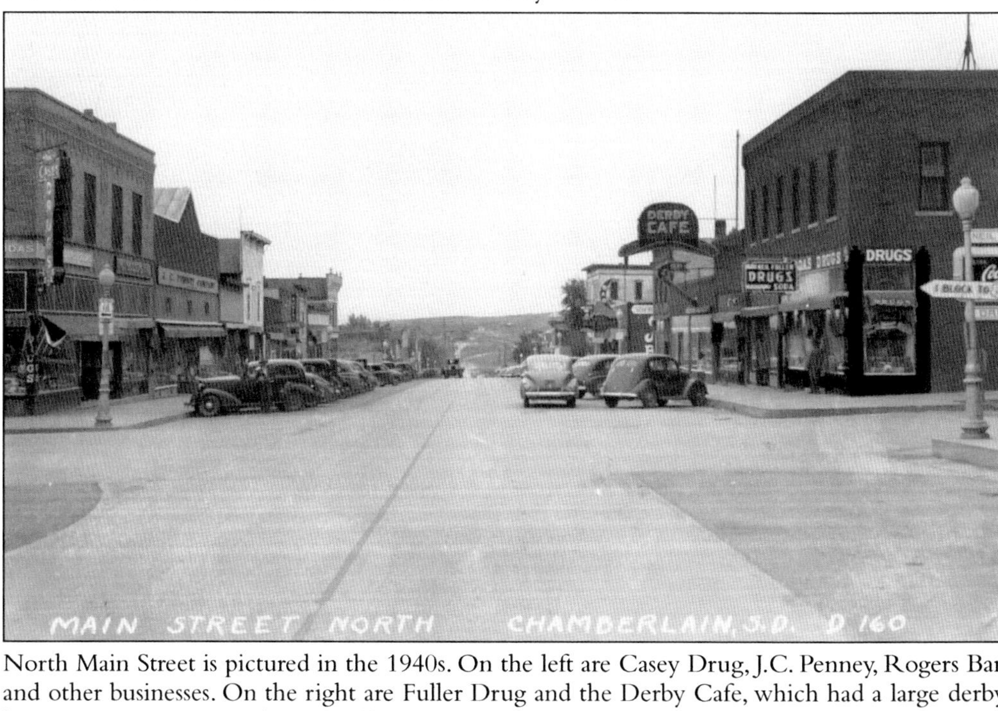

North Main Street is pictured in the 1940s. On the left are Casey Drug, J.C. Penney, Rogers Bar, and other businesses. On the right are Fuller Drug and the Derby Cafe, which had a large derby hat sign jutting out over the sidewalk. On its road signs, the Derby instructed travelers to "look for the hat" when driving down Main Street.

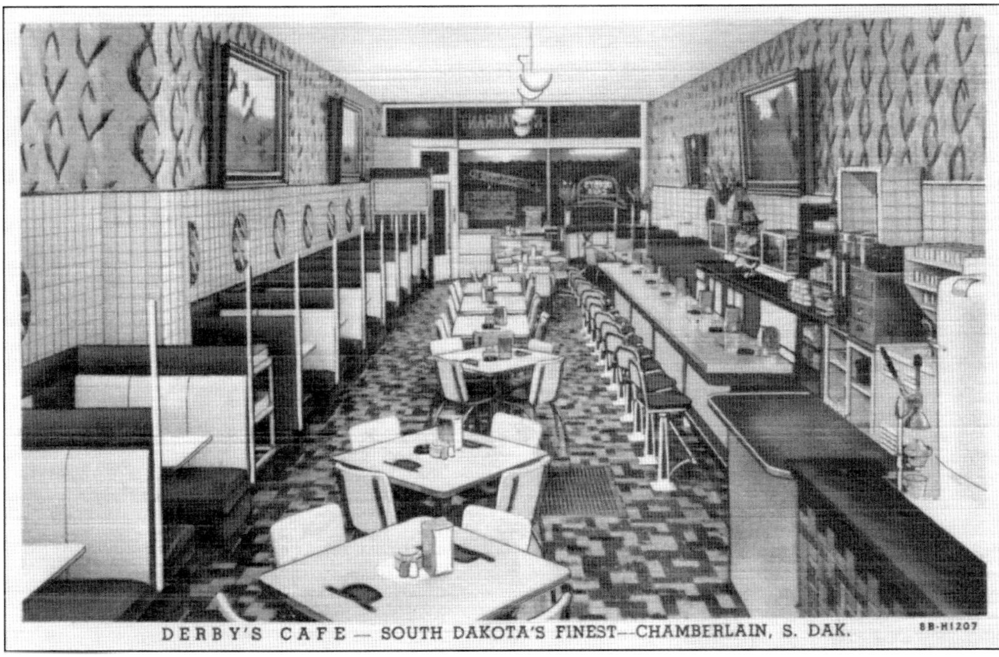

The Derby Cafe opened in 1921. Owned by Orie and Sophie Derby, it was well known for its food, especially its homemade pies. The café was a favorite stop for folks traveling along Highway 16 on their way to the Black Hills or to Pierre for state government business. Duncan Hines's *Adventures in Good Eating* recommended it, as did as the American Automobile Association. Inside were orderly booths, tables, and stools at a soda fountain. The waitresses were well trained and wore neat white uniforms and caps. (Right, courtesy Barry Betts collection.)

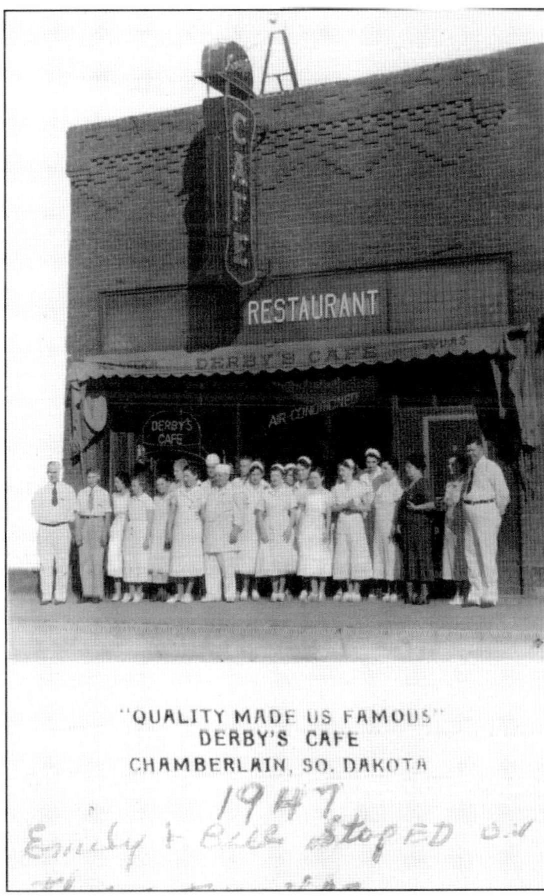

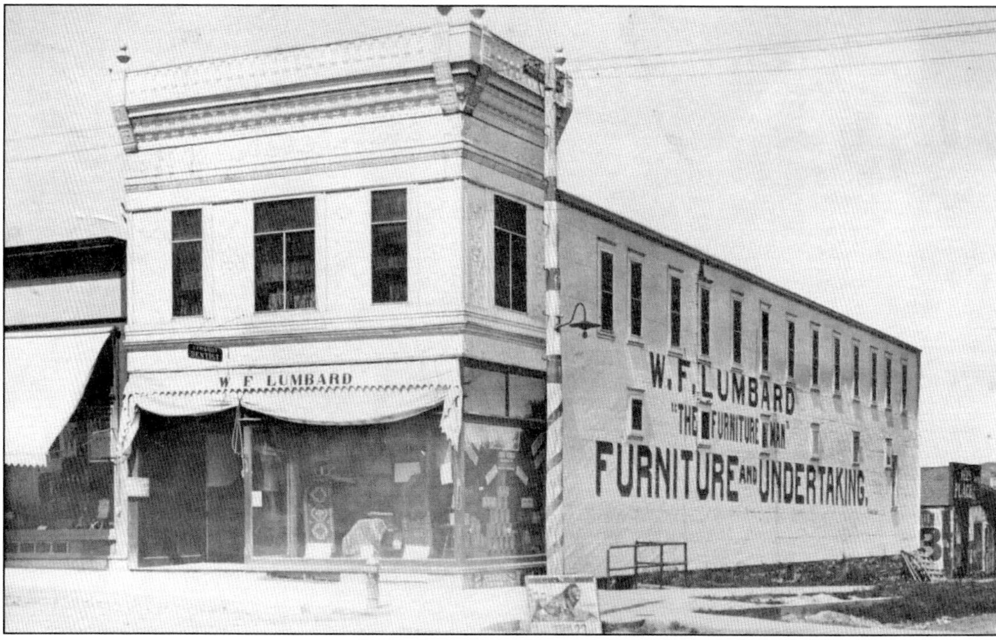

This is the W.F. Lumbard Furniture and Undertaking building, which was a very nice two-story structure with a basement. Many furniture store owners in those days were also undertakers and provided caskets. This later became the Raish Brothers building, where Chevrolet vehicles and other farm machinery were sold.

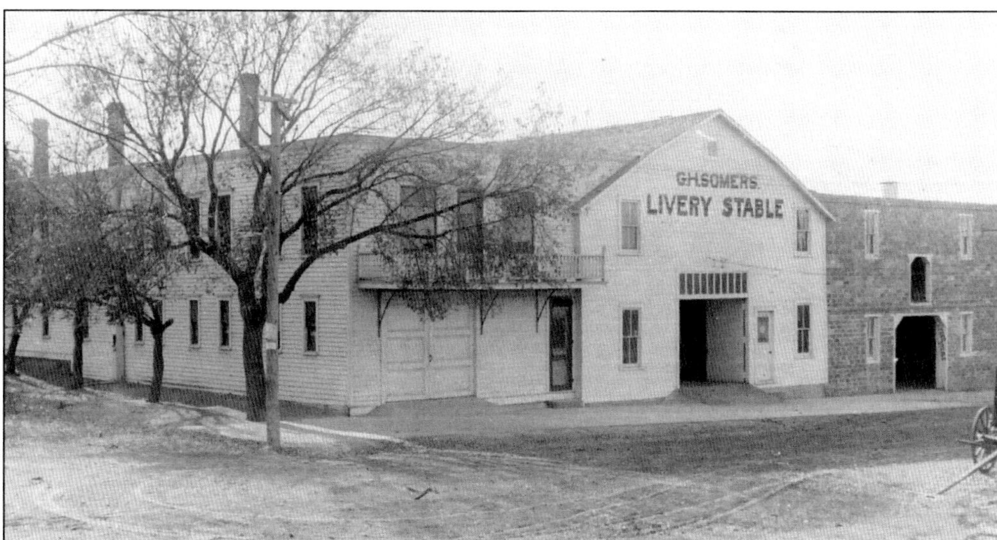

There were many livery stables in Chamberlain and on American Island. The livery stables would take care of horses for their owners. They would also rent buggies and wagons as well as horses, when needed. This large livery stable was owned and operated by Gestner H. Somers, who was also chief of police for a period of time in the early 1900s.

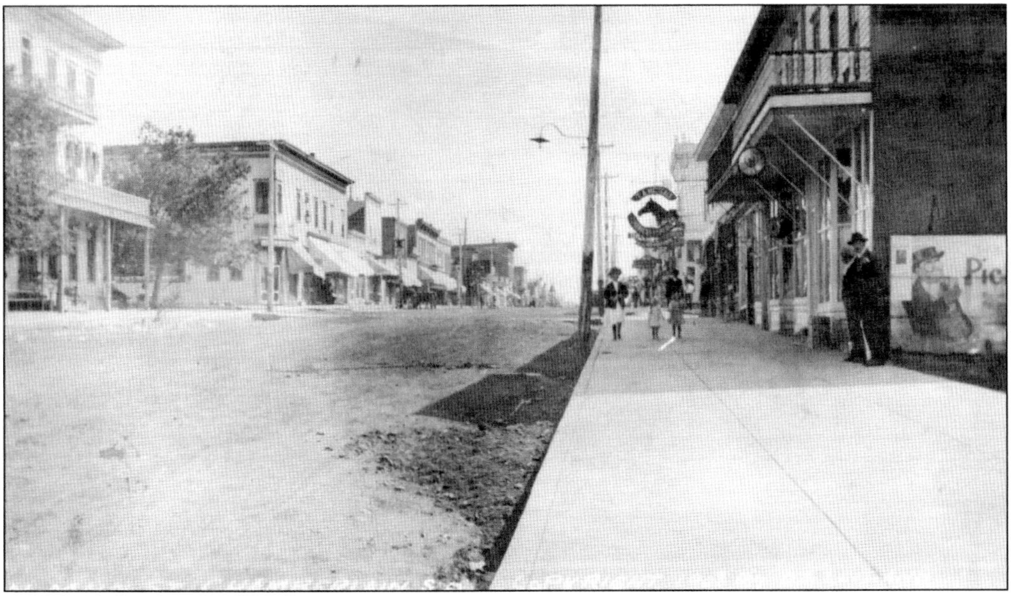

Pictured is a scene from Chamberlain's Main Street in 1908. On the left side is the Mussman House, with a bakery just past it. On the right side is a horse-head sign in front of the T.A. Metcalf Harness and Saddle Company, and a drugstore is next to that. The message on the back of this card states: "at Chamberlain and it is 12 oclock [*sic*] there is no hope of a bed it is a fright over 1500 people walking the street." (Photograph by O.S. Leeland.)

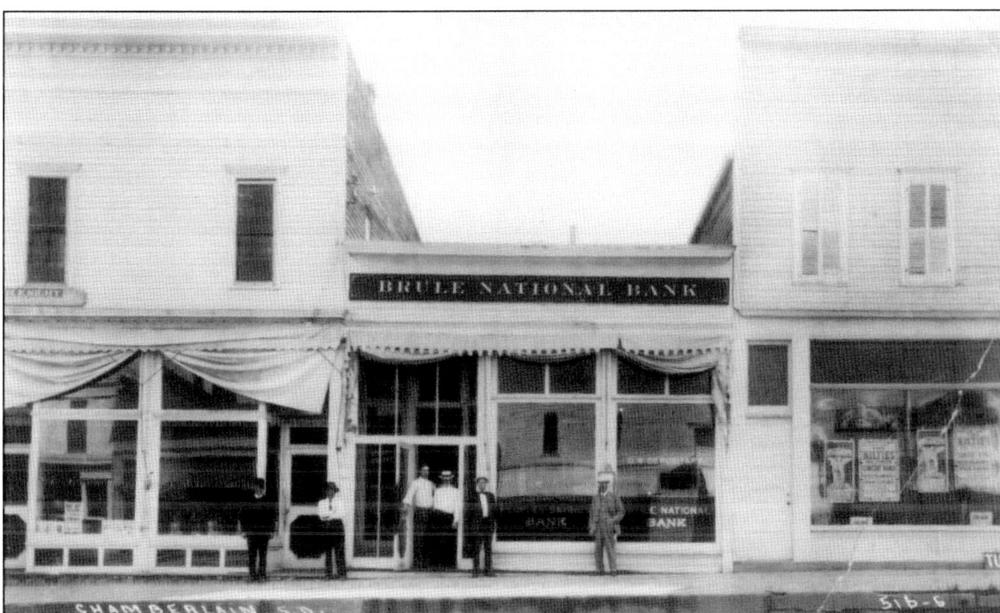

This card features the Brule National Bank, also known as the Peoples Savings Bank, in the middle. The building on the left is J.H. Knight, which was an exclusive men's clothing and shoe shop. It advertised that the finest men's clothing in the area could be bought there. The building on the right is for rent, but it does have a poster for the Kilties, a concert band.

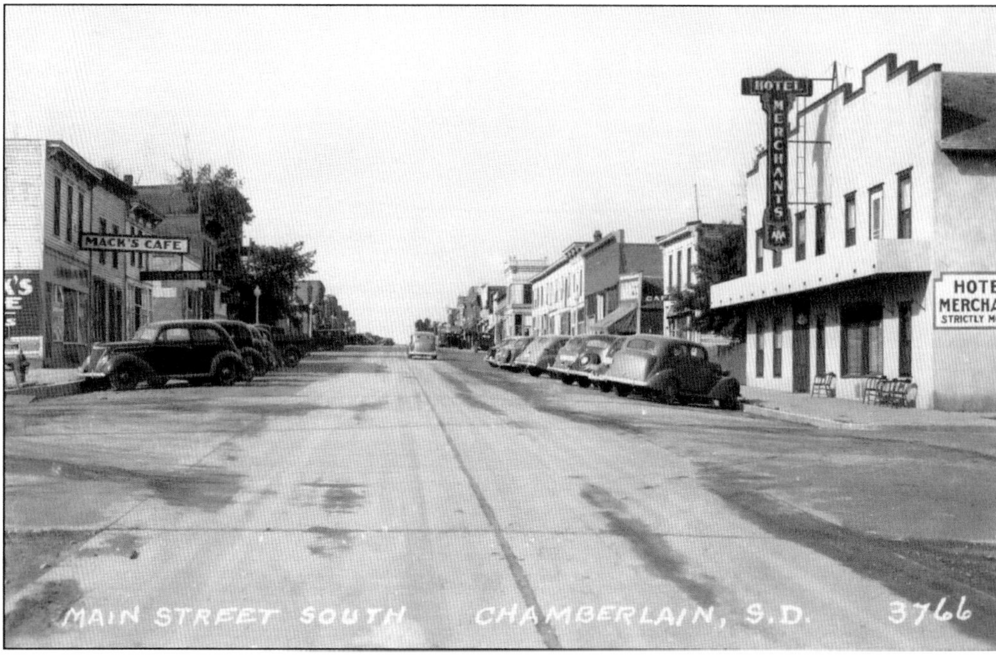

The view in this photograph looks south on Main Street and features the "strictly modern" Hotel Merchants on the right. On the left side of the street is Mack's Café, and next to it was a hide and metal store. Henry Olson operated the hide store during the typhoid epidemic.

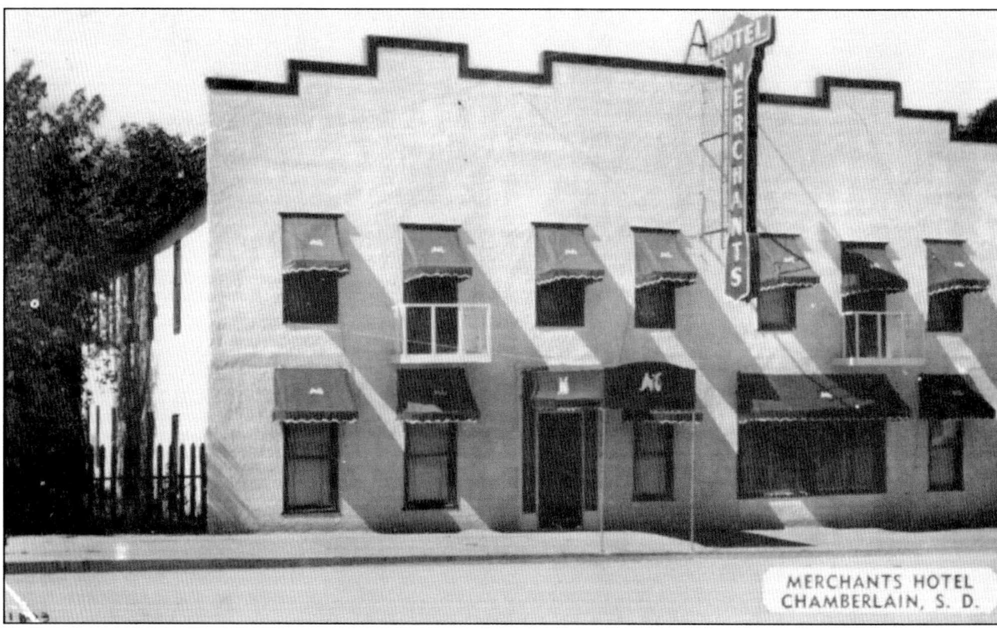

The Pilger family, who were the first white settlers in Chamberlain, was the first to own the Merchants Hotel. After spending the long hard first winter of 1880–1881 in a tent, Henry Pilger was given the first choice of lots on the town site. The hotel was built on that lot. The goal of the Pilger family was to keep the Merchants Hotel the most modern and up-to-date lodging in town. It was torn down in the 1960s.

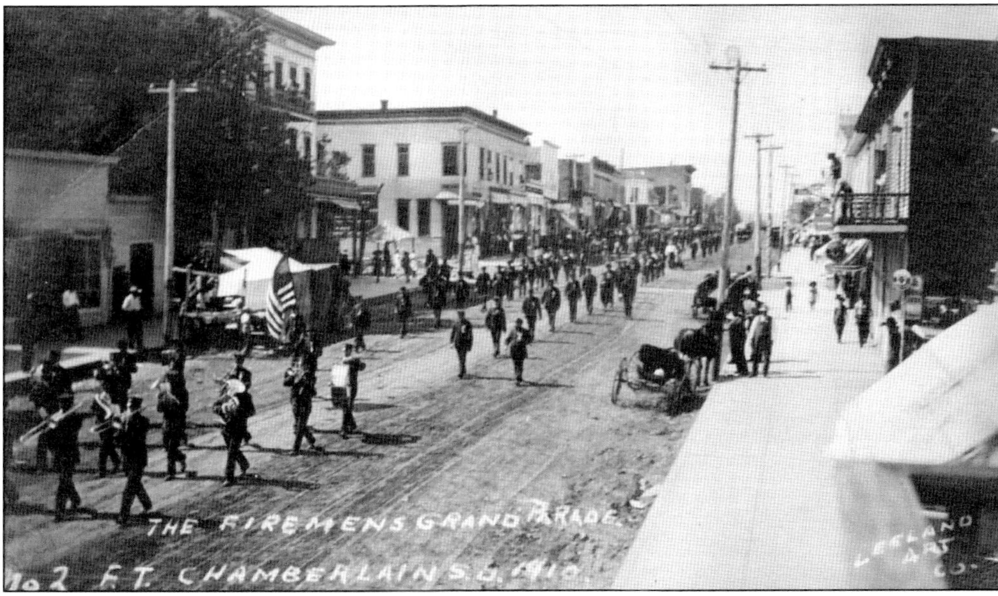

Spectators are watching the Firemen's Grand Parade No. 2 F.T. at Chamberlain from the street and from balconies on the second story of businesses. This 1910 parade was part of a state gathering of firemen and was no doubt quite an event to witness.

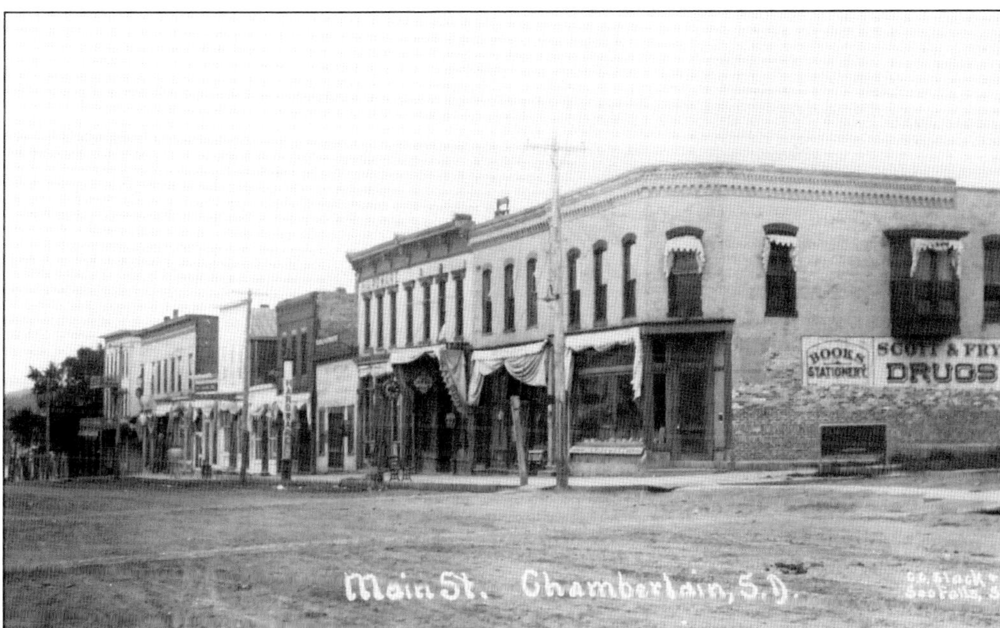

This is the original Scott and Fry Drugstore. Note the interesting balcony on the side of the building just above the sign advertising books and stationery. This building was destroyed by fire along with the cafe next to it and a hardware and implement shop. After the fire, E.F. Scott rebuilt across the street. The message on back is dated 1912, which was not long before the fire occurred.

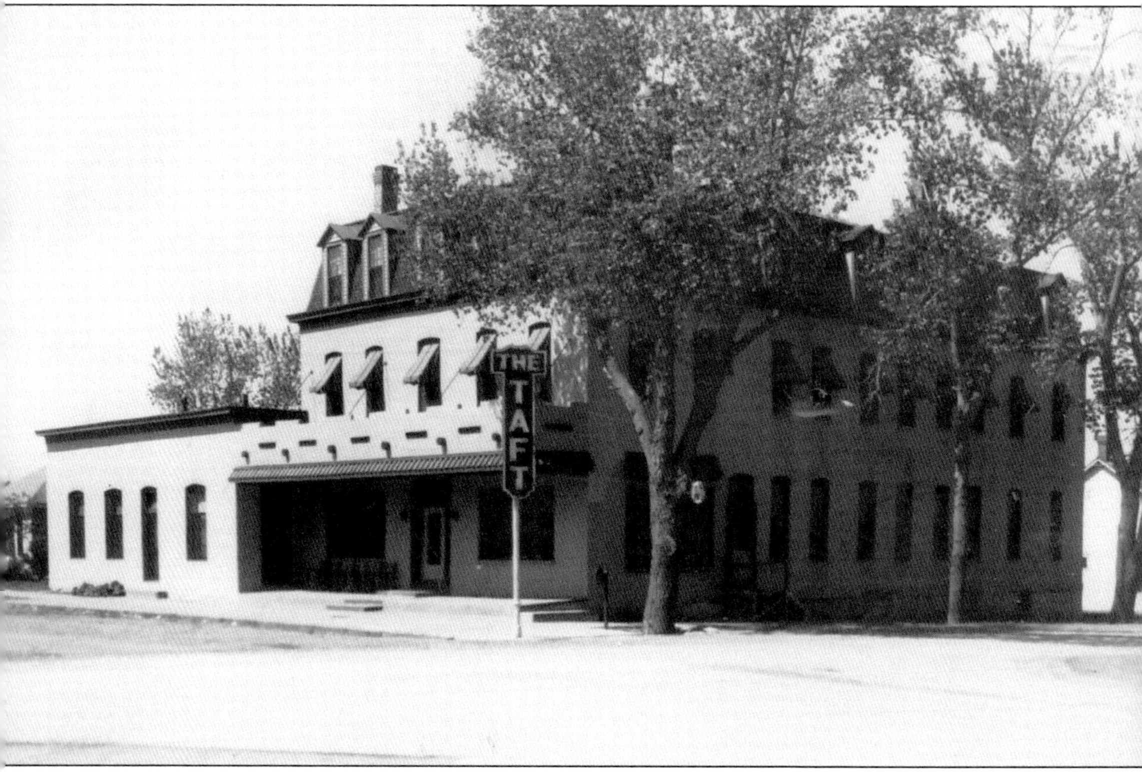

When Fort Hale was abandoned, E.B. Taft bought all the buildings and tore them down. He then brought wood, doors, and usable fixtures down the frozen river to Chamberlain and built the Taft Hotel. The grand opening of the hotel was in February 1891. Taft later added a porch on the front so visitors could sit and watch the summer activities in Chamberlain. One of the magnificent features of the Taft was its large and ornate fireplace mantle. It was said that Gen. Ulysses S. Grant warmed himself by the fireplace when it was in the officers' quarters at Fort Hale. The Taft was the finest hotel between Sioux Falls and the Black Hills for many years. In the late 1980s, it was moved close to the Interstate 90 exit to be used for tourist information and specialty shops. Sadly, it burned to the ground in 1990 before the project was finished. (Courtesy Barry Betts collection.)

Four

Around Town

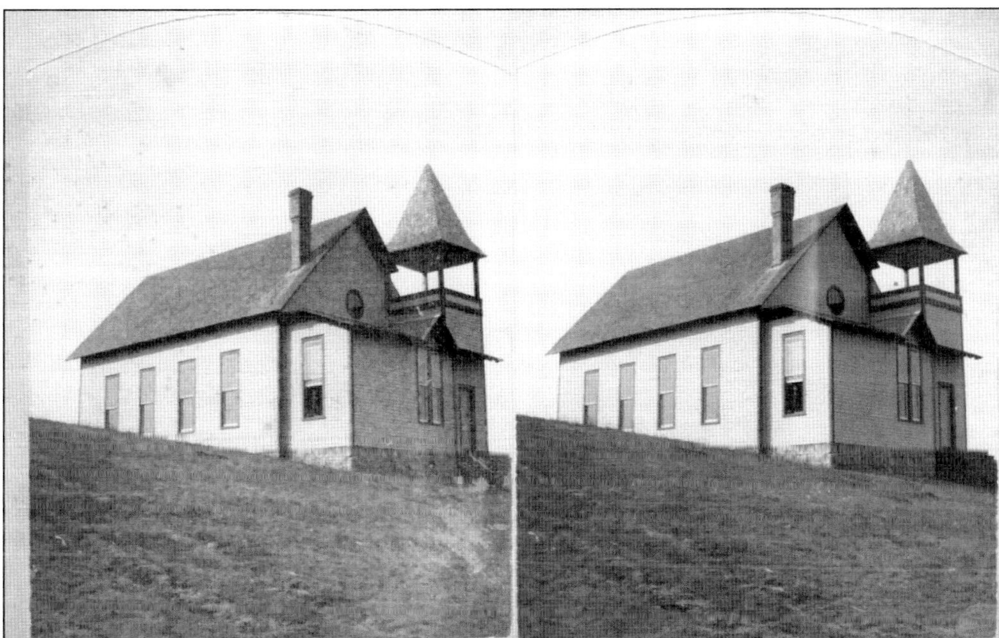

This early stereoscopic photograph is of the First Congregational Church in Chamberlain. It was built in 1881—before South Dakota became a state—at a cost of $2,050, of which Chamberlain's namesake, Selah Chamberlain, gave $300. Rev. William Thrall led the first services. (Photograph by W.H. Troth.)

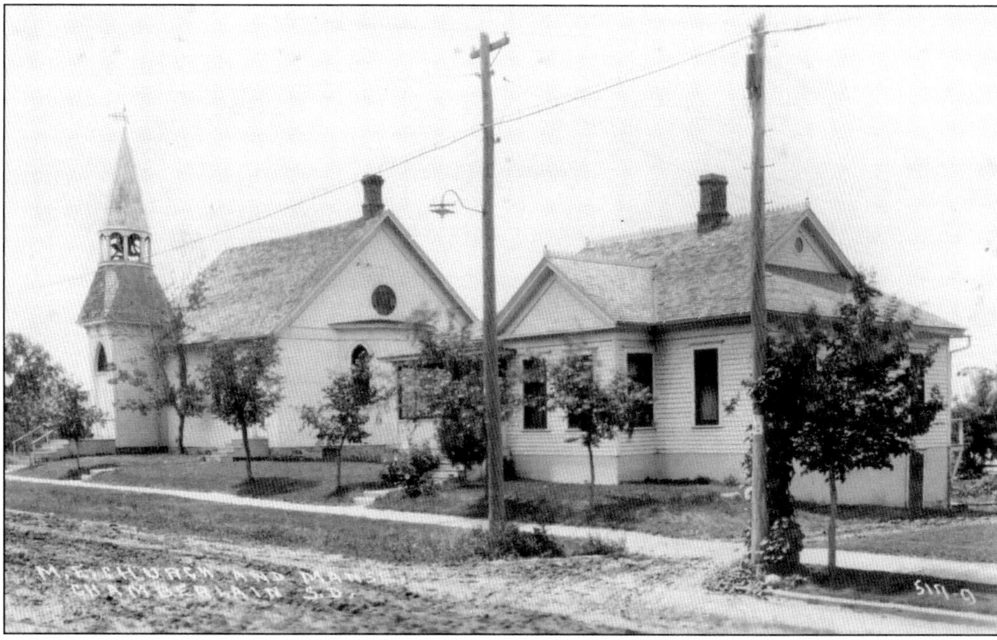

The Methodist Episcopal church and manse are shown in this early postcard. The Methodist Church was organized in Chamberlain in 1898, and the church was built in 1900. It would later merge with the Congregational Church to form the United Church of Christ. Notice the small round window and the steeple with a directional arrow on top.

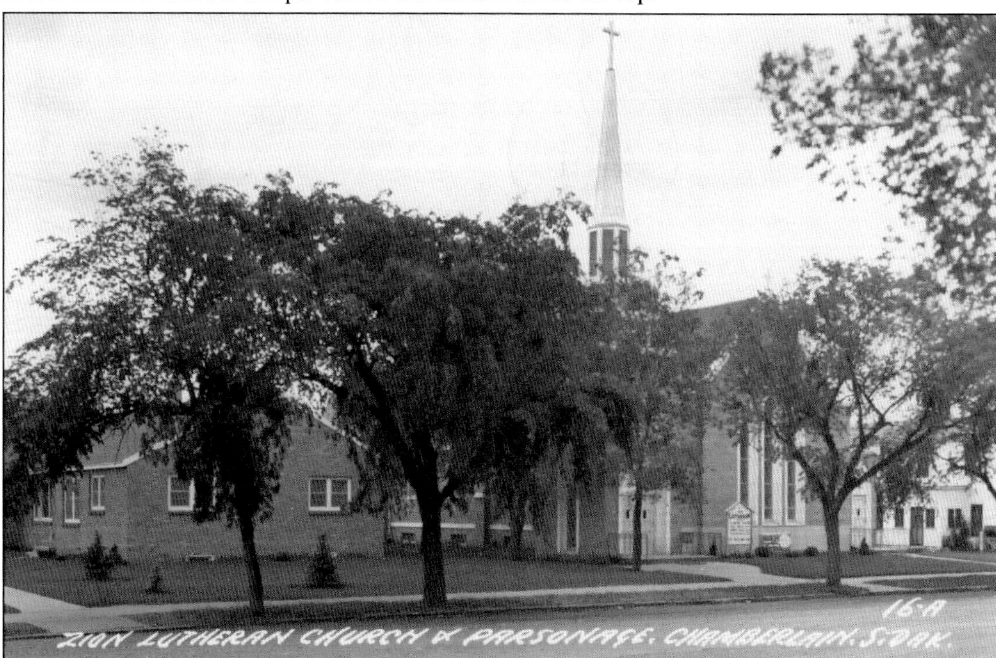

The Zion Lutheran Church was built on Main Street in 1950, and the parsonage was built in 1952. There were several Lutheran congregations in the area in the early 1900s. In 1917, Red Lake, West Point, and Chamberlain joined to form one congregation at Chamberlain. This body joined the Missouri Synod in 1920. It is still an active congregation today.

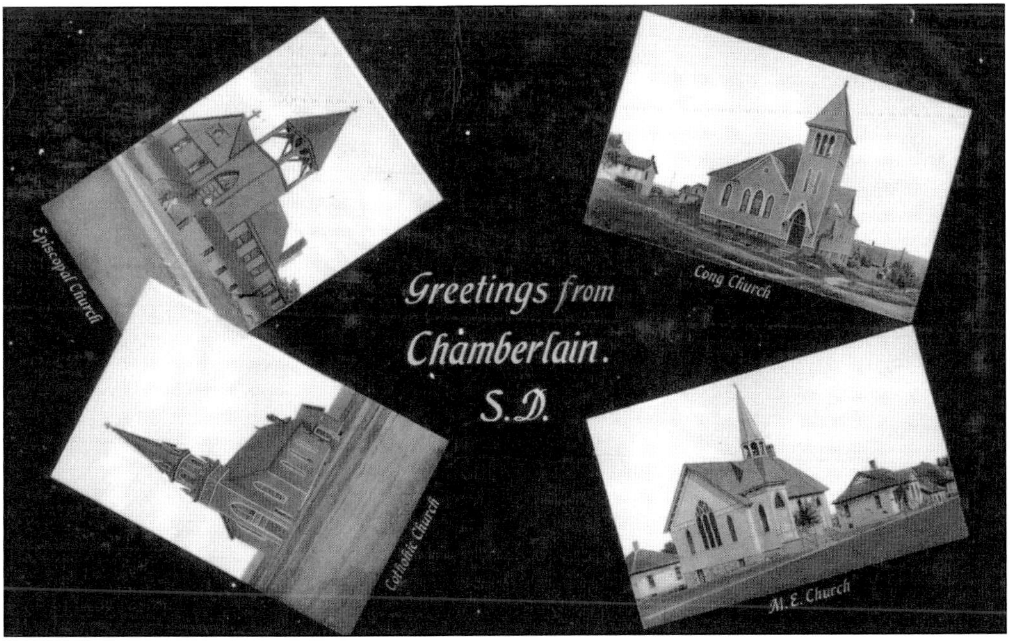

This card gives greetings from Chamberlain, South Dakota, and its churches. It shows early views of the Episcopal, Catholic, Congregational, and Methodist Episcopal churches. Of these four original buildings, the only one still standing is the Episcopal church. On the back, the following message is written: "Dear Mother, This is the best I can do in getting a church. Lovingly, Alice."

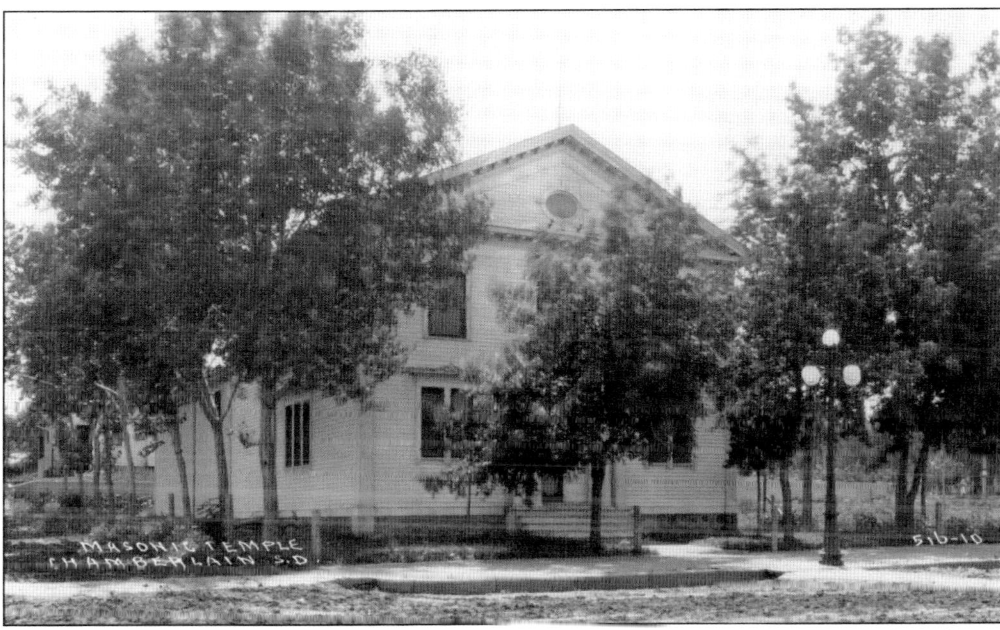

The Masonic Temple in Chamberlain held its first meeting in 1884. This postcard is of the building, constructed in 1902, that is still in use today. It is one of the oldest buildings in Chamberlain and stands on Main Street. It was remodeled in 1975 with a new carpet, kitchen, lights, insulation, and refinished furniture. This was the first major change to the structure since it was built.

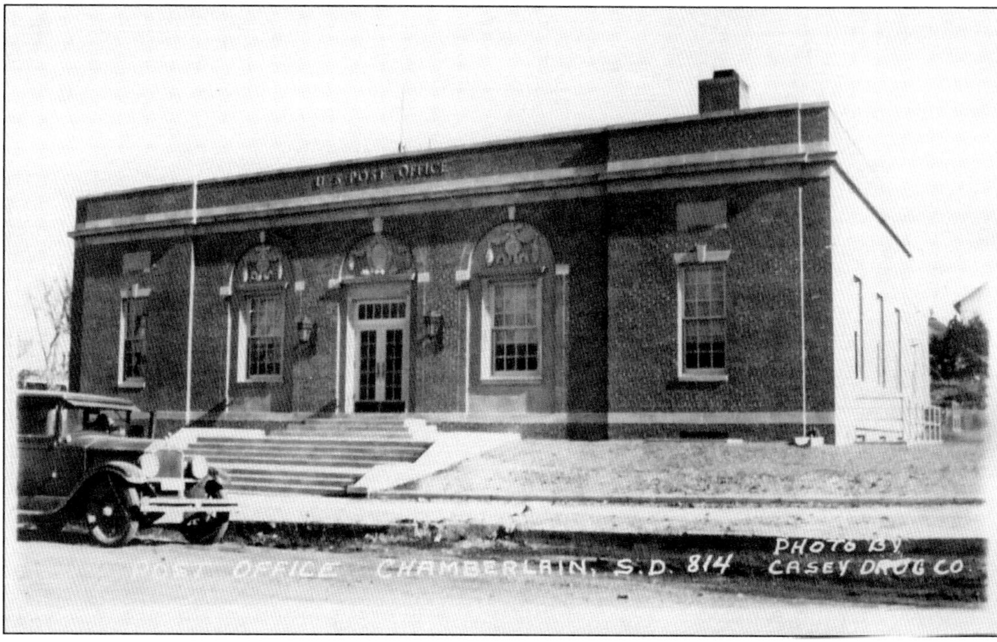

These two postcards are of the US post office in Chamberlain. Rural mail carriers have been delivering mail from the Chamberlain post office since 1916. The building was opened for business on July 1, 1928. It is still in use today, with a ramp added on the south side of the structure, and was remodeled inside in 1986. The image above shows the post office as it was in the 1930s, and below is a more recent photograph with trees having grown up around the building.

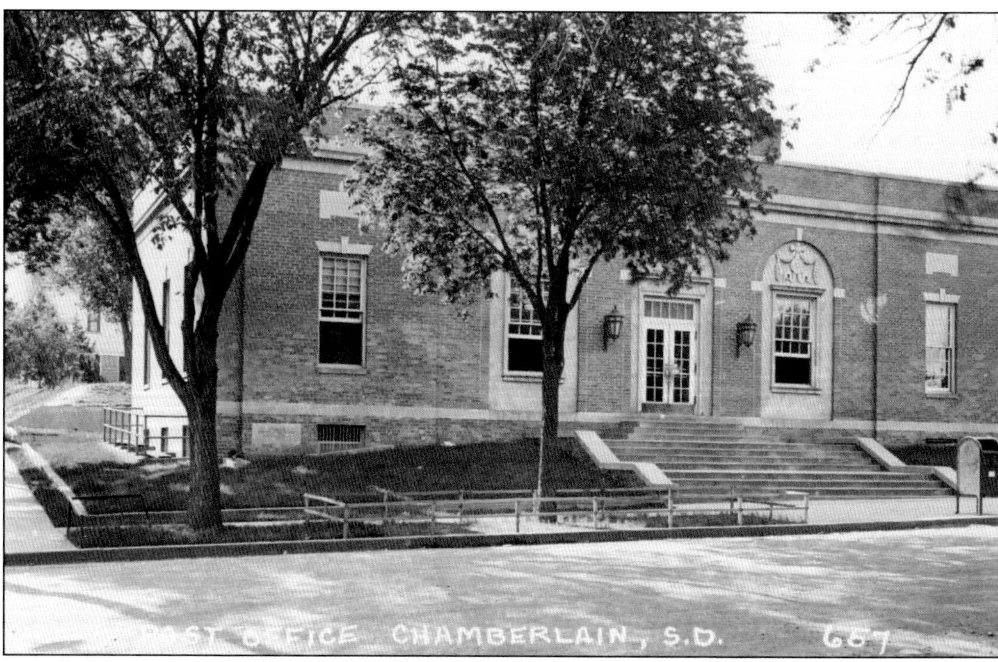

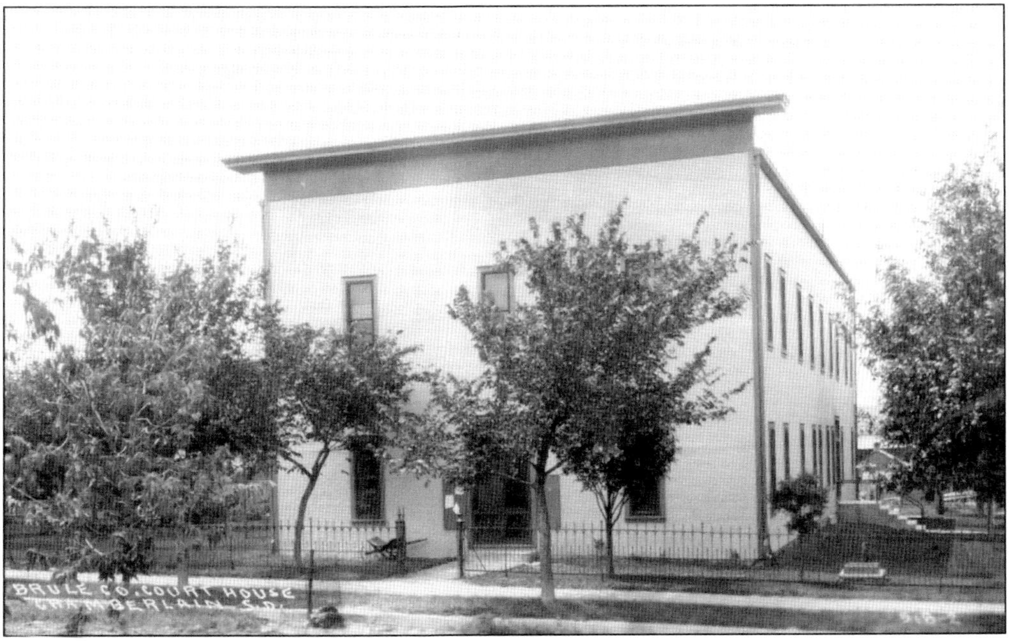

This Brule County Courthouse was built in 1925. The cast iron fence was taken down in the 1930s and later donated to the war effort. There was a movement made at one point to relocate the county seat to Pukwana because it was more centrally located. This was not accomplished, and the courthouse remained in Chamberlain. A new courthouse was built in 1958.

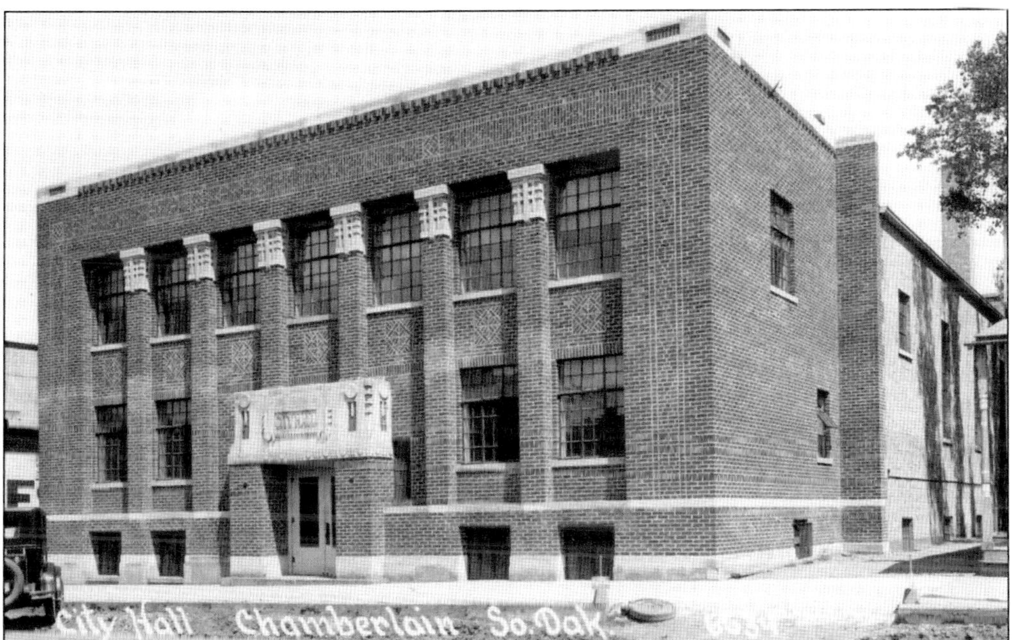

City hall was located on Main Street in Chamberlain. There was a city library upstairs and city and police offices and a small auditorium with a basketball court on the main floor. The city jail was in the basement. The building was torn down during the summer of 2012 to make way for a new community center.

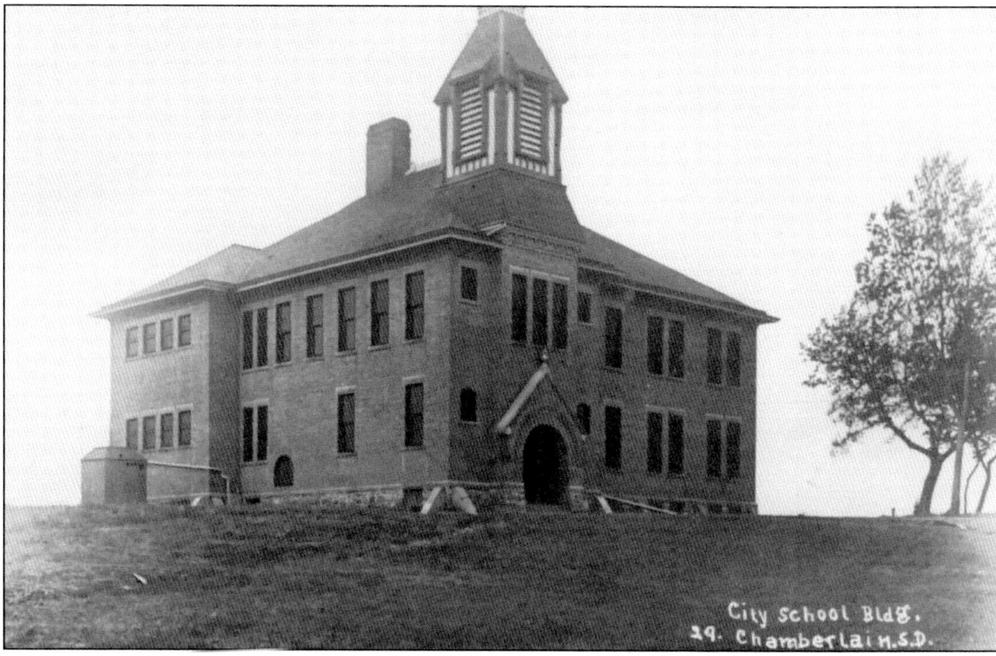

The citizens of Chamberlain have always worked to provide for the education of their young people. The first rooms for a school were provided as far back as 1883. The first year for high school classes was in 1885, and in 1891, a two-story brick school was built for both primary and high school grades. A three-story building for just the high school was constructed in 1916. These cards show two of the early school buildings. Neither of these structures is still standing.

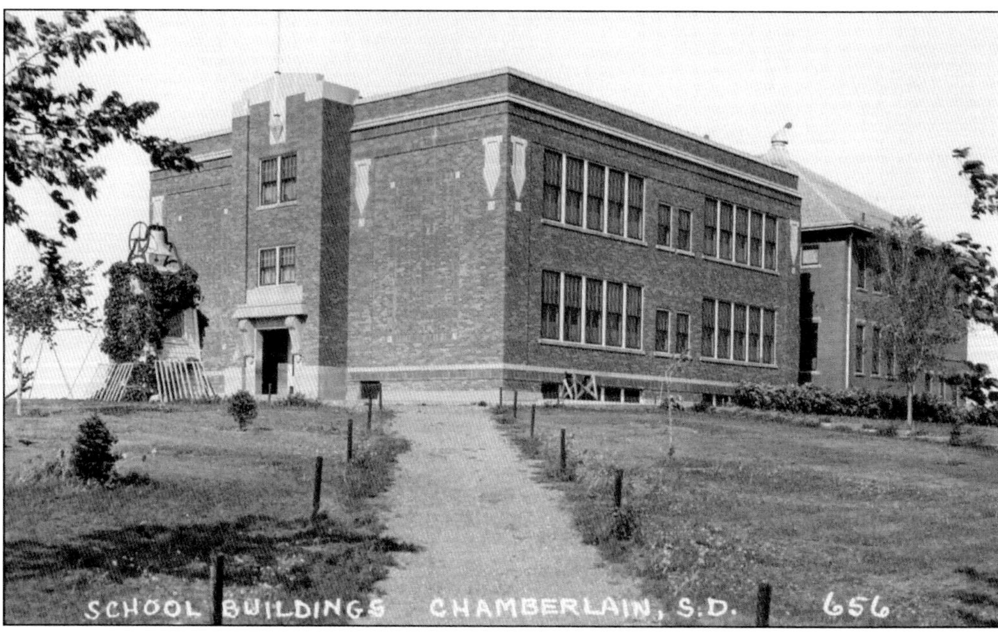

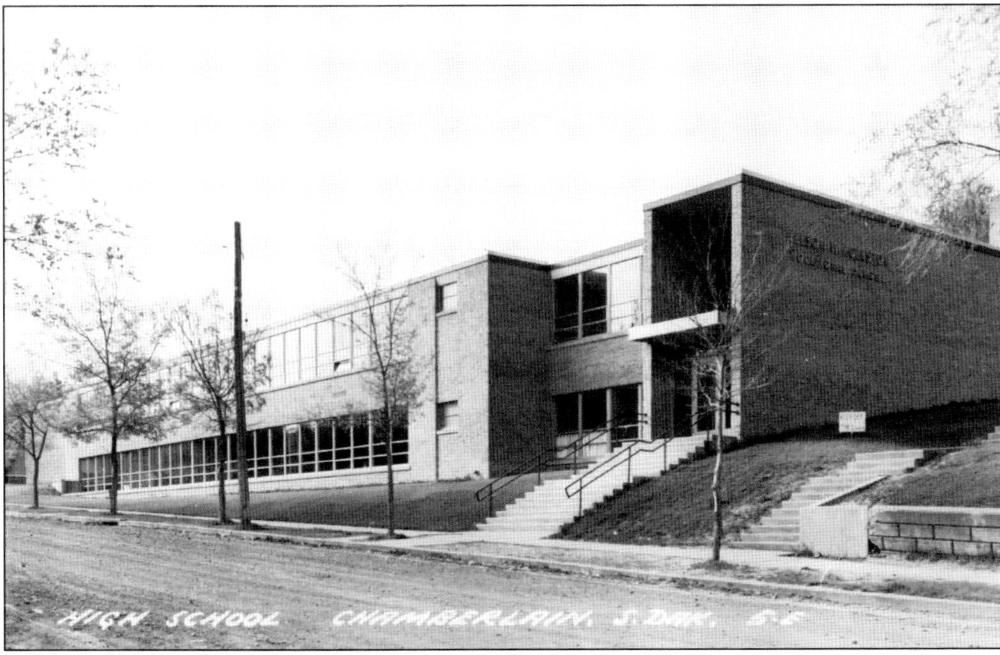

The Nelson W. Egleston Vocational High School building was completed in the spring of 1955, and high school classes started in the school that fall. Egleston was a businessman in Chamberlain for many years and left money for the new high school's construction. It was used as a high school until a new building was erected on the hill in a new development above Chamberlain in the early 1990s. (Courtesy Melanie Olson collection.)

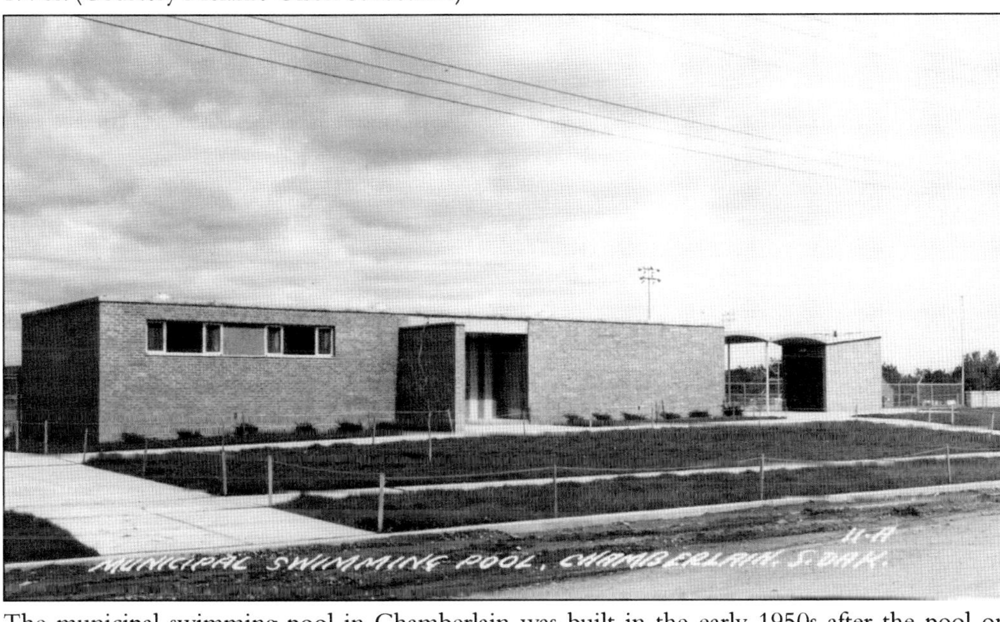

The municipal swimming pool in Chamberlain was built in the early 1950s after the pool on American Island was flooded. Funds from the sale of American Island were used to construct the pool, which is located on Main Street and is surrounded by a nice park, ball field, tennis courts, and a skateboard area. A few of the animal statues from American Island were later placed on the grounds.

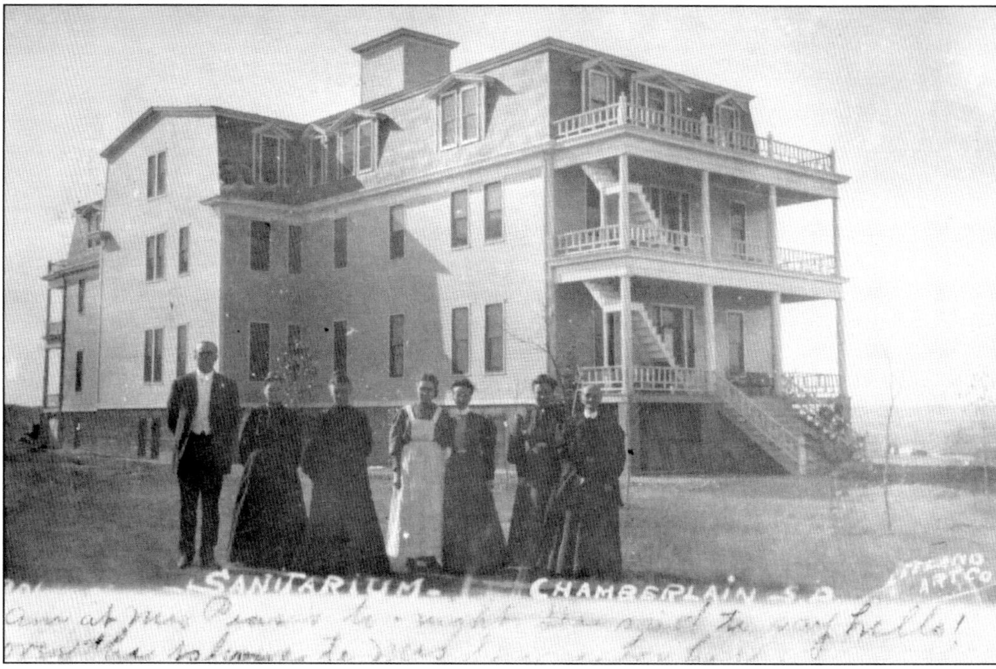

The Chamberlain Sanitarium Hospital opened in 1907. The largest hospital in the upper Midwest, it had 55 private rooms and could accommodate up to 125 patients. There was also a nurses' college on the premises. It was a first-class hospital under the supervision of the Battle Creek Institution. There were separate treatment rooms for men and women. All types of medicine were practiced, including surgery, maternity, X-rays, nose and throat, massage, solar lamps, and more. It was replaced by a new hospital in the 1950s, and the original hospital was renovated into apartments. This structure is no longer standing. The above photograph is an early one, and the photograph below was taken later, judging from the trees that have grown up around the building. (Above, photograph by O.S. Leeland.)

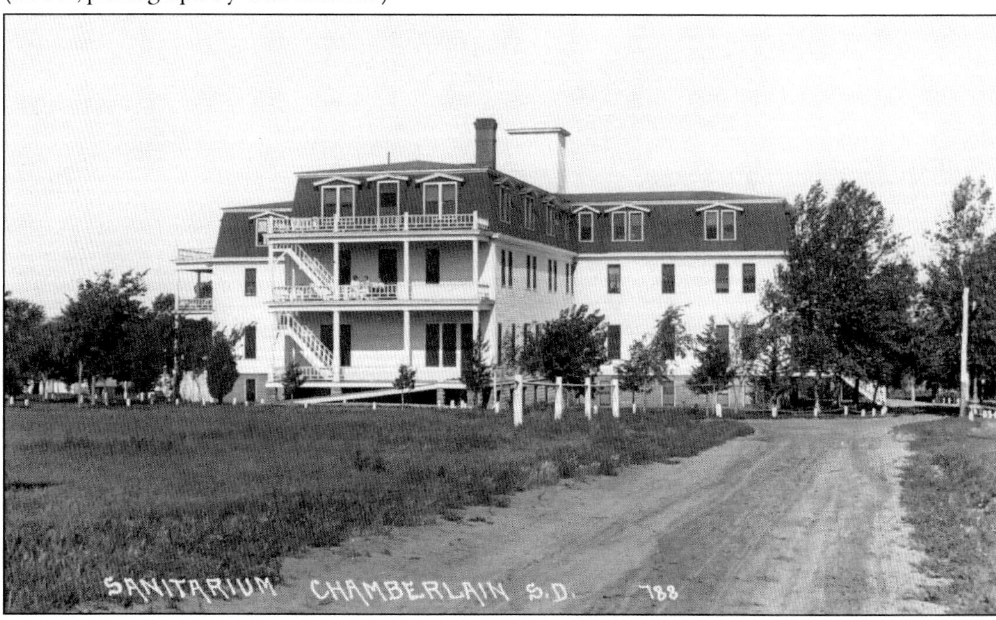

CHAMBERLAIN SANITARIUM

LOCATION The Chamberlain Sanitarium is located south of the city of Chamberlain on a plateau 90 feet above the Missouri, on the site of the old Ree village, which was visited by Lewis and Clark in 1805, when on their trip, which gave the great Northwest to the United States. The view of twelve miles of river and the great American island covered with virgin forest makes a very picturesque scene. The elevation is about 1400 feet above the sea level. This is not too high for the nervous and those suffering from heart difficulties. This elevation insures pure, fresh, bracing air, which, combined with the great number of sunshiny days, makes this one of the most healthful climates in the world.

BUILDING The building is four stories including the basement. It has been constructed for a first-class sanitarium and hospital, and is very conveniently arranged for that work. The rooms are large and well ventilated and lighted, neatly furnished, giving them a cheerful and homelike appearance. The building is heated by steam, is electric lighted and has a telephone in each room.

METHODS The institution possesses the best features of a first-class hotel and all the medical advantages of a modern scientifically equipped hospital and sanitarium. The means used are nature's most powerful remedies. Complete bath rooms, where sprays, electric, vapor, sitz, medicated and Russian and Turkish baths are given. Massage, electricity, dietetics, exercise, the resources of medical and theraputic appliances of all kinds. The Surgical department leaves nothing to be desired. There are complete labratories for special examination, maternity wards, and a limited number of rooms for old people who wish a comfortable home. A fully equipped electrical department including the X-ray, Static, Faradic, Galvanic and Sinusoidal currents. Also photophores and a solar lamp is maintained. A throat and lung department for catarrh of the nose and throat is equipped with the latest appliances.

Rates are moderate and uniform. Particulars made known on inquiry. Carriage will meet all patients when notified of time of arrival. Address,

CHAMBERLAIN SANITARIUM, or
Dr C. P. Farnsworth, Chamberlain, S. D.

This is the inside of a 1908 postcard sent to possible customers of the Chamberlain Sanitarium. It tells all one needs to know about the location, building, and methods of treatment. At the time, the sanitarium was under the direction of Dr. C.P. Farnsworth. When folded, the card shows a view of the sanitarium on one side and could be addressed with a message on the other side.

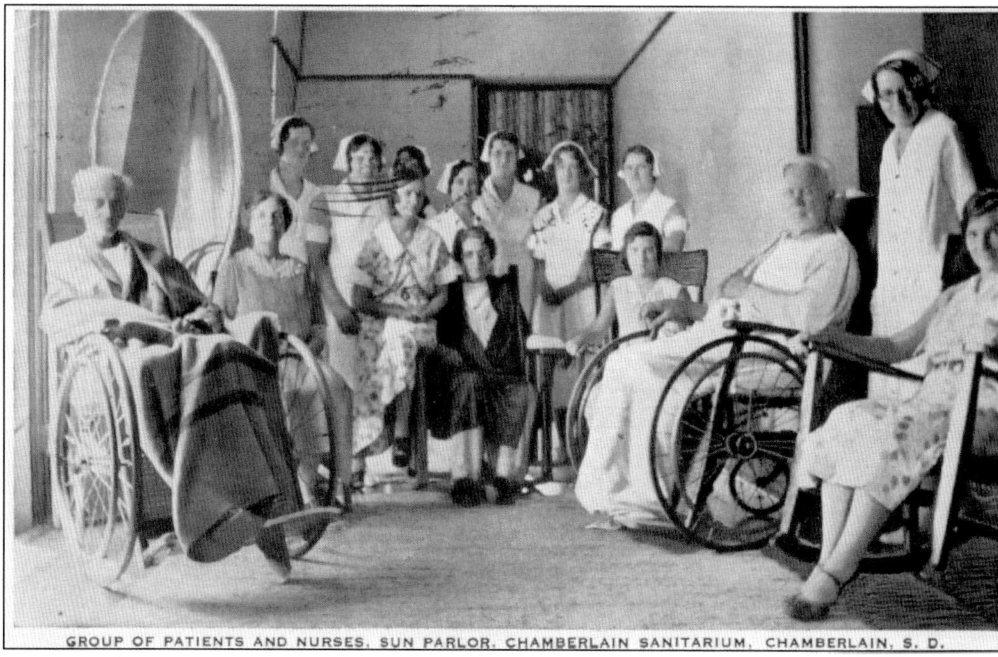

A group of patients and nurses enjoys the sun parlor of the Chamberlain Sanitarium. This card was mailed in 1932 as an advertisement for the hospital. It extended a warm welcome to all who were sick and in need of care. Rates at that time ranged from $2.50 to $4.50 a day, depending on the level of care or desire for a private room. Notice the old-fashioned wicker wheelchairs and the nurses' uniforms with crisp white caps.

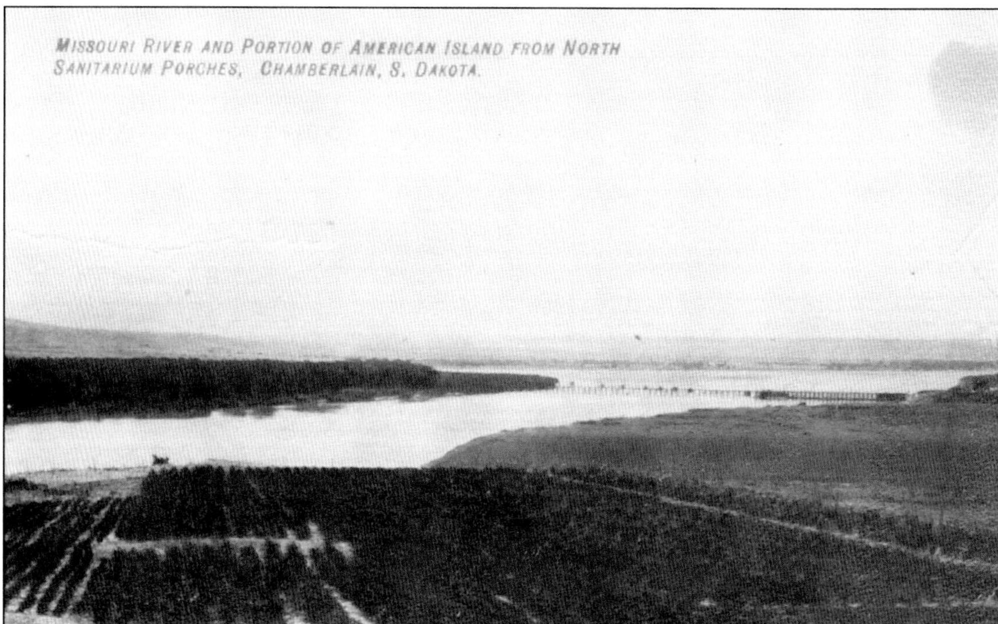

This 1908 view of the Missouri River and a portion of American Island could be seen from the north porches of the Chamberlain Sanitarium. The pontoon railroad bridge is in the distance. This must have been a beautiful view for patients recovering at the hospital.

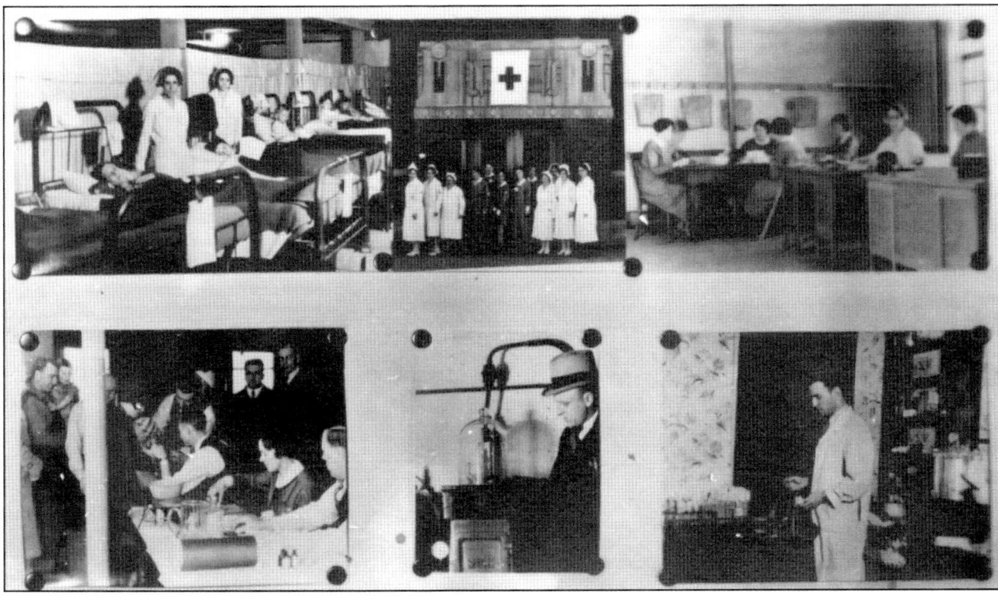

In early 1933, a typhoid epidemic hit Chamberlain. This postcard shows pictures of patients, doctors, nurses, and machines used in the treatment of this horrific disease. Besides the hospital, the city hall was also used to house patients, and the Red Cross was on hand to help. More than 30 people died, and the water supply was determined to be the cause. A new water filtration system was put in place in 1934. (Photograph by Fred Legler.)

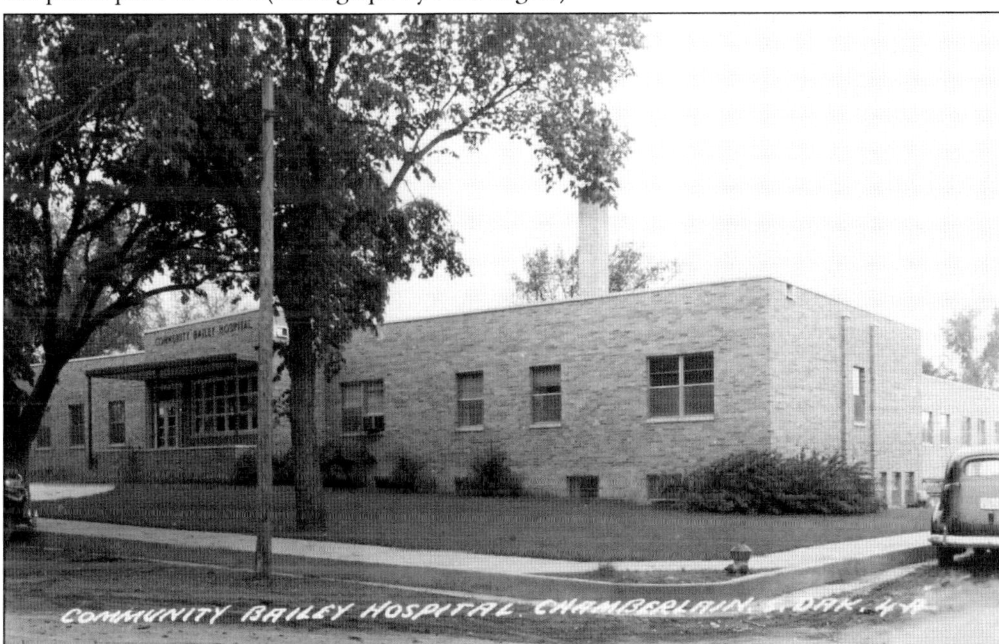

Community Bailey Hospital was built in the early 1950s, replacing the Chamberlain Sanitarium. It was in use until a new hospital was built on top of the hill in 1982. The building was sold and is in use now as Chamberlain Academy, which is a facility for at-risk youth. The author, Alice Arhart Olson, started her nursing career in this hospital under the direction of Robert Beckwith and Lydia Crawford.

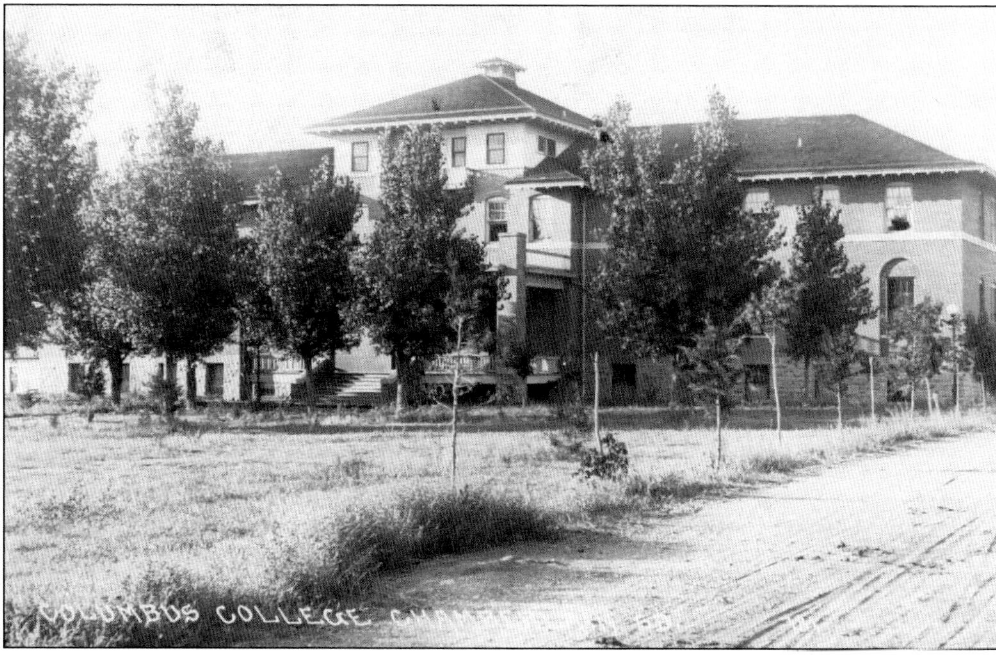

Columbus College was the first Catholic College in South Dakota. The buildings and land were purchased from the federal government. It served as a college for young men, especially those who wanted to study for the priesthood. It later served as a boarding school for high school boys. The college was moved to Sioux Falls in 1921, and the buildings and grounds were sold to the Sacred Heart Fathers in 1927. The buildings and grounds are still being used as St. Joseph's Indian School. The card above is of the main building of Columbus College. The card below shows the main building from a distance with a footbridge in the foreground.

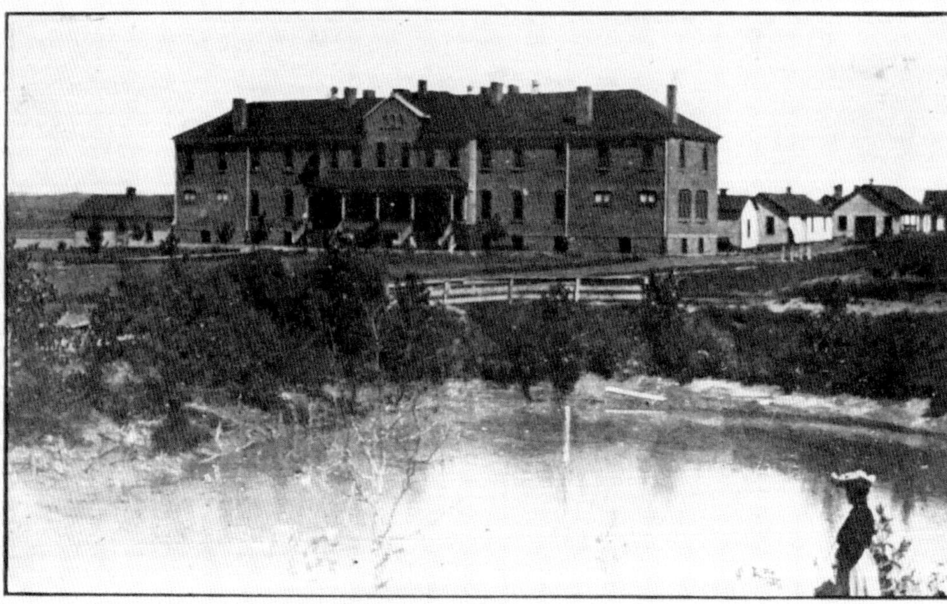

COLUMBUS CATHOLIC COLLEGE, CHAMBERLAIN, S. D.

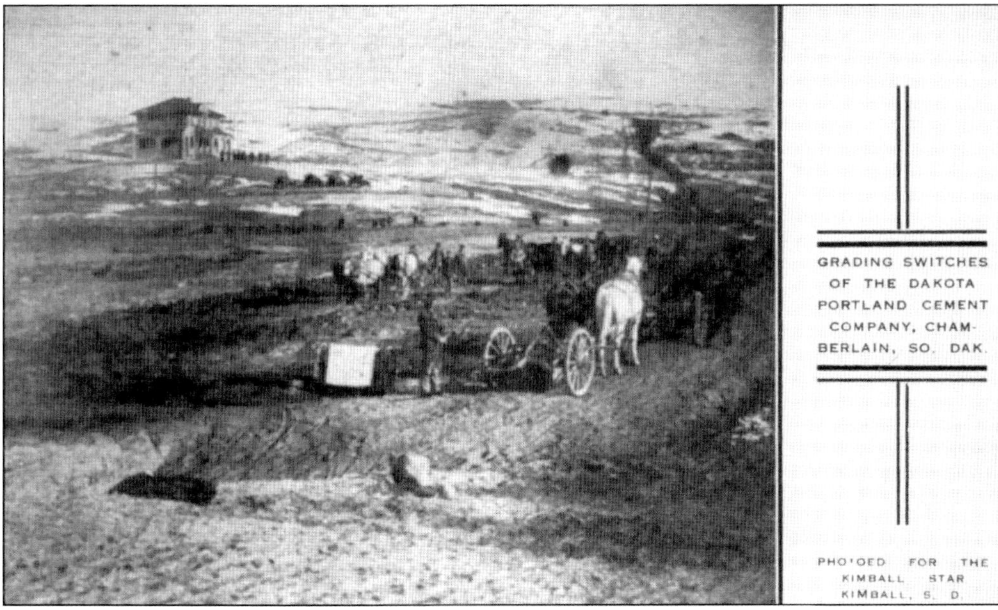

A structure was built in 1903 and used for the offices of the Dakota Portland Cement Company. It is located just north of American Creek and is now a private residence that looks much as it did originally. The house is not as far inland now as it was in the days before the dams were built on the Missouri River. The card above, postmarked in 1914, depicts the grading switches, which were areas for the railroad to build and haul the chalk stone to the plant to be ground up for cement. The cement plant ceased operations in 1919, after which Rapid City jumped on the chance to start one there.

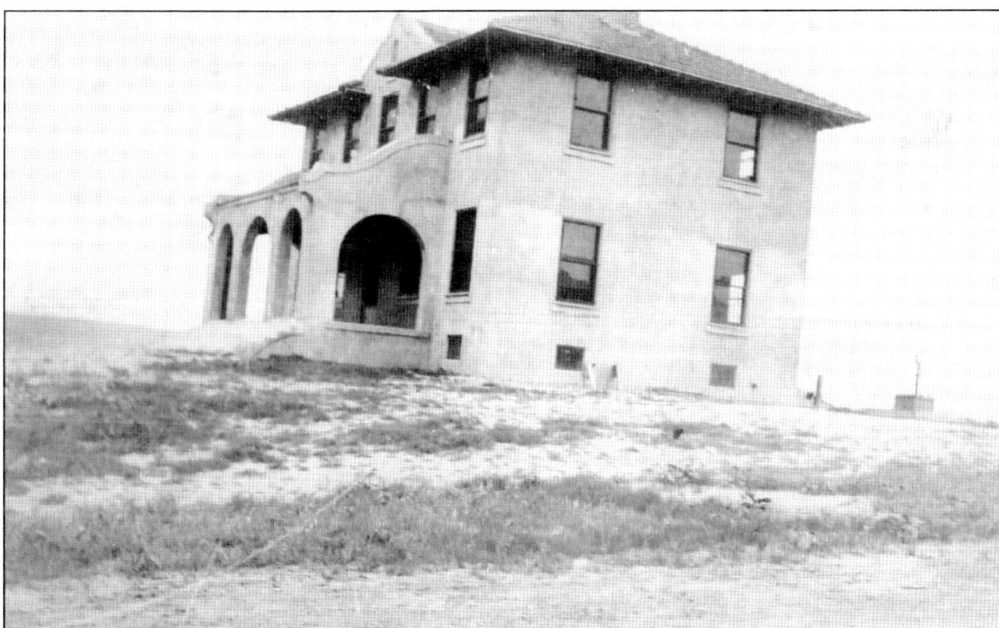

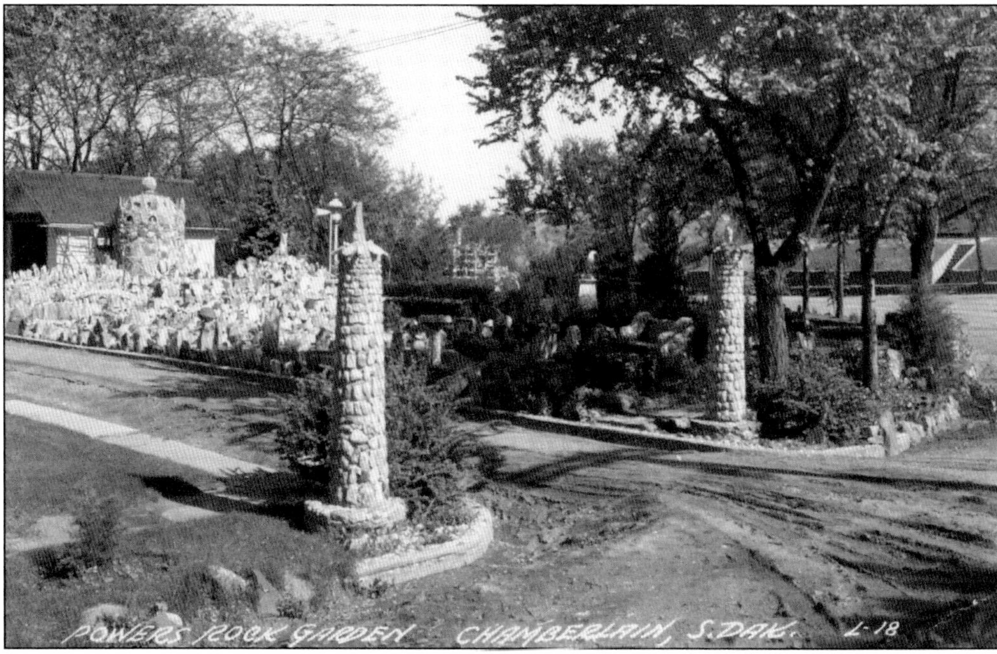

The Powers Rock Garden was a unique part of Chamberlain for many years. These lawn ornaments made of local rock were created around 1930. Although most of the formations have been removed or have fallen apart due to age, evidence of the rock garden is still visible.

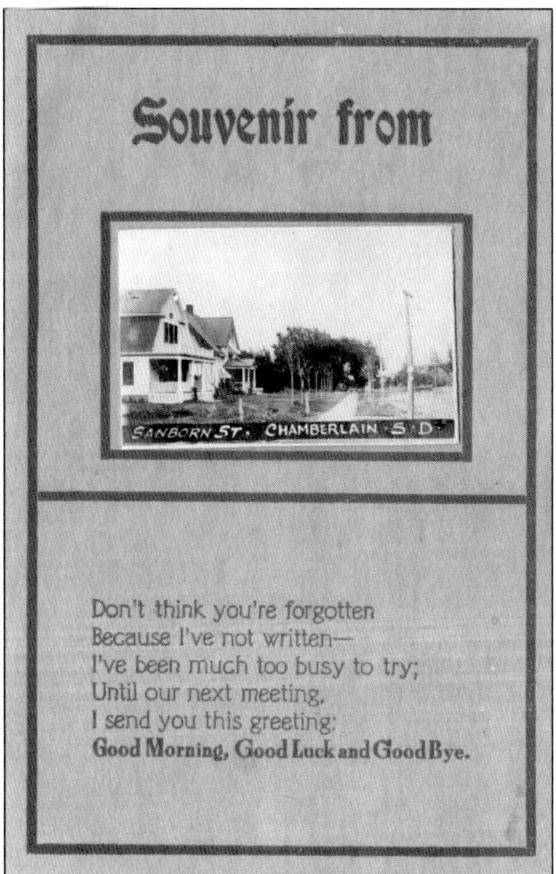

This standard postcard includes a small, glued-on photograph of Sanborn Street in Chamberlain. These cards could be used in any form and fitted with any photograph to make a souvenir. There is always a poem or saying printed in the bottom section.

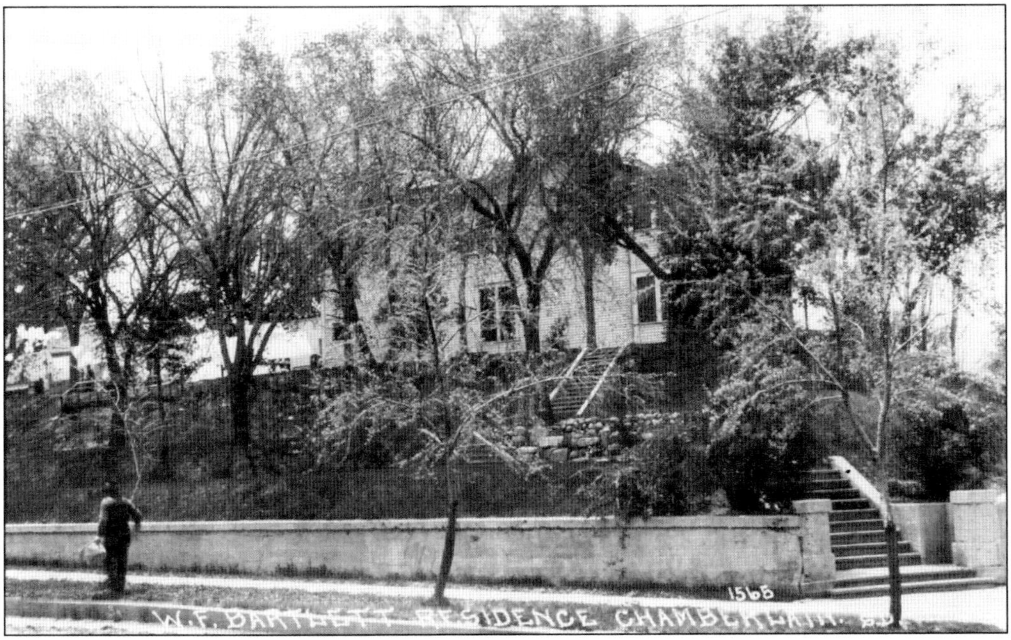

The large W.F. Bartlett residence is situated high on a hill overlooking the town and the Missouri River below. The house still stands today and maintains many of its original features. Dr. Bartlett was a chiropractor and used up-to-date medical devices for his patients.

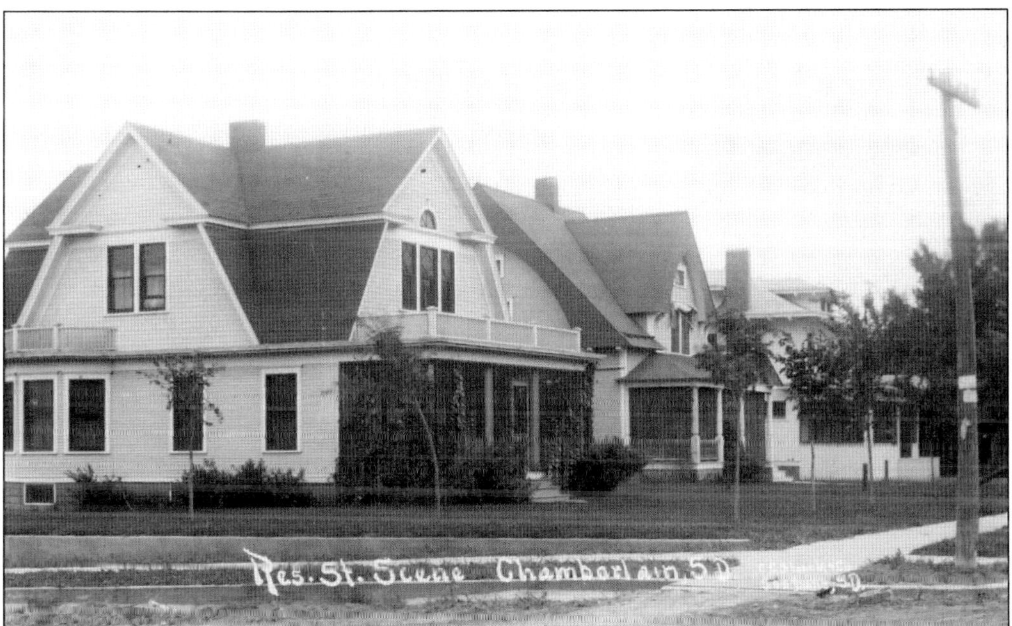

This is a view of one of the residential streets in Chamberlain. The date on the postmark is not visible, but a 1¢ stamp was used to mail it. The writer tells of "taking in the sights" and riding a steamboat over to the island.

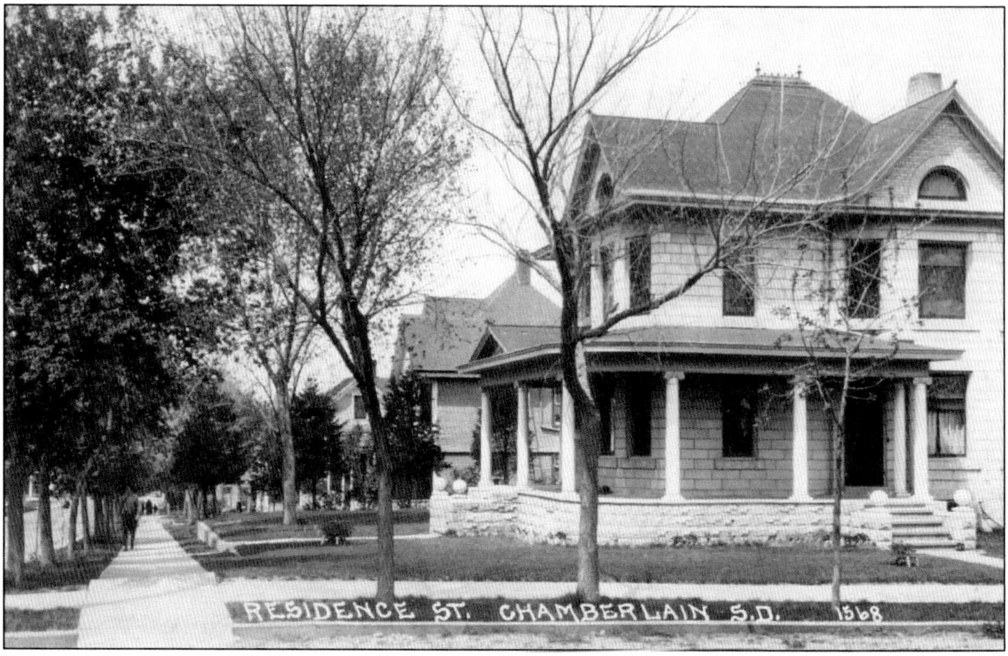

These are two different views of the Lawler Avenue home of J.Q. Anderson, who was a well-known farmer of sheep and cattle. He also served two full terms in the South Dakota Legislature. This was one of the older homes in Chamberlain before it was torn down. Notice the beautiful open wraparound porch with pillars.

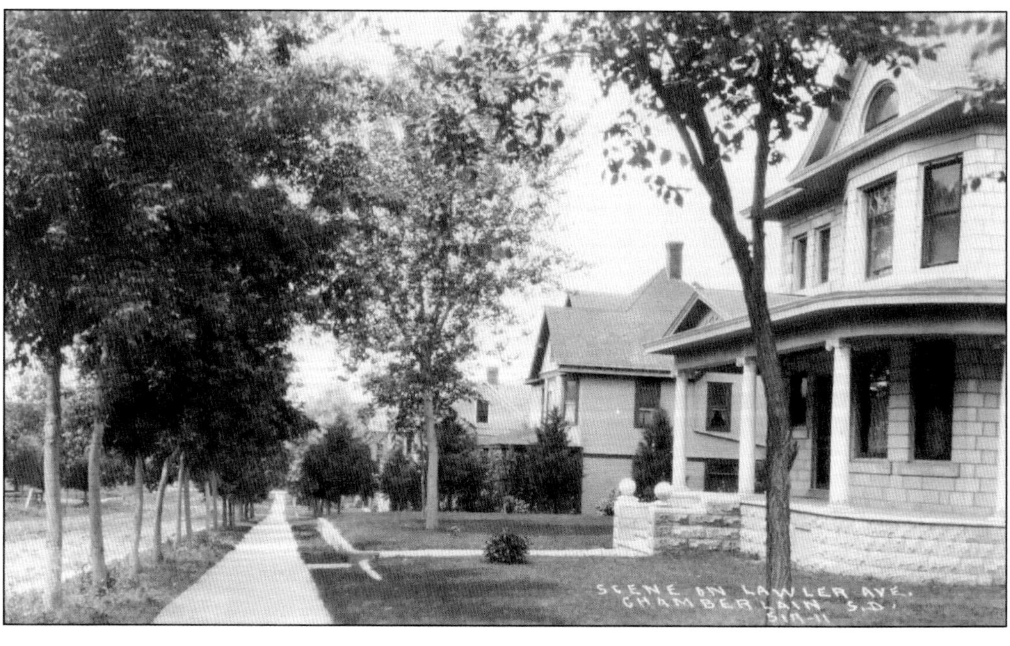

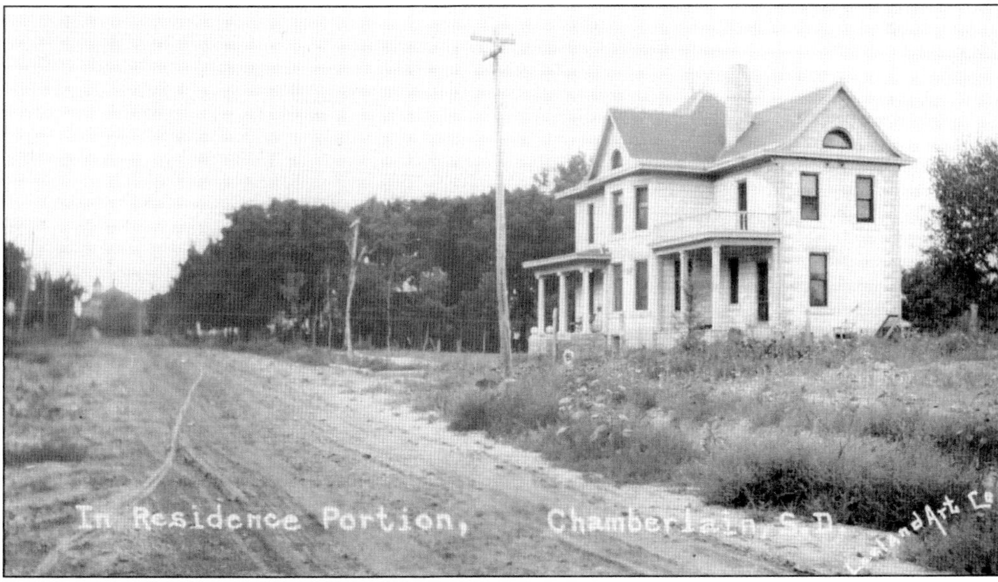

This is a nice, large three-story home that appears to be several blocks from the school, which can be seen in the distance at the end of the street. There is a cistern next to the house for water, and power lines run alongside the dirt street. The card is dated 1908. (Photograph by O.S. Leeland.)

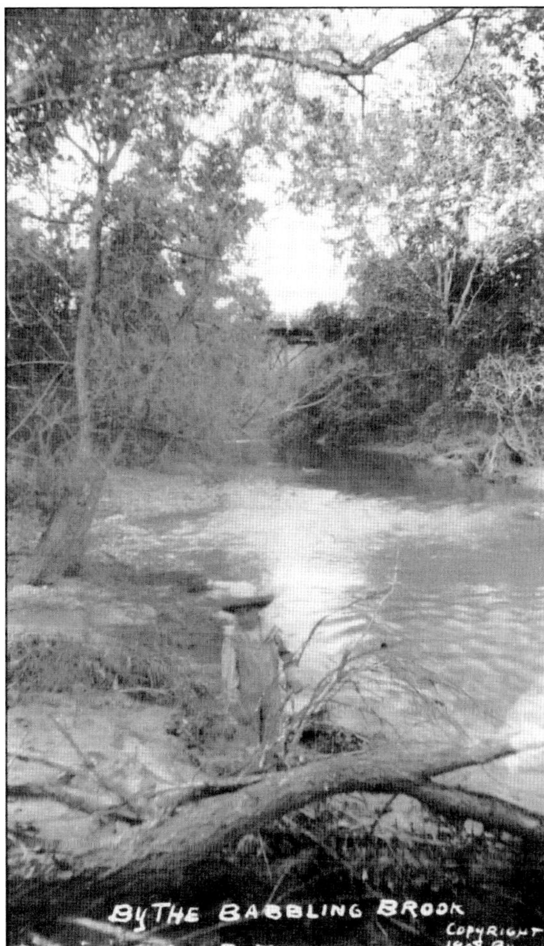

"By the Babbling Brook" is the title of this postcard. It shows the flowing spring by American Creek. The American Creek Bridge is just visible through the trees along the creek. This card is also postmarked 1908. (Photograph by O.S. Leeland.)

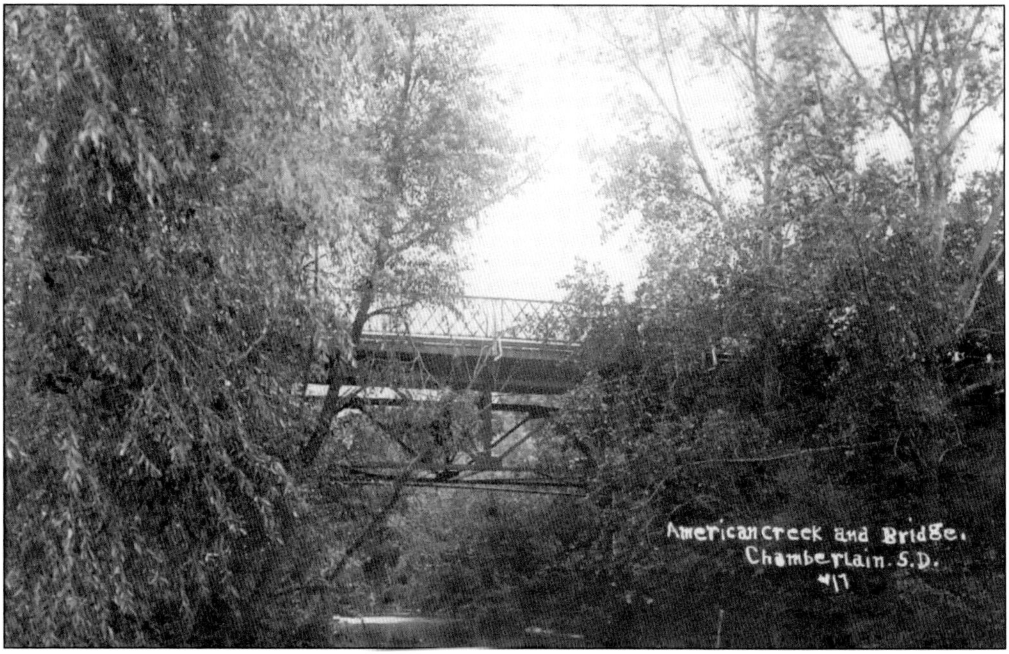

These two cards are different views of the bridge over American Creek at the north end of Main Street. F.M. Raush of the Iowa Bridge Company erected the steel bridge. The card above was mailed in July 1916. The card below shows a car crossing the bridge. The writer tells about being so hot that she is going to sleep on the porch. She also writes about going over to the island on the ferry and that she may go to the bathhouse on the other side. Notice the railing and support for the bridge in both views. This bridge met its demise when the artesian wells ran wild a few years later. It was replaced by a cement bridge.

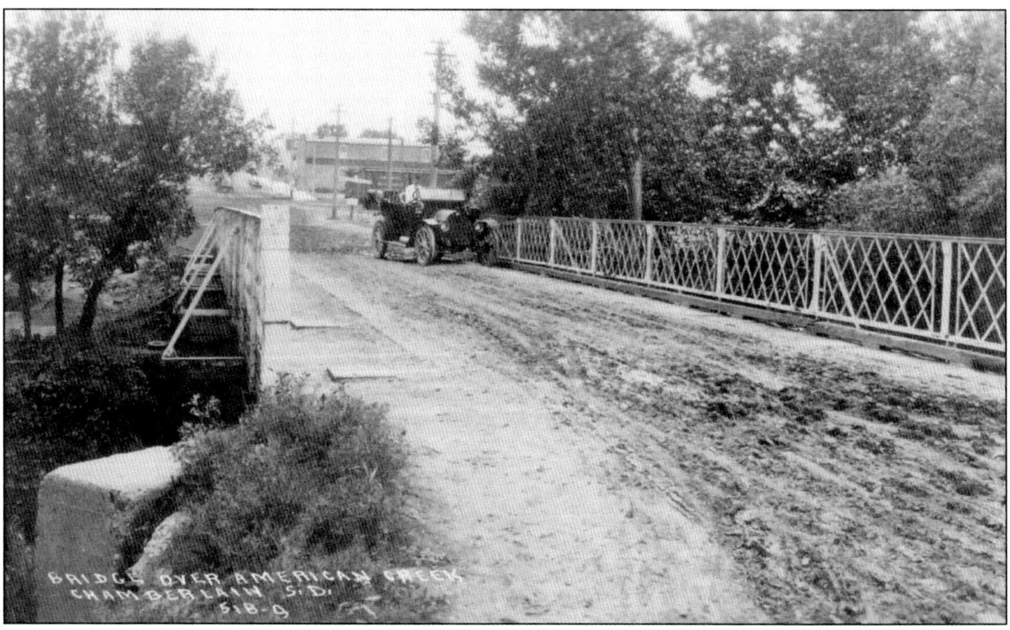

Five

Neighboring Area

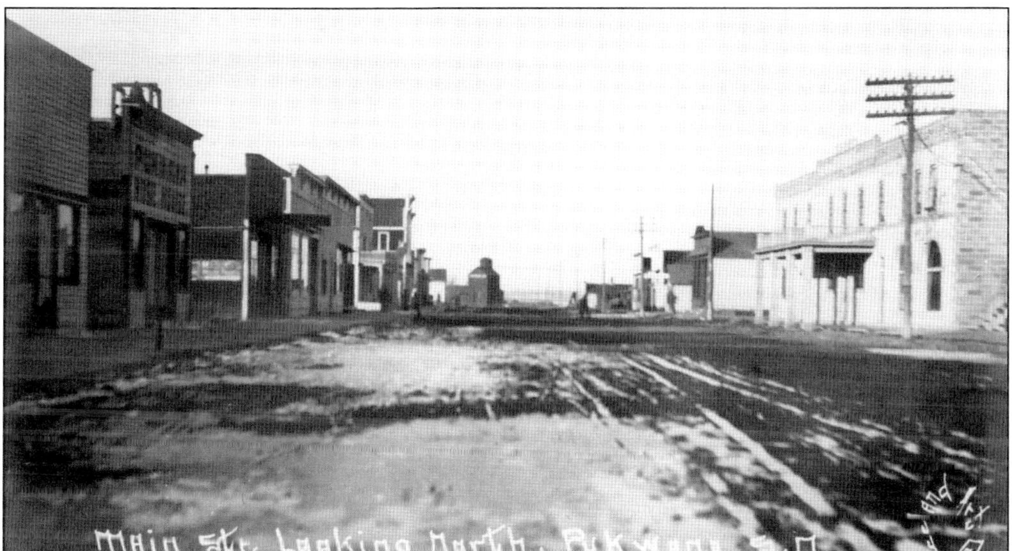

Pukwana had a thriving Main Street in the early 1900s. This 1911 postcard is of Main Street looking north. On the right side of the street is the Stransky Building. Across the street is the Pukwana Fire Department, with its large bell on top of the building. (Photograph by O.S. Leeland.)

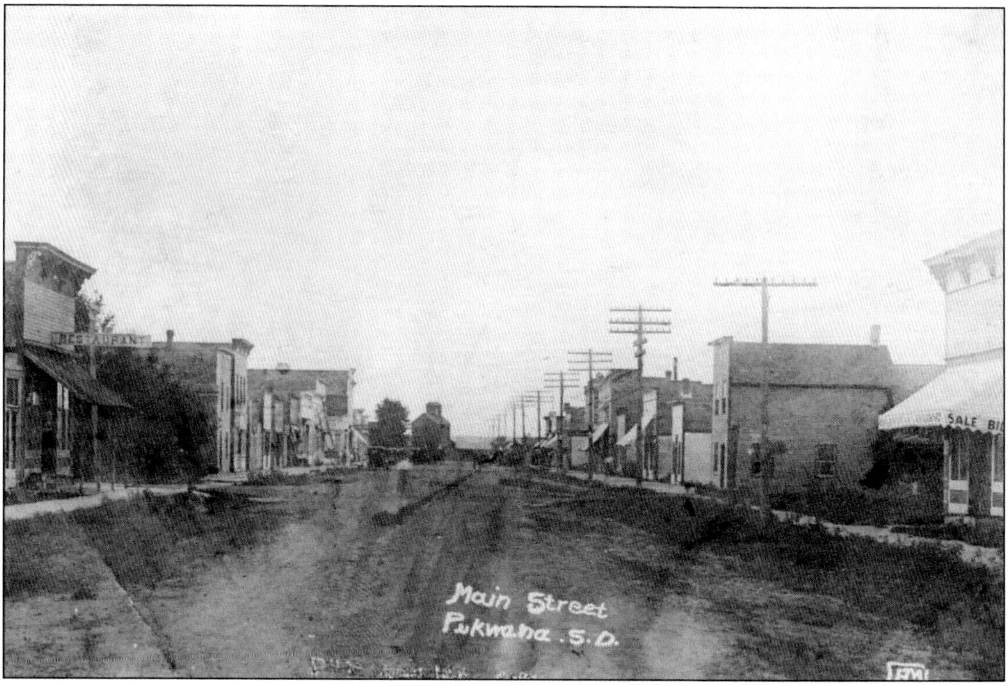

Pukwana came into existence in the 1880s. The name *Pukwana* is from Henry Wadsworth Longfellow's *The Song of Hiawatha* and means "smoke from a pipe," such as one smoked by the Great Spirit. These two cards are from the early days of Pukwana. The card above shows a restaurant on the left and a grain elevator in plain sight at the end of the street next to the railroad tracks. The street scene below also shows the business district. There is a furniture store on the left, with the fire department building down from it. The large fire bell is on top of the fire department.

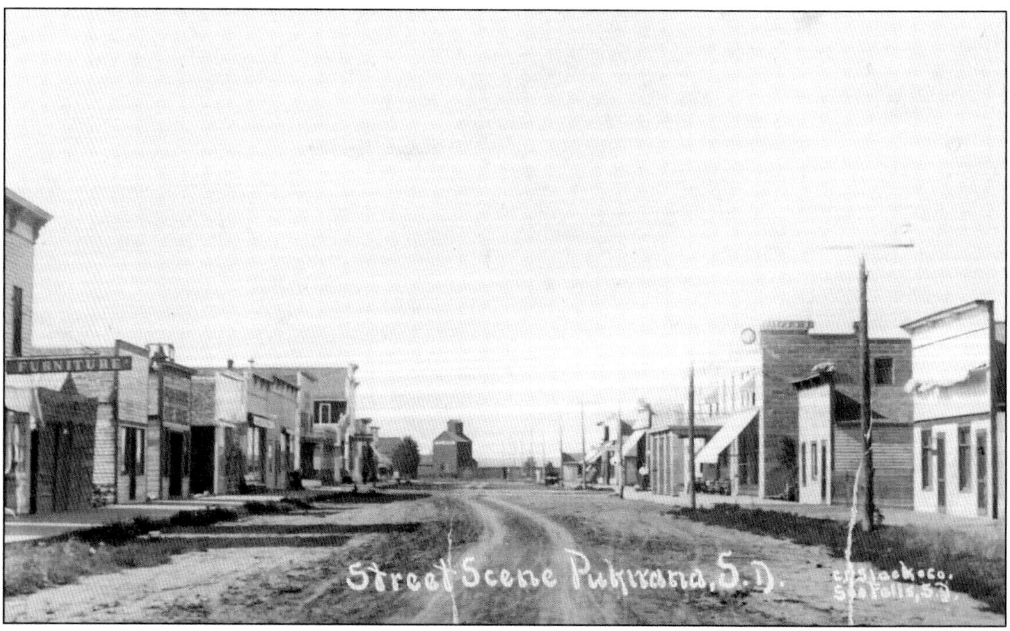

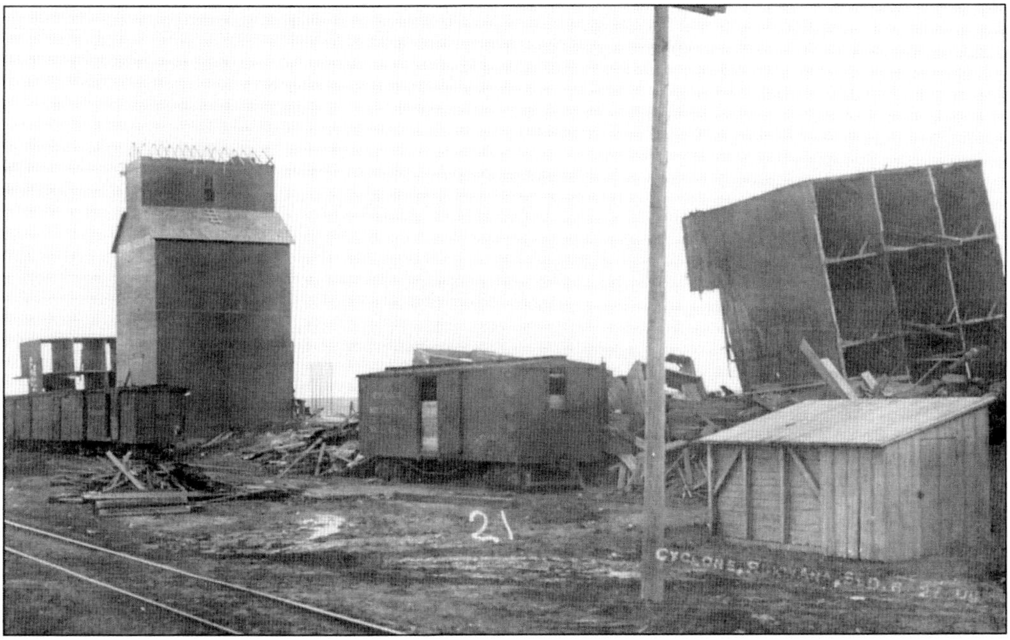

A tornado hit Pukwana on June 27, 1908. The storm came from the northwest in the afternoon. Many of the buildings in town were damaged. In the above photograph, the top of the tallest elevator has been blown off and another elevator lies toppled over next to it. The card below is of the Murry residence, with the house blown over and the owners and townspeople standing next to the rubble. Even with all the destruction throughout the town, no human lives were lost. Unfortunately, many animals were killed.

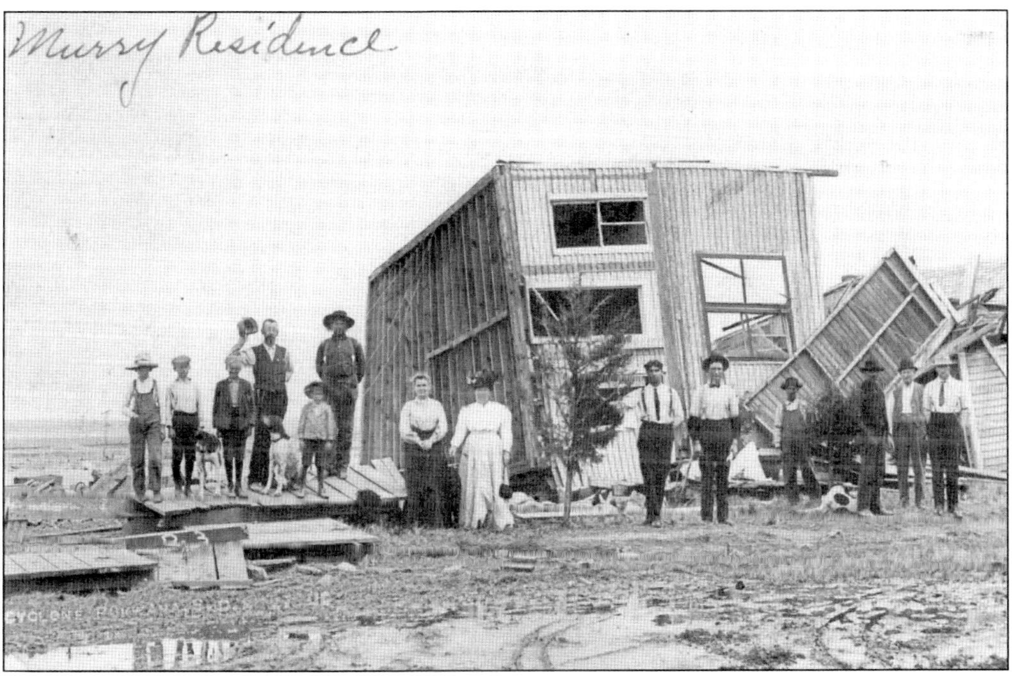

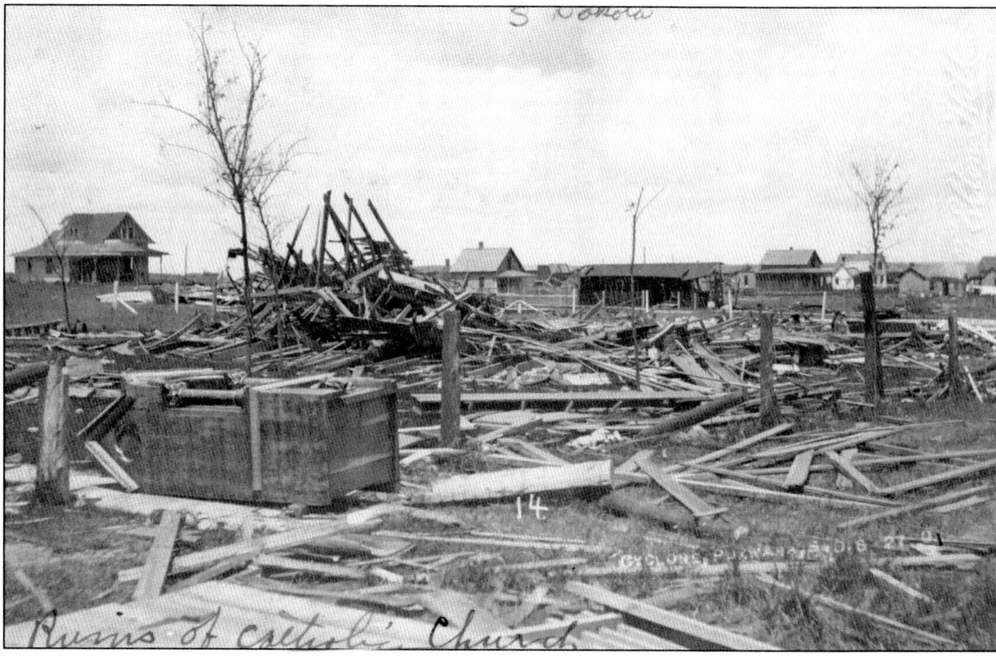

The Catholic and Methodist Episcopal churches of Pukwana were both destroyed by the tornado. Above is what was left of the Catholic church. It had just been painted a light green color, and pieces of this color wood were found many blocks away. Below, the Methodist Episcopal church has been reduced to a pile of rubble. Both of these cards were mailed in 1908. The population of the town at that time was 164. Other buildings damaged by the tornado were the Pukwana feed barn, a rooming house, and most of the homes in town.

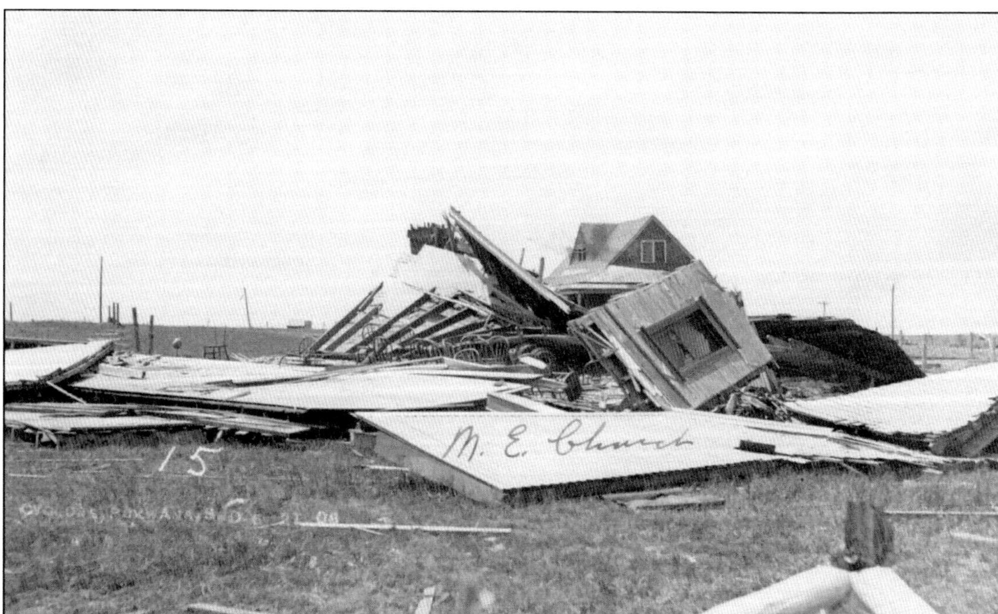

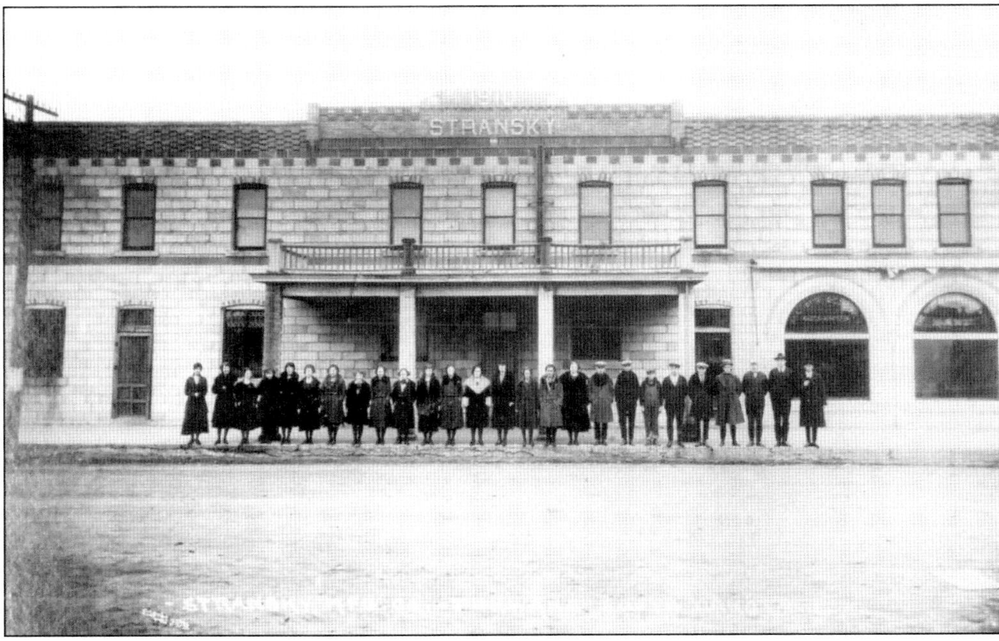

Some of its employees are pictured standing out front of Pukwana's Stransky Building. The year 1910 is plainly seen at the top of the building. J.A. Stransky was an inventor, and Stransky Manufacturers was most well known for the visible vaporizer. It was advertised that the device would bring gas costs down to 5¢ a gallon. Stransky also invented and manufactured another device called the "devil dog," which would make the horn go off if someone was rocking the car. The Pukwana Post Office did so much business due to Stransky that Pukwana was one of the smallest towns in the United States with a first-class post office. Below are some of Stransky's prize-winning Percheron horses that had been imported from Belgium. (Below, photograph by O.S. Leeland.)

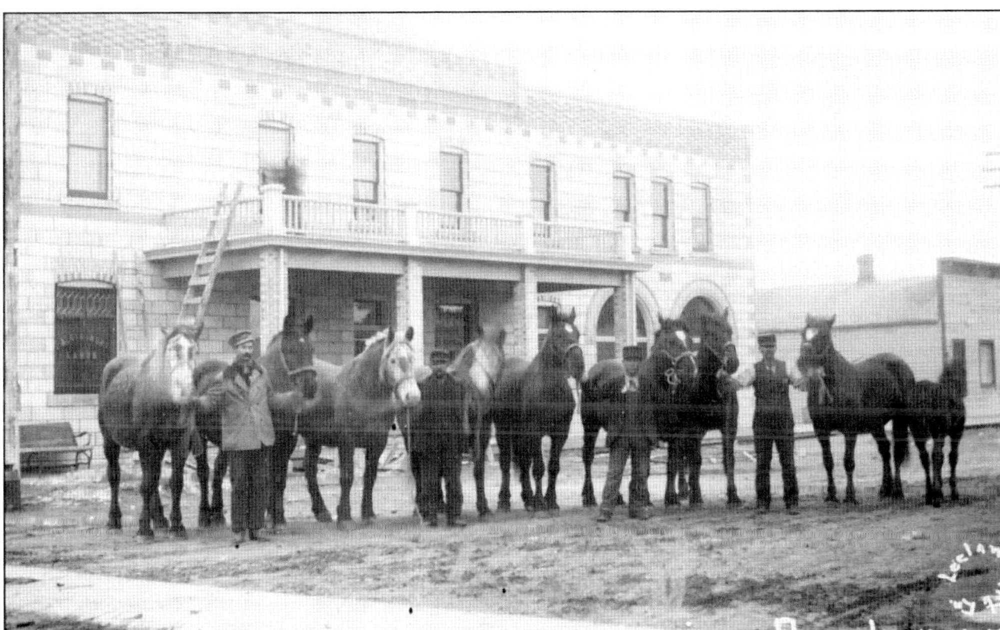

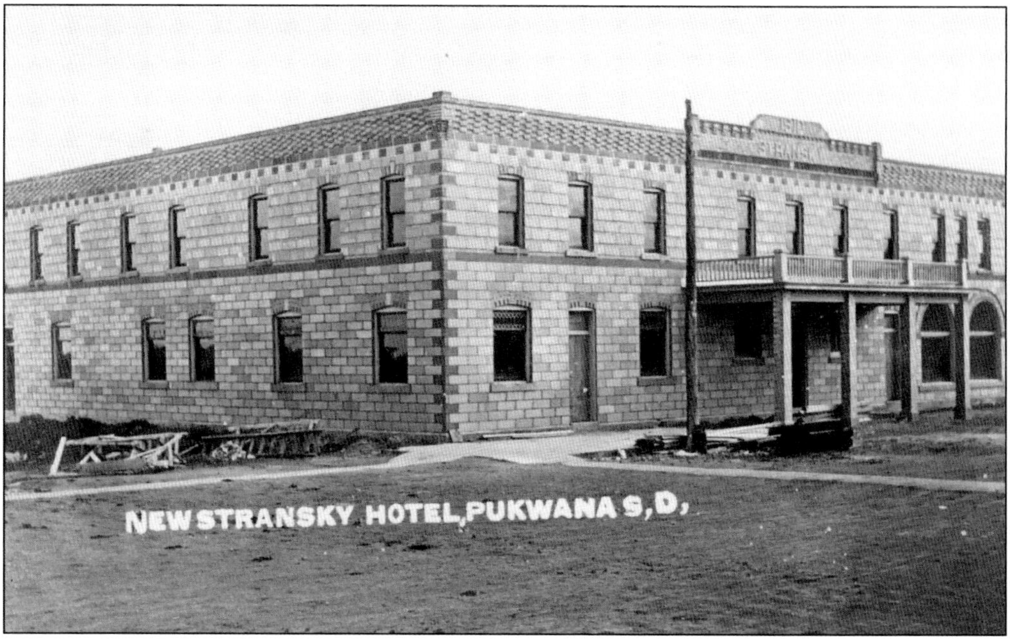

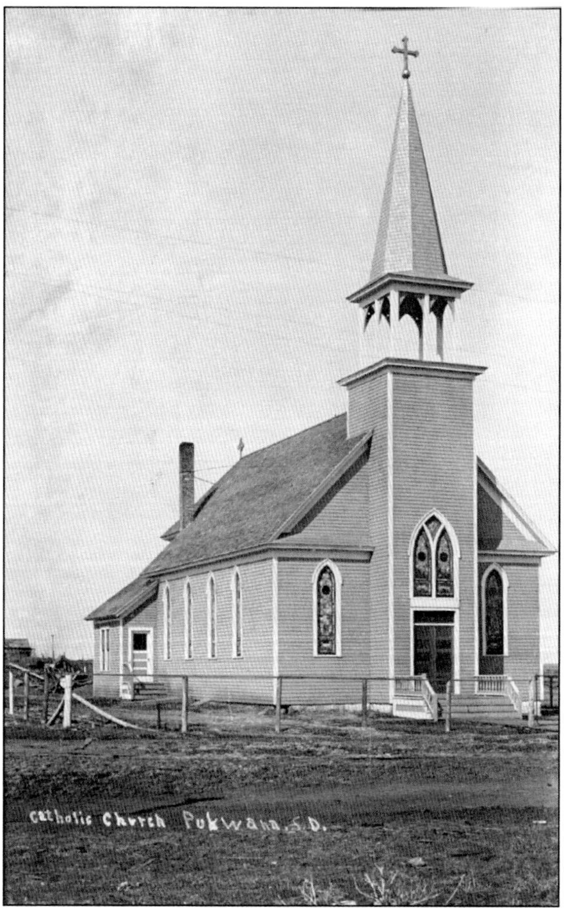

J.A. Stransky operated a hotel on the main floor of this building, with a café in one corner and a bank in another. Part of the message on the back of this card reads, "This is the new hotel in Puk. It's a dandy." High school students boarded here during the late 1930s and early 1940s while going to school. The building still stands today.

The Catholic church in Pukwana was called St. Anthony's in 1904. In 1909, the Pukwana church became a mission church. Until 1914, priests from Columbus College in Chamberlain were in charge of the church. It featured a tall steeple and beautiful stained-glass windows that can be seen in this photograph.

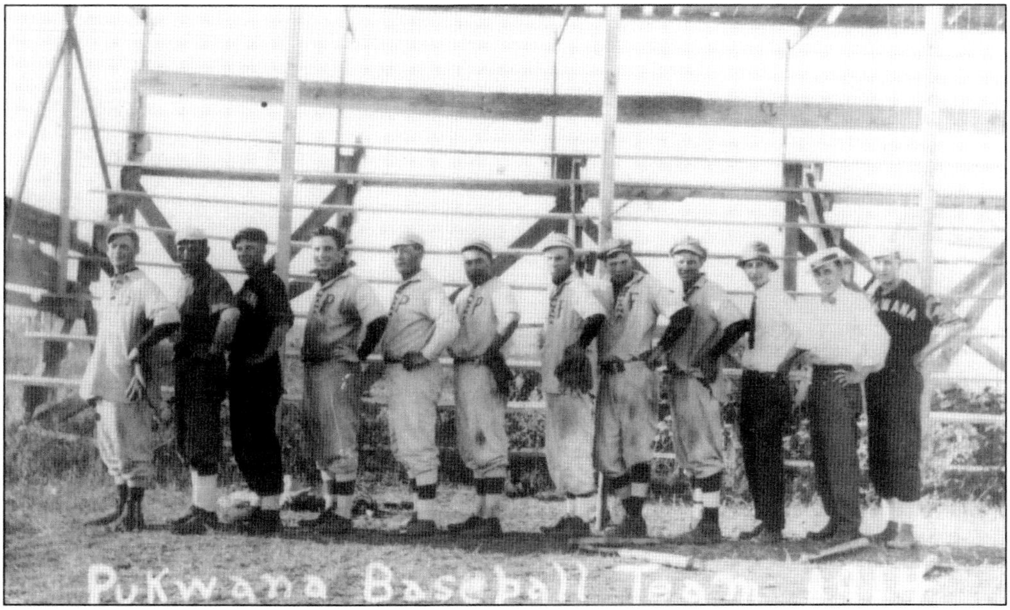

The 1914 Pukwana Baseball Team is pictured here. This looks to be the starting nine players with the manager, third-base coach, and one reserve player. A large grandstand is behind the players. They are wearing two different types of Pukwana baseball uniforms, and many of the players are also holding three-finger gloves.

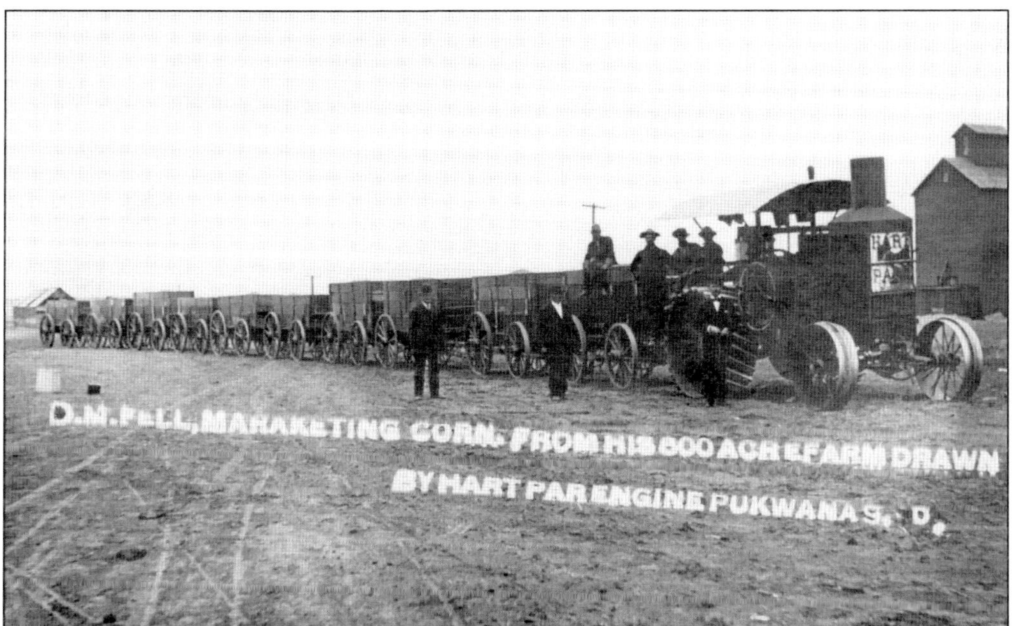

This card was sent by D.M. Fell and has a July 1909 postmark. Fell is bringing corn to market from his 800-acre farm. His Hart Par engine is pulling the row of wagons. The elevator at Pukwana is seen behind and to the far right. Not all farmers could afford such an engine at that time, so it was definitely a photograph-worthy sight.

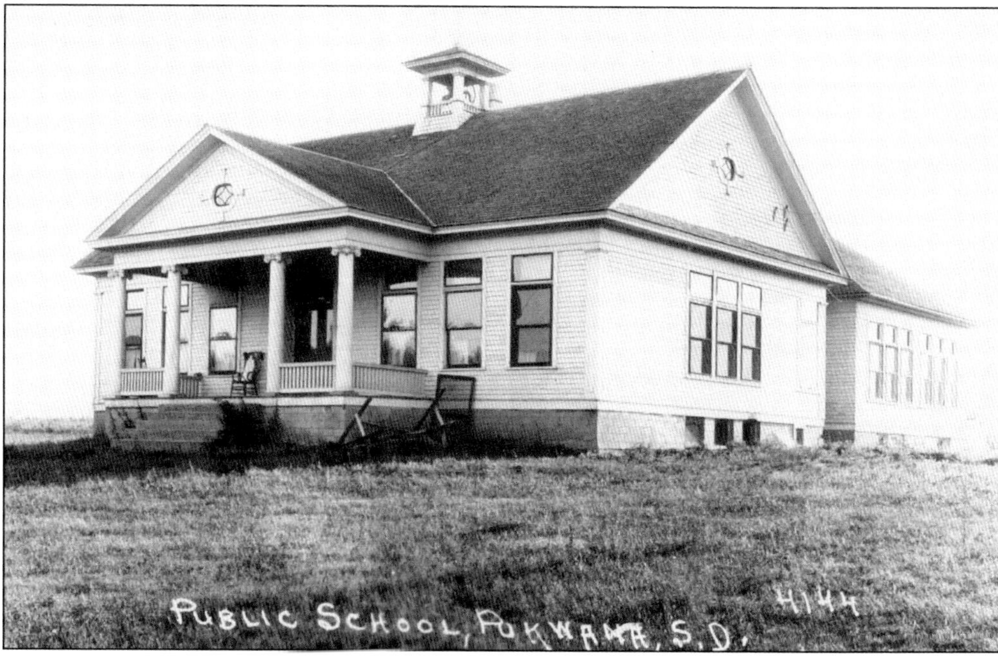

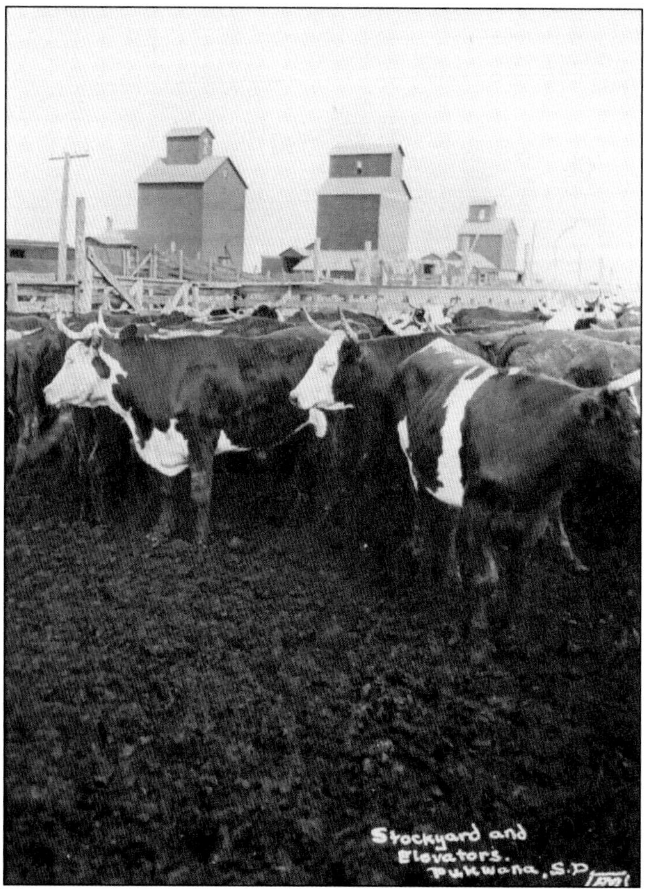

The first school in Pukwana was a large two-story building. It was damaged in the tornado of 1908 and replaced in 1910 by a two-room grade school. High school was provided starting in 1921, and the first graduating class was in 1926. During the 1930s, a dormitory was available in the Stransky Building, which made it possible for rural students to attend high school. The last graduating class at Pukwana was in 1964. A grade school continued, but eventually all students were sent to schools in Chamberlain or Kimball. (Courtesy Melanie Olson collection.)

The stockyards at Pukwana were quite large, and cattle were shipped out on the railroad that was located next to the elevators. Notice the horns on the cattle pictured. A good amount of grain from around the surrounding area was also shipped out on the railroad from the elevators.

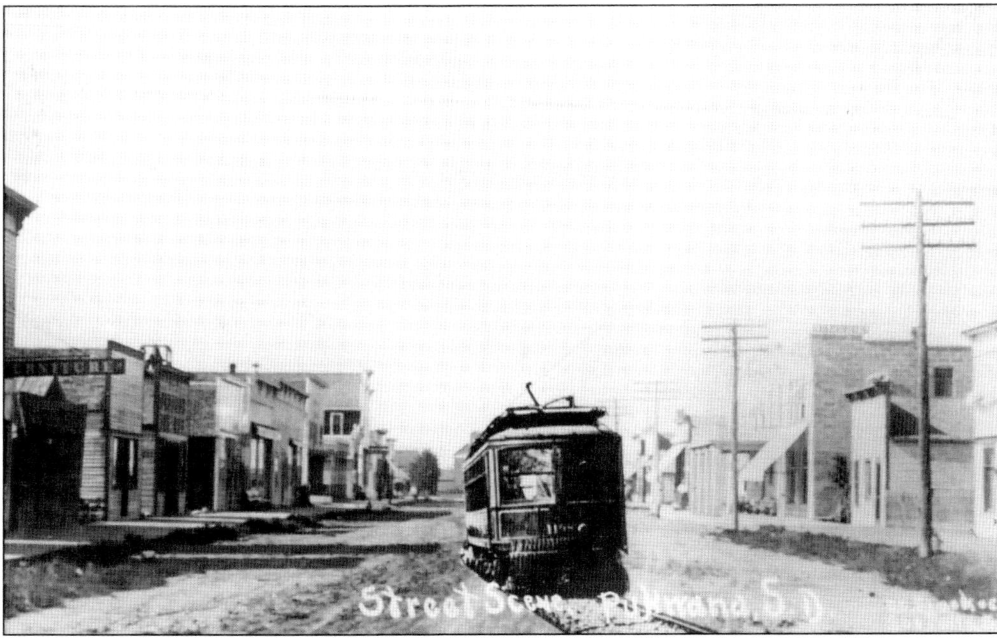

This is a "fantasy" card of Pukwana. It shows a streetcar coming down the tracks in the middle of Main Street. Of course, the small town of Pukwana did not have a streetcar. One has to wonder how many people who received these cards believed what they saw in this photograph, dated 1912.

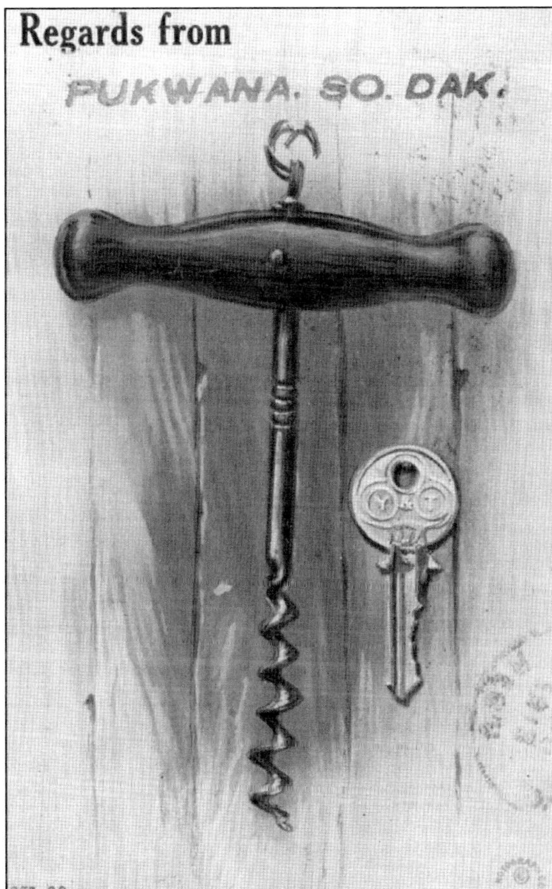

This postcard was a standard card that was used by many different towns and cities. The name of the town and state would be stamped on it beneath "regards from." The rustic bottle opener and key seen here are different from the usual flowers or country scenes on most standard cards. This postcard was postmarked in 1913.

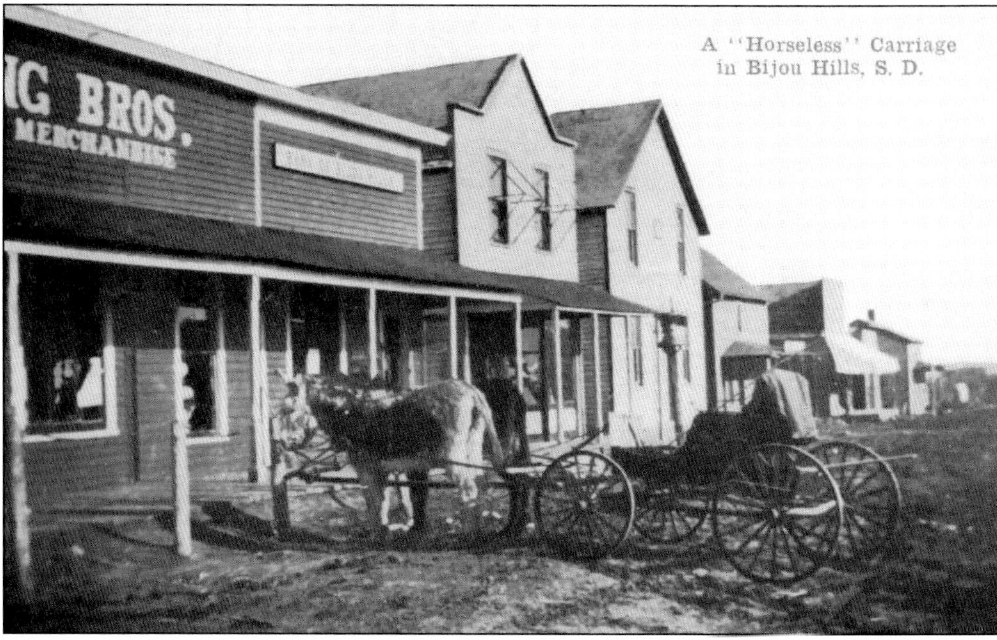

Bijou Hills, South Dakota, was located approximately 25 miles south of Pukwana. Bijou Hills's name came from a French fur trader who lived in the area. The Bijou Hills Post Office was established in 1877. In the view above, a "horseless" (mule-drawn) carriage stands in front of the Thwing Brothers Merchandise store. Next to it is the Bank of Bijou Hills. The card below shows a similar scene as above, but from a different angle. The Bank of Bijou Hills is in the center. A general store is to the right. Notice the gaslight post out front. This card was postmarked in 1907.

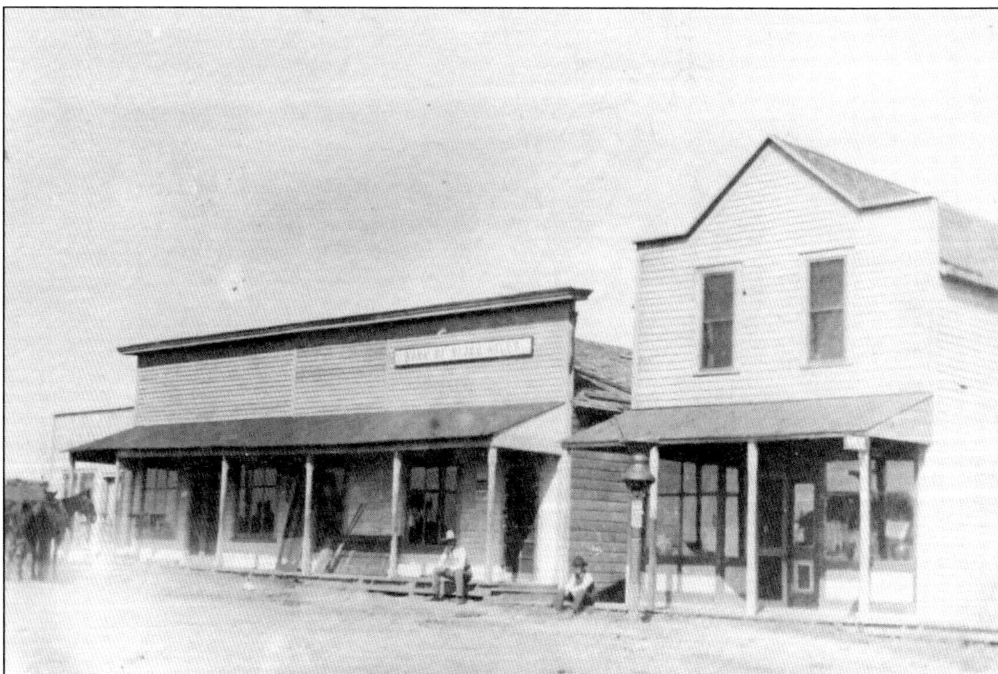

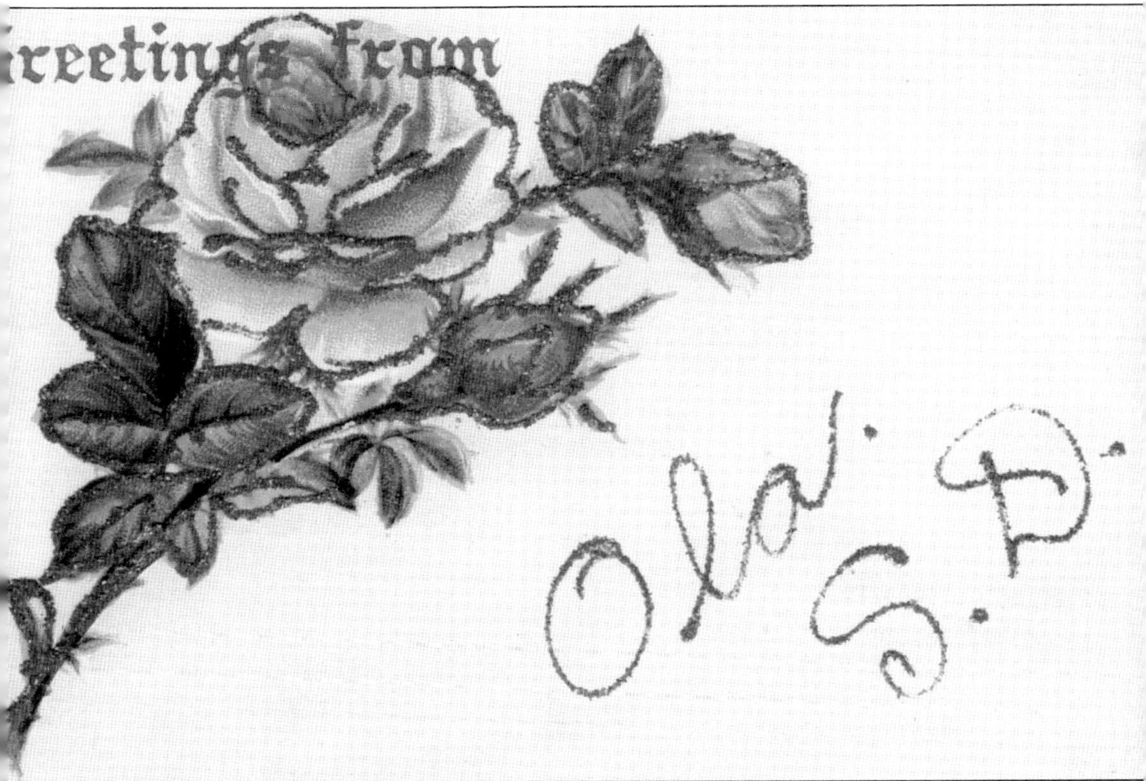

A standard postcard announces greetings from Ola, South Dakota. Ola was named in 1881 when the post office was established there and the government wanted a short name given to it. Ola is approximately 15 miles southeast of Chamberlain. There were so many people with Scandinavian roots in the area that Ola seemed an appropriate name. In the early 1900s, Ola was known for its band. Starting in 1903, the band played off and on until the 1920s. At one time, Ola had a barbershop, pool hall, general store, town hall, harness shop, and more. Today, there are only the Ola Hall and St. Olaf Lutheran Church left standing. The church is still active. Nowadays, Ola is home to the Ola Players, who perform a play every year in November. The proceeds are used to keep up the Ola Hall for the use of future generations.

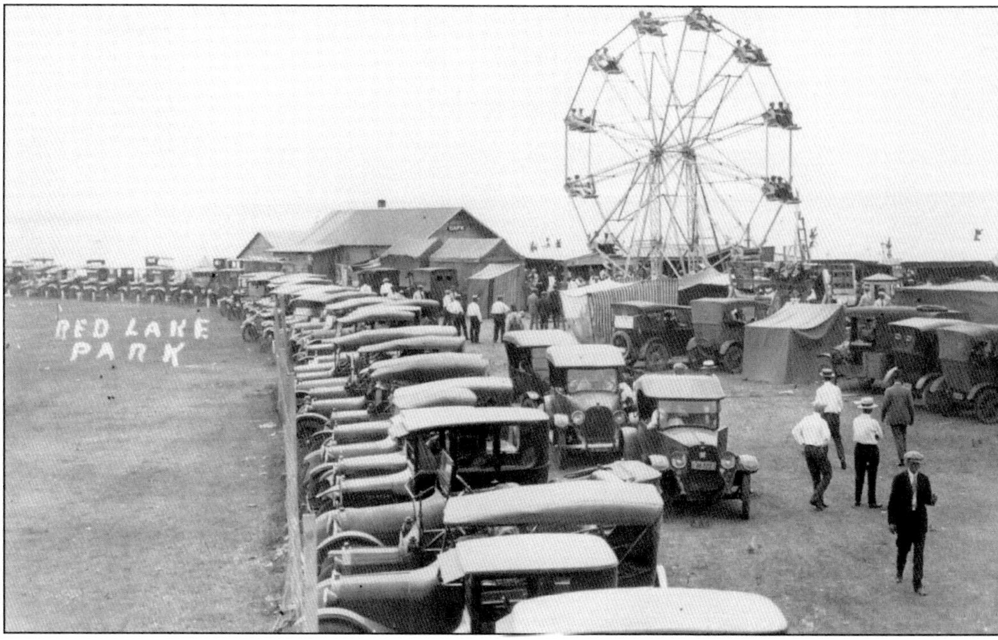

These two real-photo postcards from the 1920s are of Red Lake Park. Red Lake is located south of Pukwana. There was never an actual town of Red Lake, although there was a post office in the area on and off between 1880 to 1915. The Ferris wheel shown could take three people in each seat for a thrilling ride. The larger building in the back is a café. Many cars are parked around the edge of a baseball field for a comfortable view of the game. There are even tents set up for some to stay over several days during the festivities. (Both, photograph by Kuchera.)

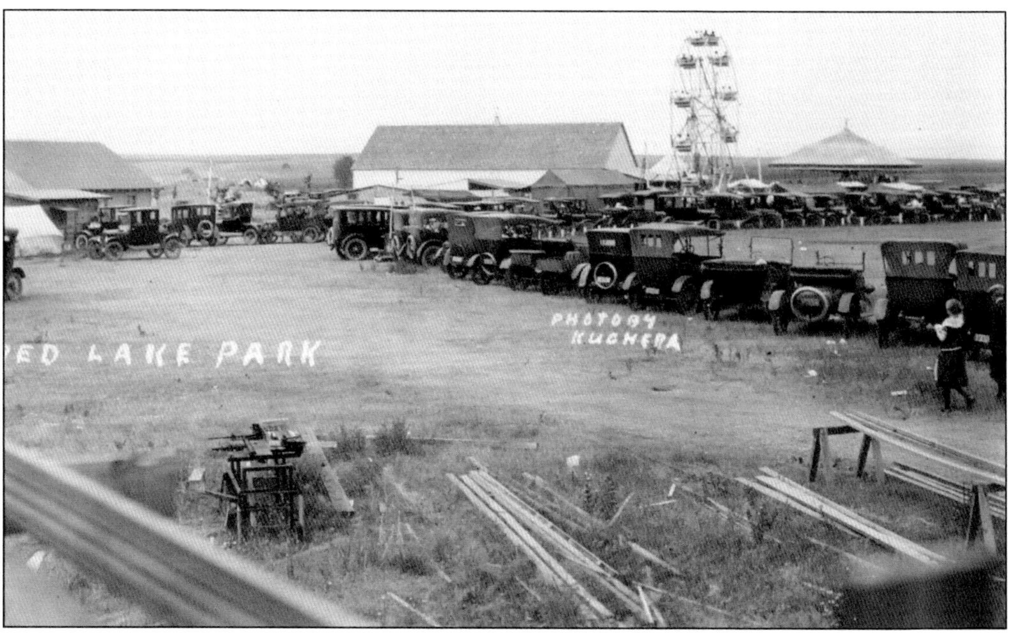

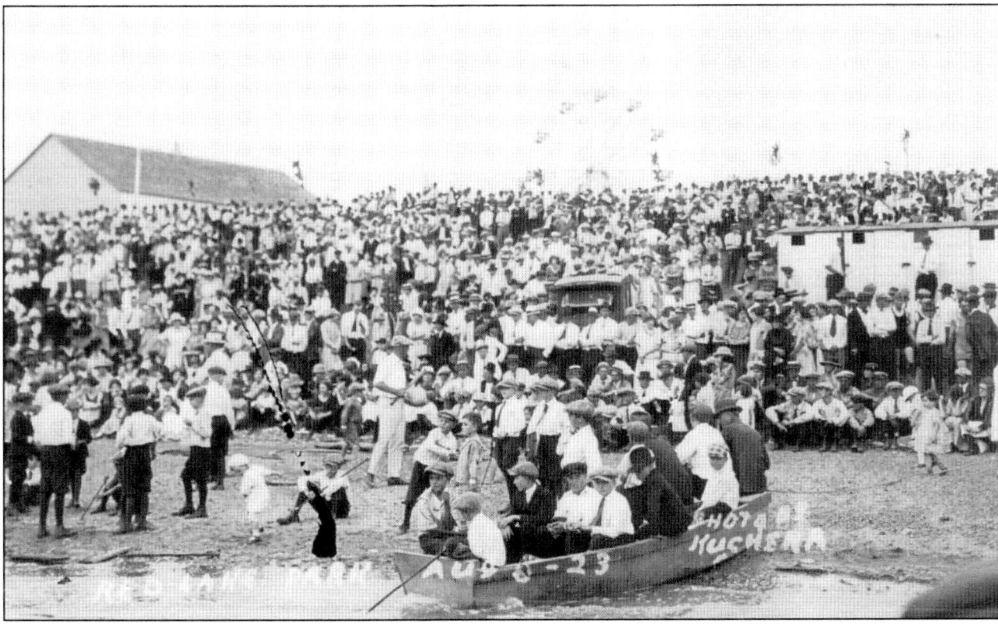

This large crowd of people is at Red Lake in August 1923. This celebration was obviously the place to be. Everyone is well dressed, with most of the men wearing ties. It looks as if the crowd in the back is watching the men and boys in the front while they are fishing. Possibly, a fishing contest is underway. (Photograph by Kuchera.)

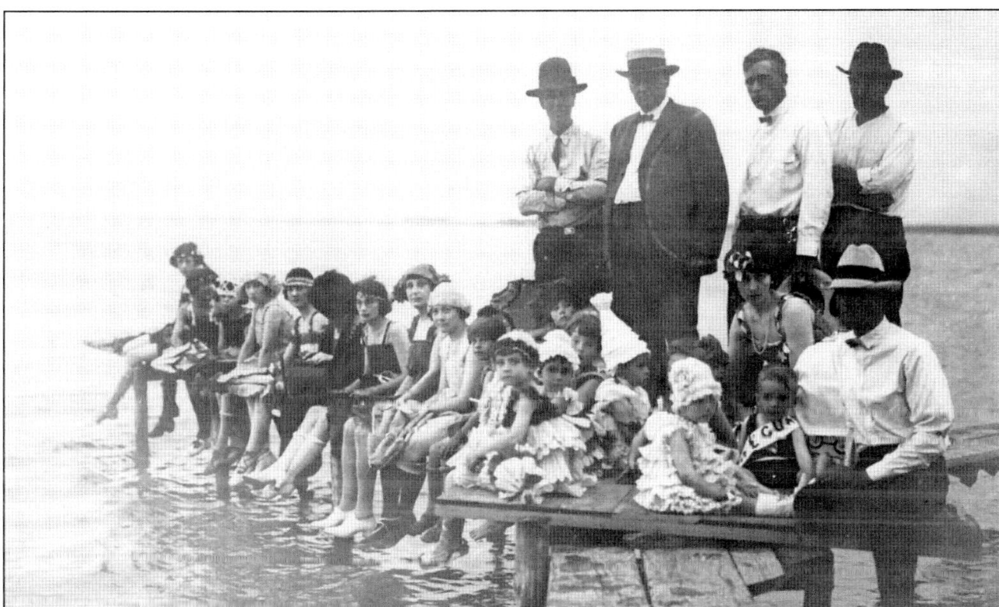

This real-photo postcard shows a group of people cooling themselves on the dock at Red Lake. There was a roadhouse near the east end of the lake built by Peter Nelson. In 1876, Lt. Col. George Armstrong Custer stayed at the Nelson Roadhouse on the way to his demise at Little Bighorn.

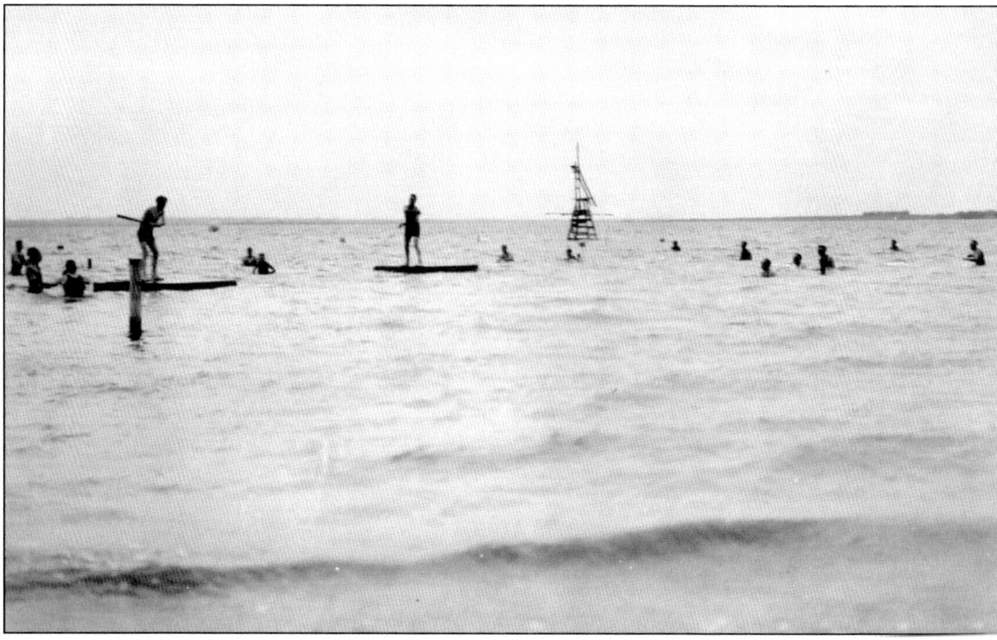

A group of young people is playing a game of baseball on Red Lake in this unusual real-photo postcard. There was a crude diving board and dock where the batter would swing at the pitch that another participant would throw. Although it was likely a fun game, many baseballs must have been lost.

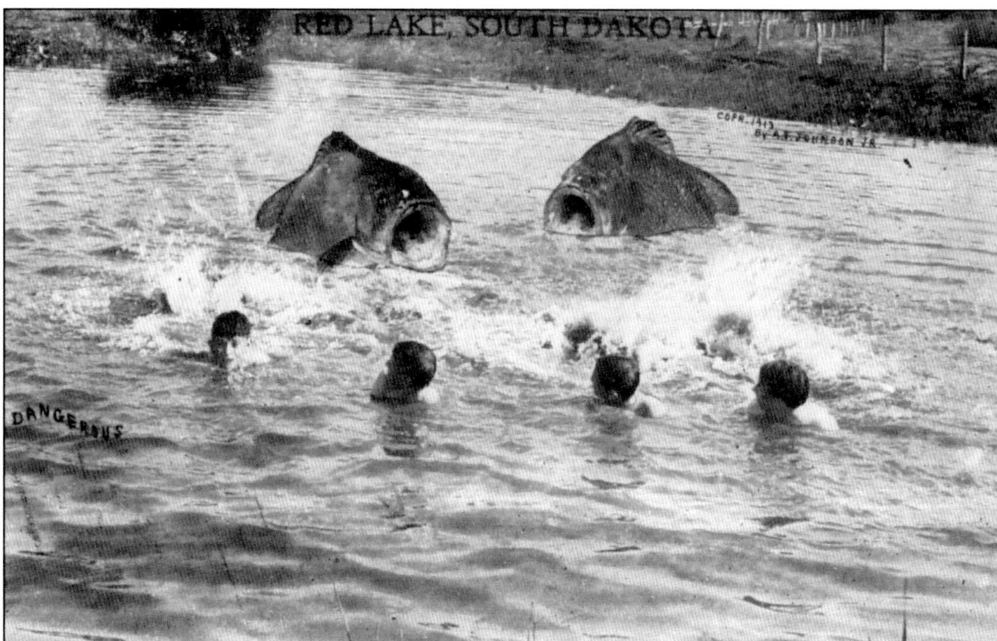

This fantasy postcard shows a couple of "big mouth" bass going after four young swimmers. "Red Lake, South Dakota" is stamped across the top of the card. To the left side is the caption, "Dangerous." Although this is not a real photograph of Red Lake, it was probably a popular card to send to friends and acquaintances.

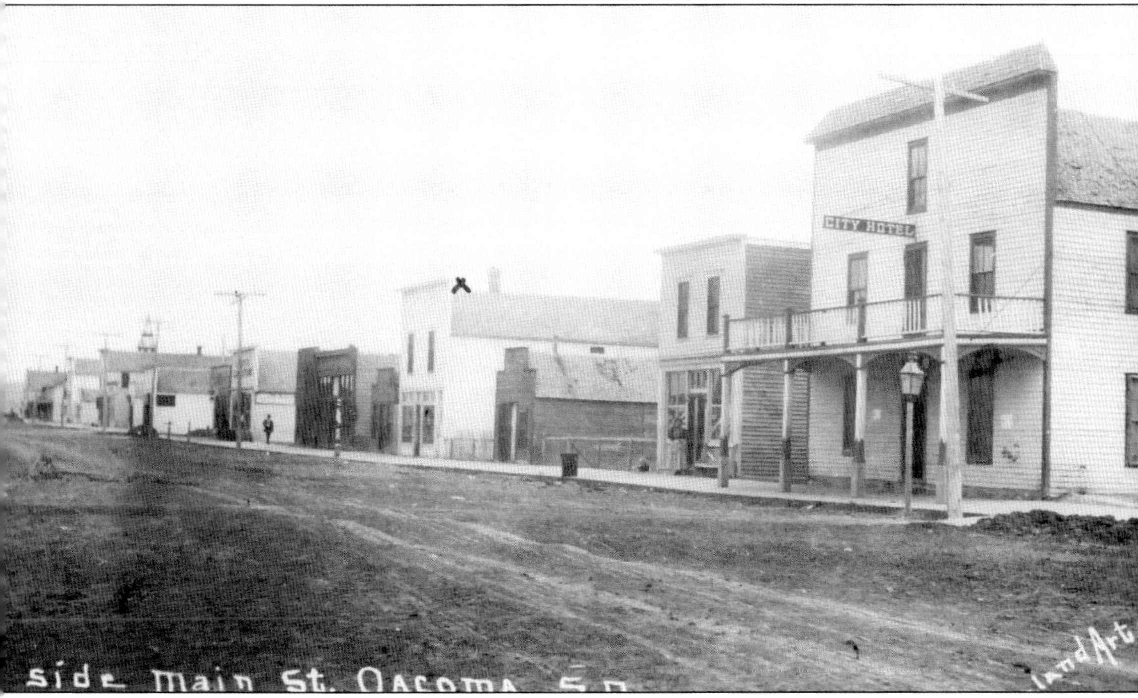

Postmarked in 1911, this card shows the east side of Main Street in Oacoma, South Dakota. Oacoma was once called Gladstone. It is located almost directly across the Missouri River from Chamberlain. The name *Oacoma* comes from the Sioux word for "in between." This is appropriate, as Oacoma lies in between the Missouri River and the bluffs. The name still fits Oacoma nowadays since it is the in-between stop for those going west to the Black Hills. The first post office was established at Oacoma in 1890, and the town itself was organized in 1893. It was a thriving town with many businesses, including a grocery store, drugstore, livery, newspaper, hotel, café, and saloon. The city hotel with a gaslight out front is in the foreground. The steeple of the church can be seen at the far end of Main Street. (Photograph by O.S. Leeland.)

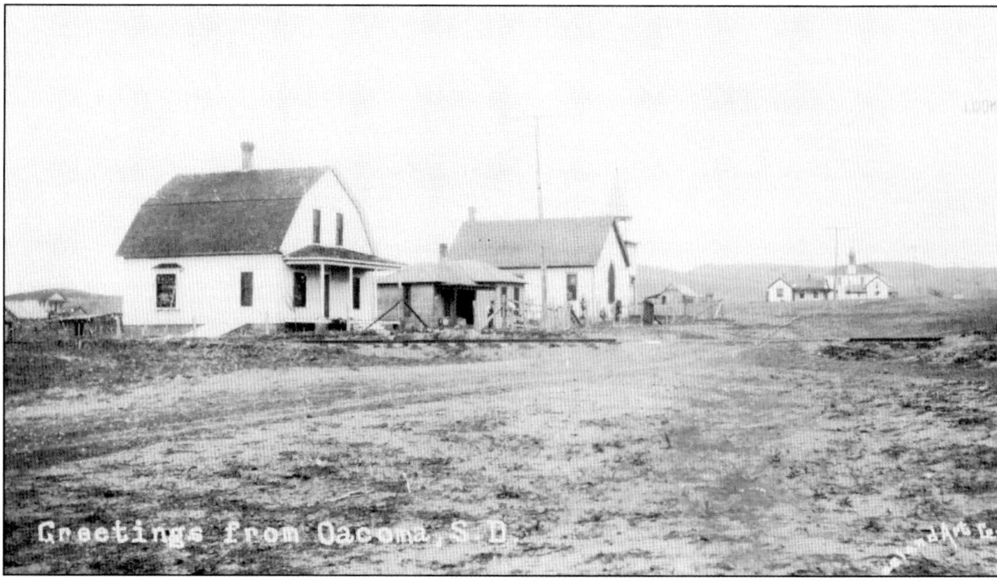

Both of the cards on this page feature Oacoma. The first view announces "Greetings from Oacoma, S.D." It shows some homes and the church and was postmarked in 1914. A better view of the Christian Church of Oacoma is pictured below. Written in pencil are the names of the pastors. A large bell is in the round-roofed bell tower. This church was one of the oldest buildings left in Oacoma when it was sold to the Old West Museum in 1975 and moved to that site. It was later donated to the Chamberlain Area Historical Society and moved to a location near the Oacoma cemetery, where it still stands. (Above, photograph by O.S. Leeland.)

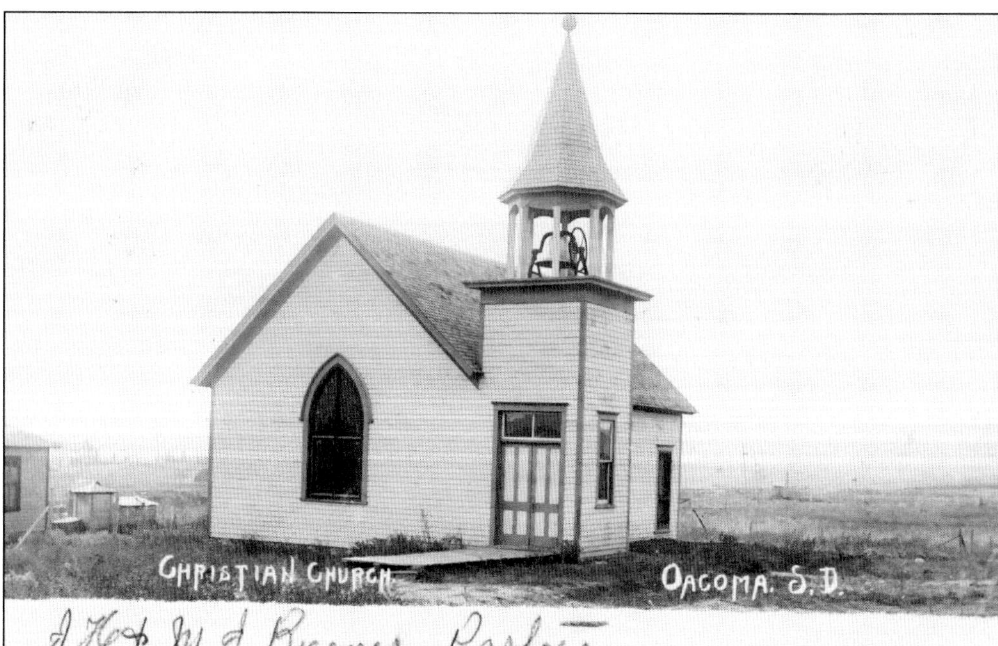

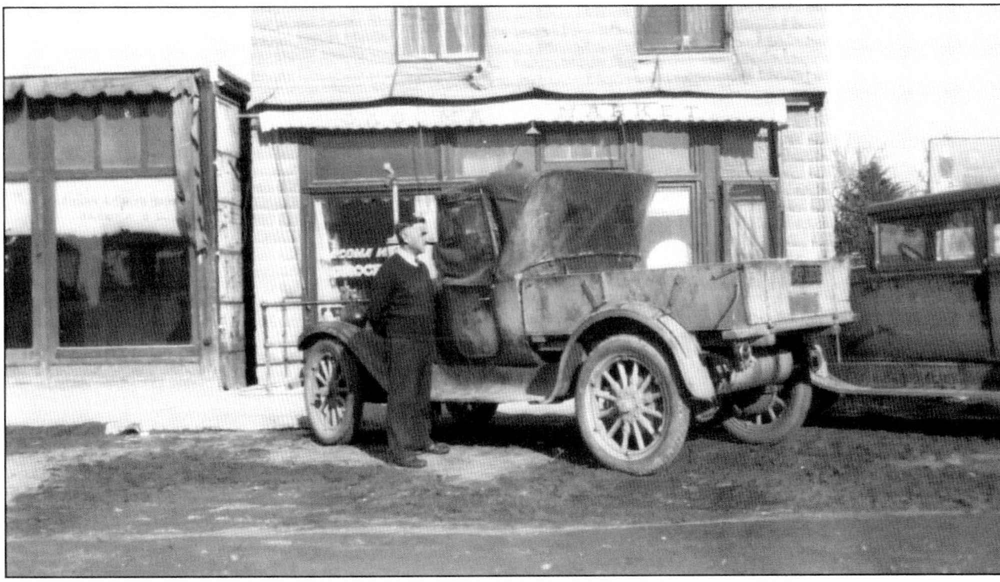

In 1919, Albert Mueller and Alfons Wetterer bought the Beaman and Strong Dry Goods store at Oacoma and changed the name to the Oacoma Market. Later, Albert would become sole owner, and following World War II, his son Alfred would go into business with him. In the early 1950s, when Highway 16 changed its route, Al and his wife, Veda, had the insight to move their business closer to the highway. Al's Oasis is seen below in the early days. Over the years, it has expanded little by little and has become a favorite stop for travelers on Interstate 90. It is still owned by the Mueller family. (Both, courtesy Al's Oasis.)

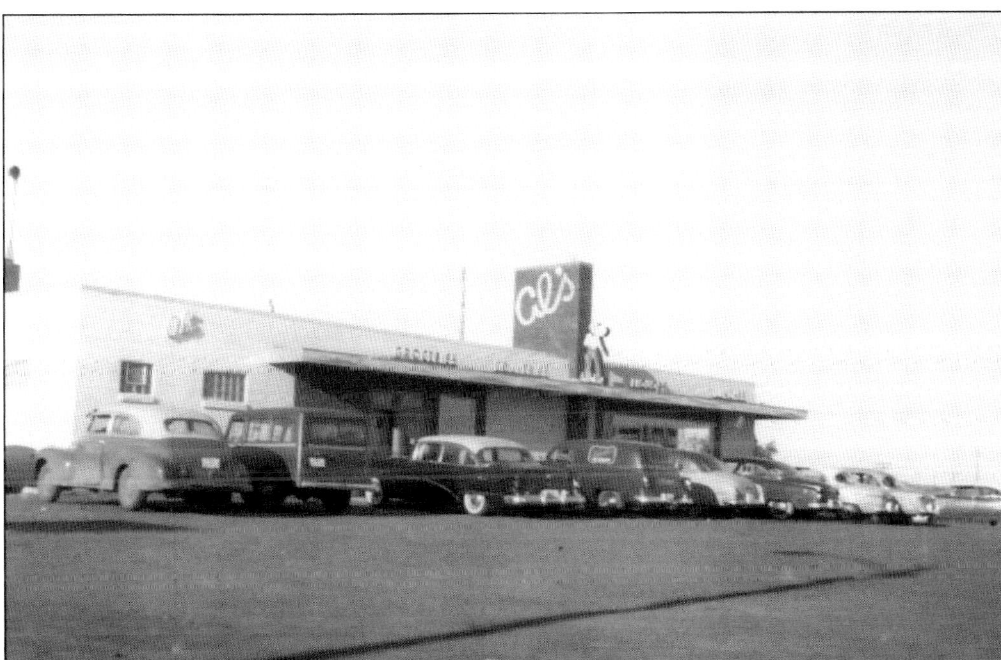

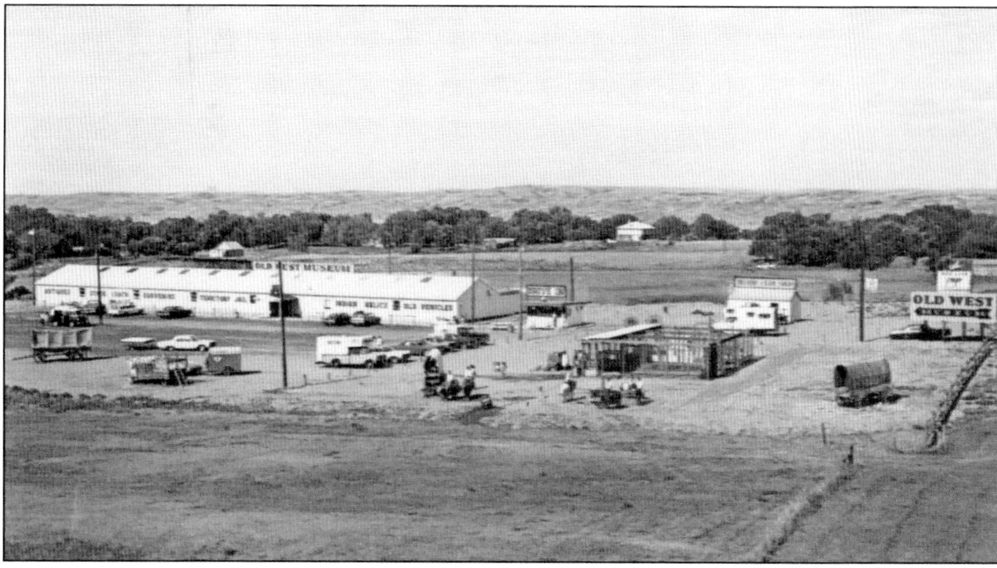

Gene and Alice Olson opened Old West Museum in the spring of 1969. The museum was open for 29 years before they retired. It was an attraction with a little bit of everything, including a main street, cars, tractors, Western and Native American artifacts, horse-drawn vehicles, and items of local significance. The museum started with one large building and over the years was enlarged to make room for expanding collections. A live buffalo and Texas longhorn were also kept on the grounds. The Olsons raised Texas longhorn cattle when they ranched south of Chamberlain before they started the museum. Charley the longhorn, shown below, had his photograph taken by many visitors. The Olson's son and daughter-in-law, Greg and Melanie Olson, now operate an antique mall called Old West Trading Post in the same location.

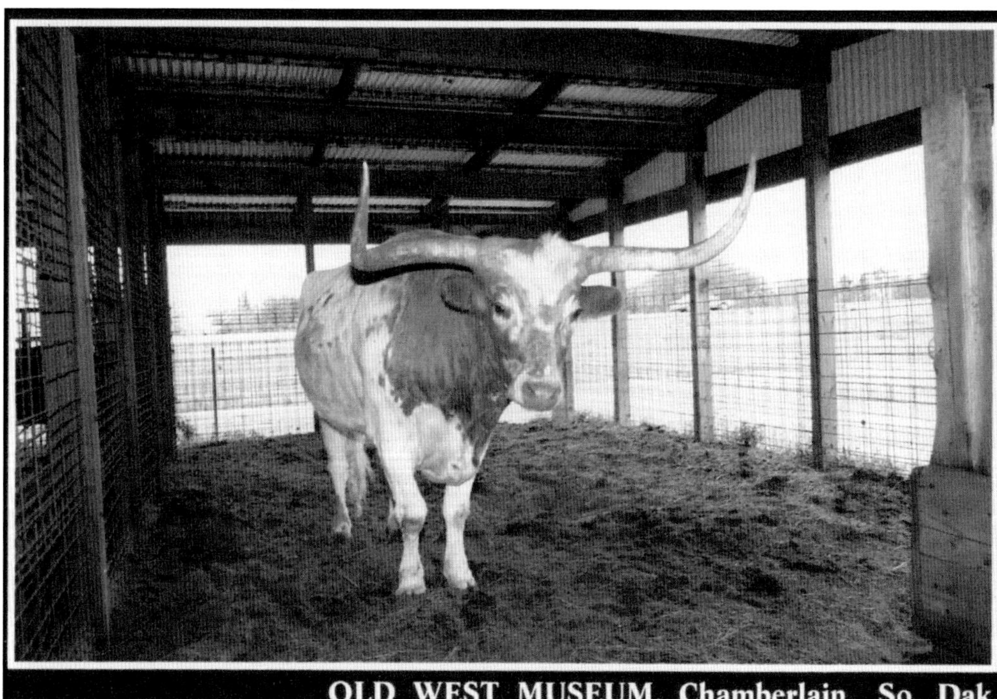

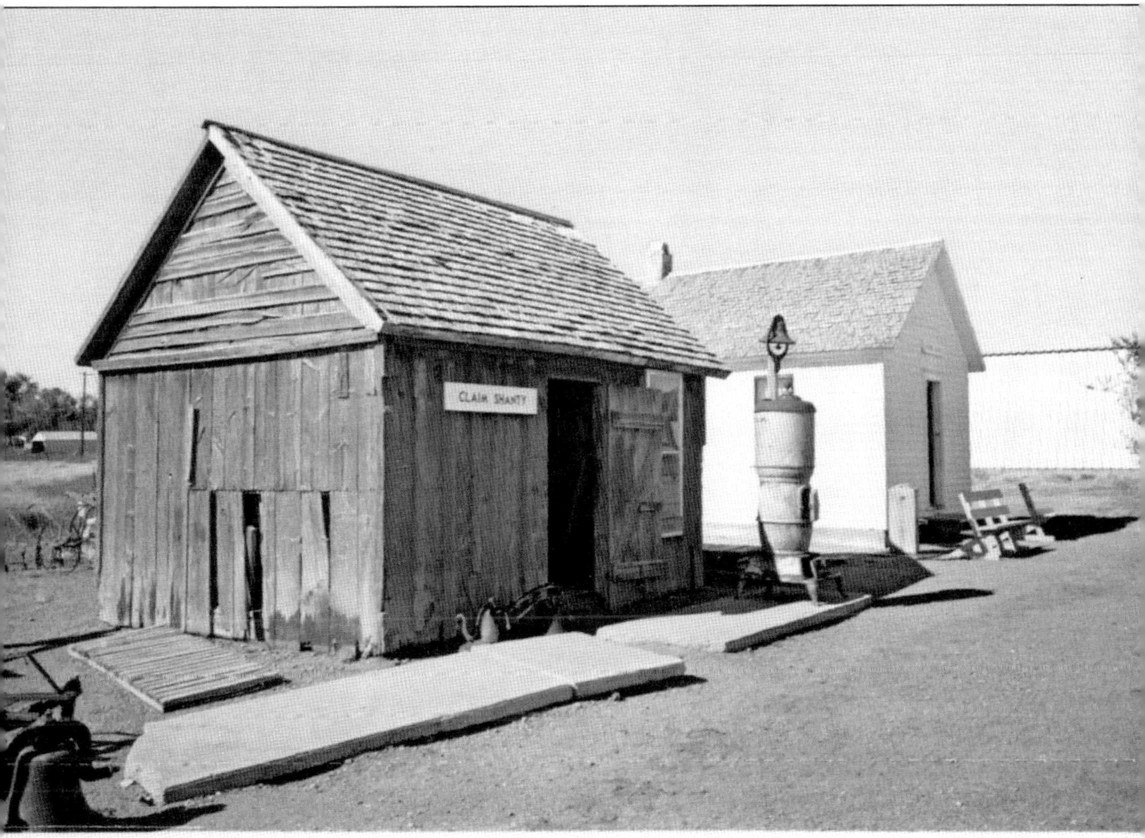

880 Claim Shanty *Old West Museum*

This original Brule County claim shanty was part of the Old West Museum of Oacoma's display. Close to 140 years old, it still remains on display at Old West Trading Post. The shanty was originally located on the southwest quarter of Section Four in Cleveland Township. The Peter Olson family lived in it for a year when they claimed their homestead. Many times, these shanties would be moved from quarter section to quarter section to be used when someone else claimed land. This 12-foot-by-15-foot shanty still has the original shingles and was built with square nails. Over the years, it remained in the Olson family and was moved from place to place and used as a chicken coop and storage shed before becoming part of the museum. The building pictured just beyond the shanty is a one-room schoolhouse that originated near Lane, South Dakota. It is different from many one-room schoolhouses because it does not have an entry or porch, but rather opens directly into the schoolroom.

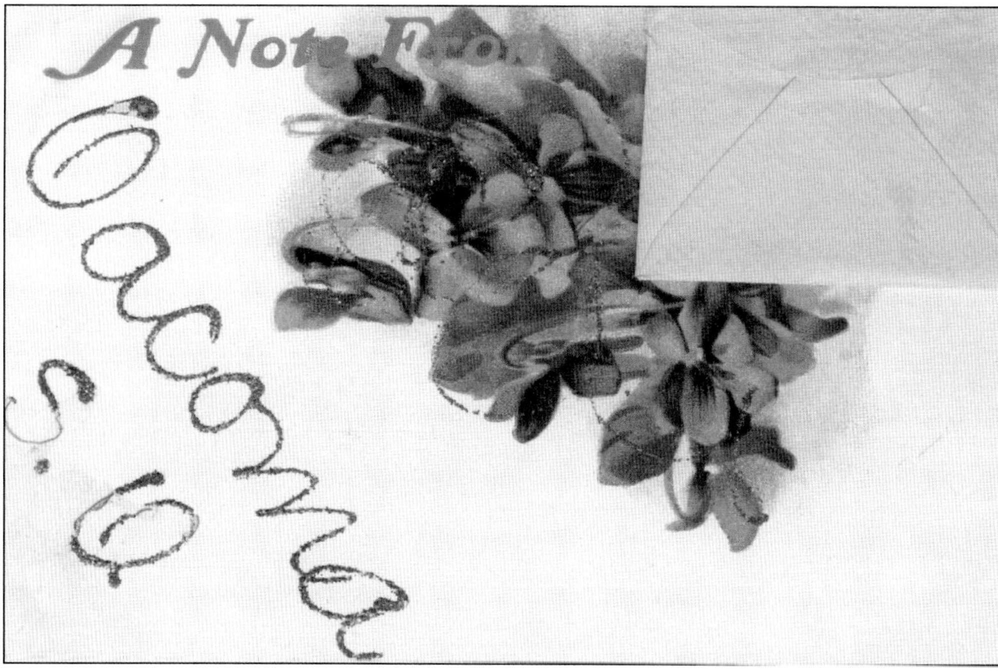

This is a standard postcard with "Oacoma, S.D." written on it in glitter. These standard postcards were especially popular with small towns. This one is a little unusual because it has a tiny envelope added to it for the sender to include a small note. There is actually a tiny handwritten note inside the envelope as well as a note on the back of the card.

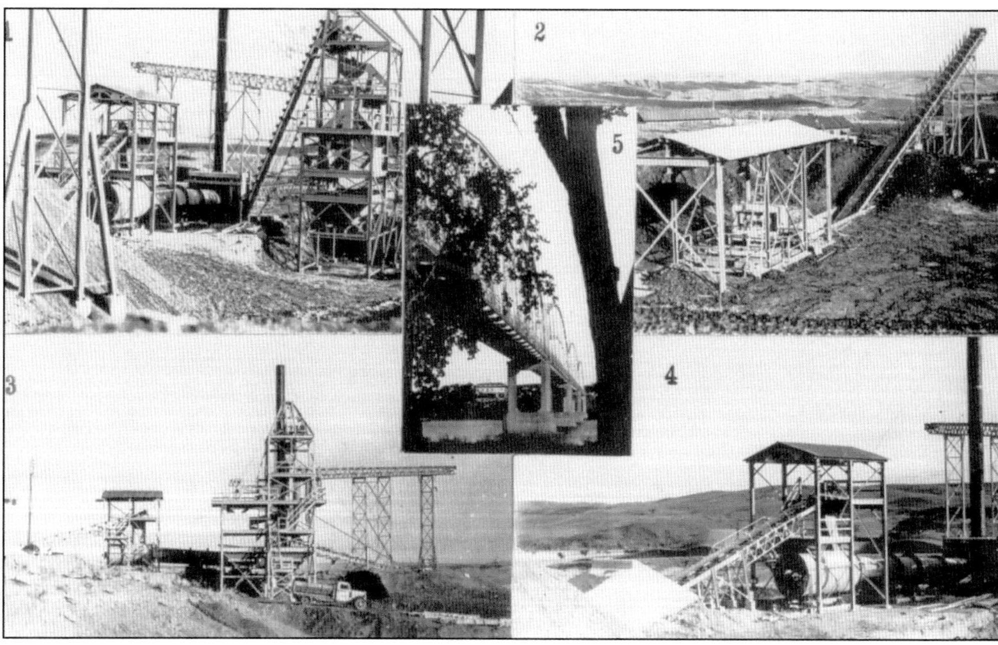

This manganese test plant was located two miles west of Oacoma. The hills in the area around Oacoma have a good amount of manganese-bearing shale and clay. There was a test working to recover it, but it ended up costing too much in time and money, so the plant did not last very long. The remnants of some of the cement shafts can still be seen in the hills today.

Six

Farm and Ranch

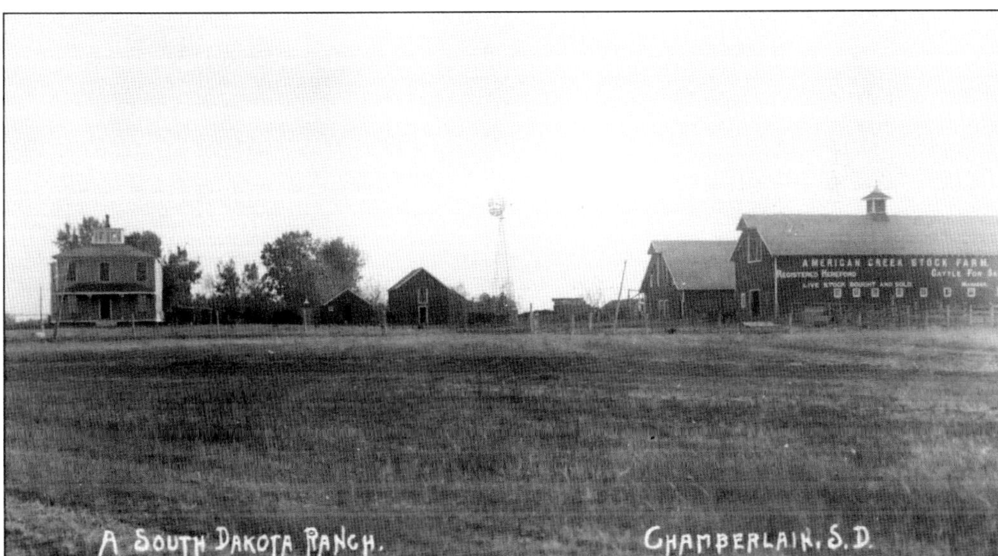

This is the original Sloatman ranch headquarters. It was at the top of the hill east of Chamberlain. Years ago, the farmers would announce the name of their farm and specialty by painting it on the barn. On the side of this barn is written, "American Creek Stock Farm, Registered Hereford Cattle for Sale." A beautiful home, granary, windmill, and other outbuildings give evidence that this was a prosperous ranch.

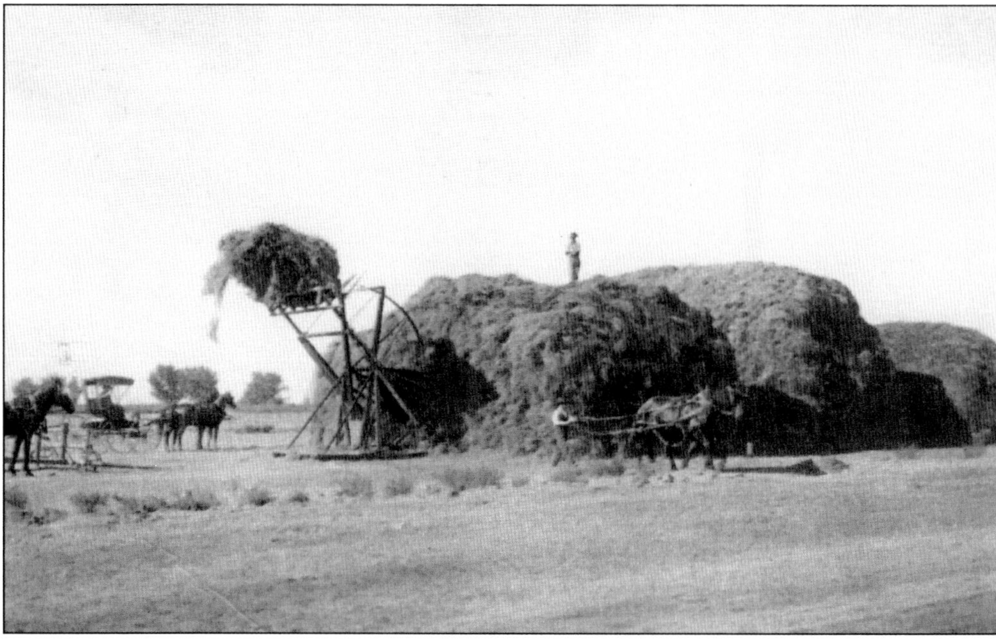

Alfalfa stacking was a common sight on farms in the Chamberlain area around 1914. The horse team on the left just loaded the stacker while the team on the right is now raising it and putting the alfalfa on top of the pile. The team of horses with the buggy is possibly driven by one of the women with lunch for the men. This was a hot and dusty job—especially working on top of the stack.

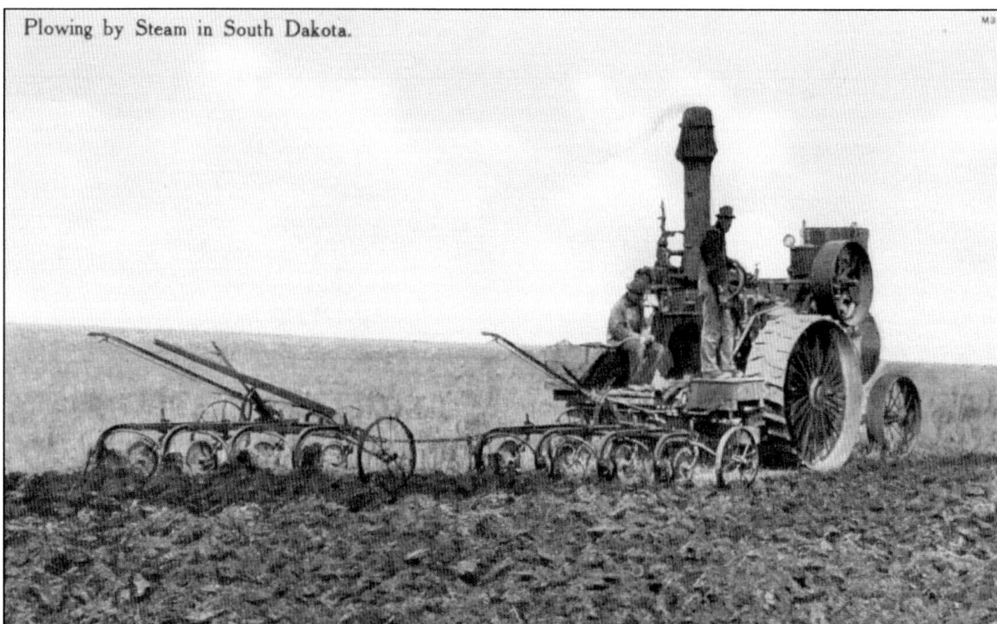

A steam tractor plowing a field in South Dakota is the subject of this card. This steamer is pulling an eight-bottom plow, which made the work a lot faster than using horses and a one- or two-bottom plow. One man had to get up earlier than the others to start the tractors in the morning since it took quite a while to heat up the water to make the steam.

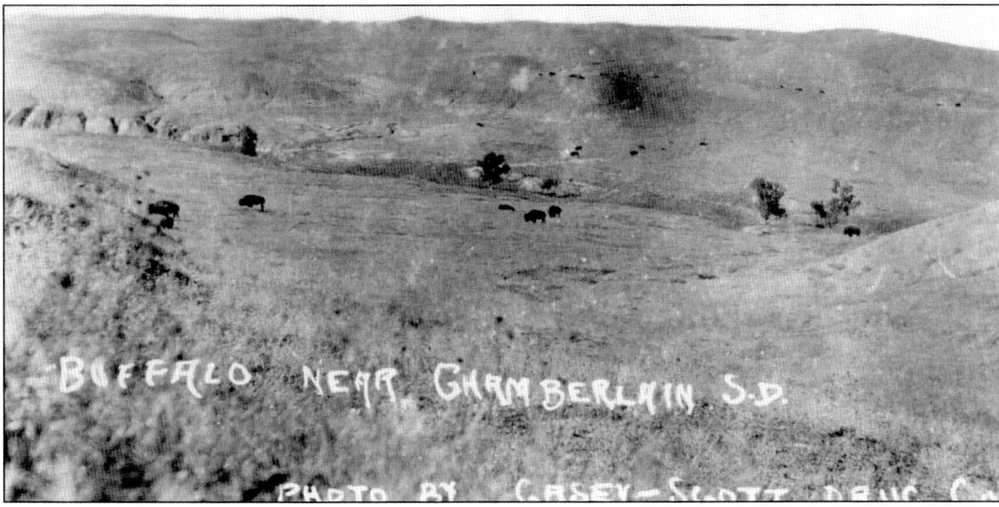

This view shows some buffalo roaming the foothills along the Missouri River near Chamberlain. As is evident, there were not many trees in the area. Almost all the trees not by the river or a watering hole were planted by hand. No fences can be seen in this photograph, so the buffalo could roam a great distance.

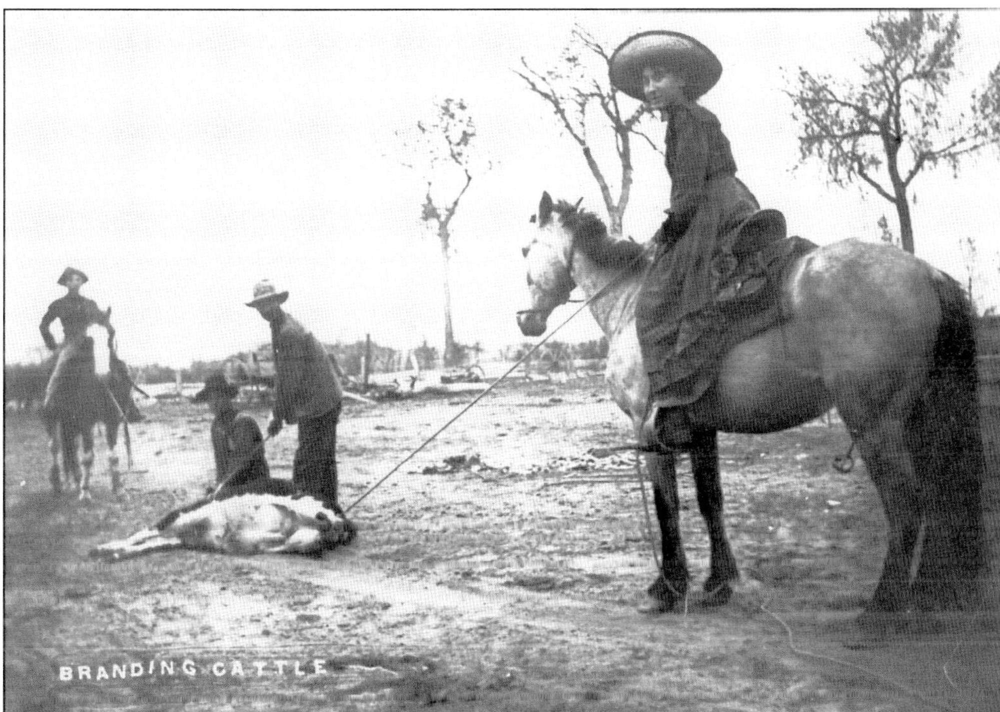

Branding cattle in central South Dakota is the subject of this postcard. This card was postmarked March 14, 1911, and the message states, "This is one that was taken last spring. Mildred is on the first horse and papa is branding and I am on the other horse do you remember Jim well that is the one I am on."

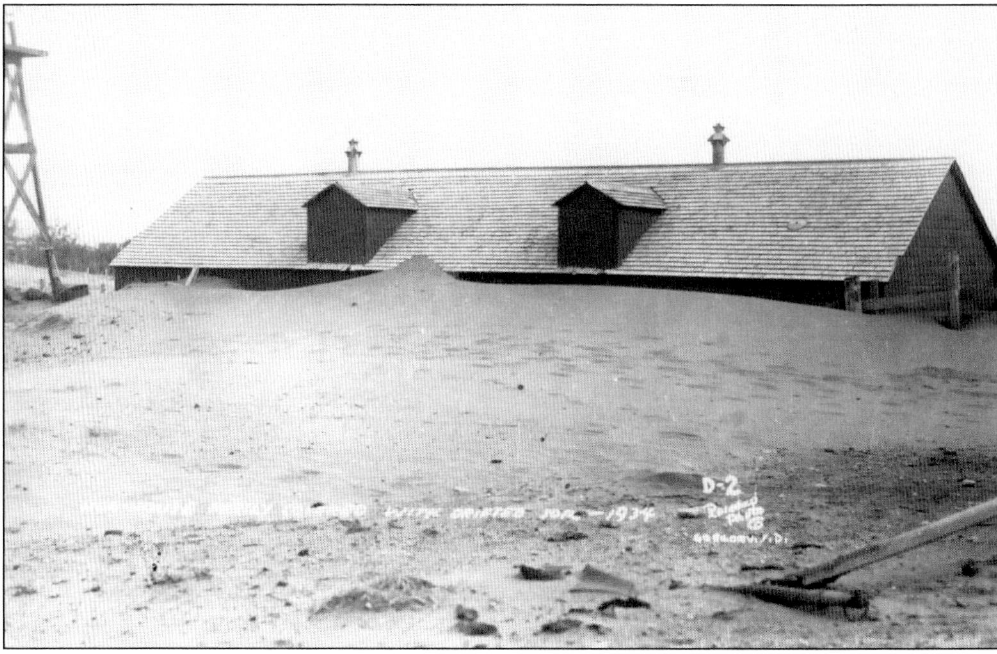

These two cards show what the dust bowl was like in the 1930s. Above, a hog house is pictured almost covered with drifted soil in 1934. Below, a 1935 photograph shows drifting soil that is covering a chicken house and a shelterbelt of trees. During the 1930s, almost 75 percent of the artesian wells in the Chamberlain area went dry. The dirt would blow through every crack in a house or barn. Some days were so dark due to the dust that lamps needed to be lighted to see inside. It was even hard to take a breath many days. This was a hard time in the Chamberlain area.

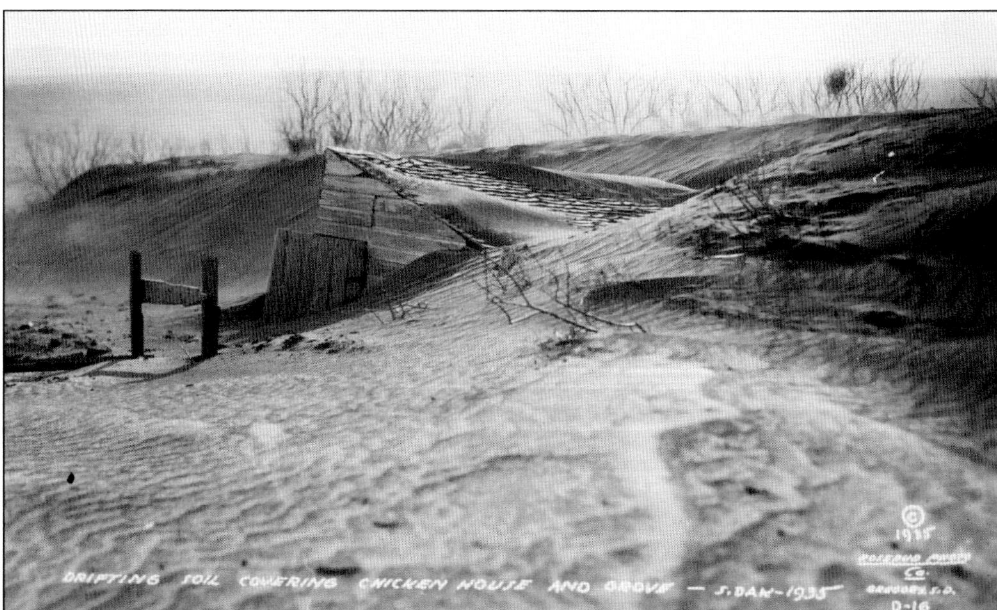

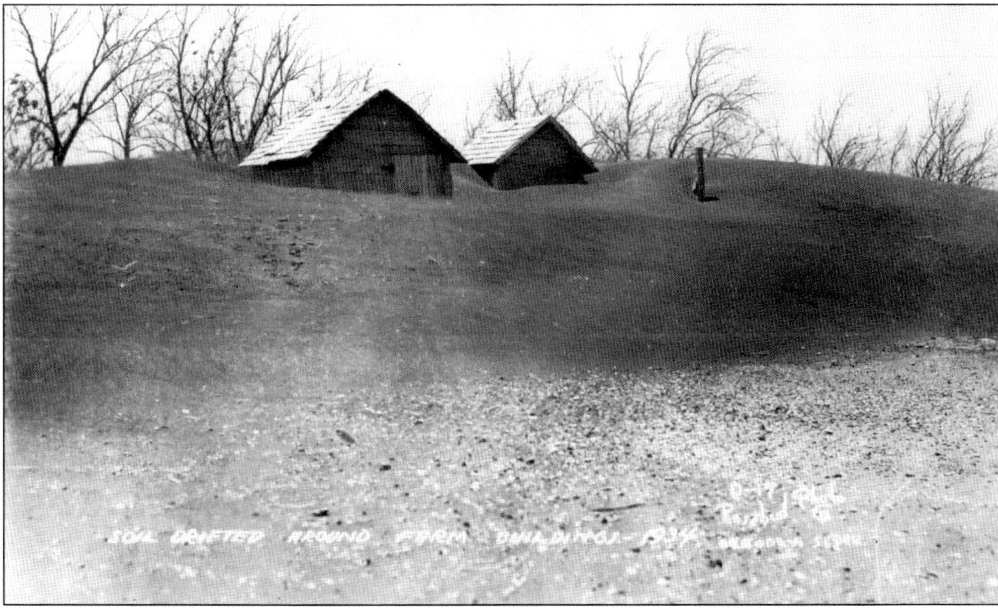

Soil that had drifted around farm buildings is shown here in 1934 during the dust bowl days. The Civilian Conservation Corps (CCC) was one of the government programs implemented during the 1930s to make jobs available. The CCC camp on American Island was active planting trees, building dams, doing roadwork, and making other improvements in and around Chamberlain.

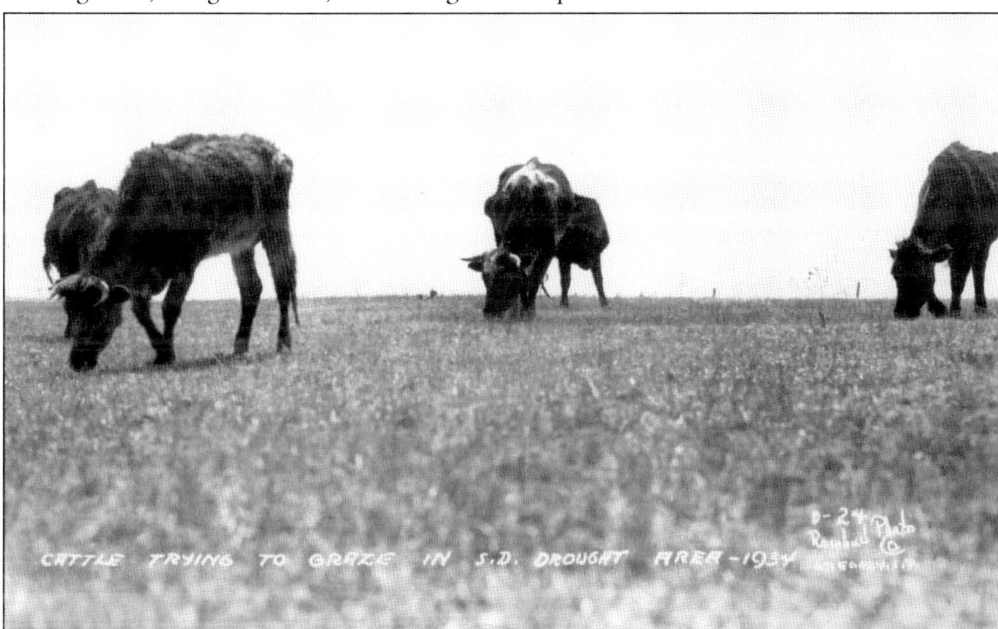

Cattle trying to graze in the South Dakota drought of 1934 is the story of this postcard. During the "dirty '30s," almost all pastures were grazed down and cattle feed sold for a premium. Many thistles were harvested for cattle feed. Most of the cattle in the Chamberlain area were sold to the government and either hauled away to canneries or killed. The cattle that were killed were taken west of Pukwana and buried in a trench. The hides of the animals were sliced to guard against theft for profit.

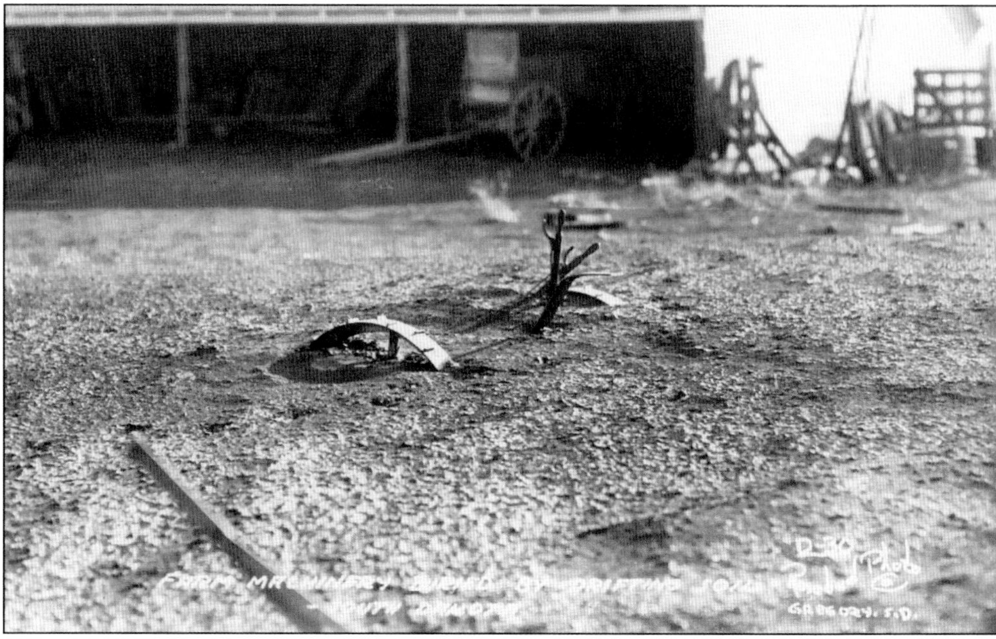

The dust bowl devastated central South Dakota. The photograph above shows farm machinery buried by drifting soil. Notice the iron wheels just sticking up over the dirt. Below, drifting soil after a dust storm covered a hog house in 1935. Grasshoppers were also a big problem during the early 1930s. They were known to eat whole fields of corn and wheat as well as pastures. They would sit on fence wires and make them look like thick ropes. The grasshoppers would eat the bark off of trees, and even newly washed clothes on the line would have holes where the insects would chew on them. They were even known to gnaw on rubber automobile tires. When a strong wind blew them against a house, the grasshoppers would sound like hail.

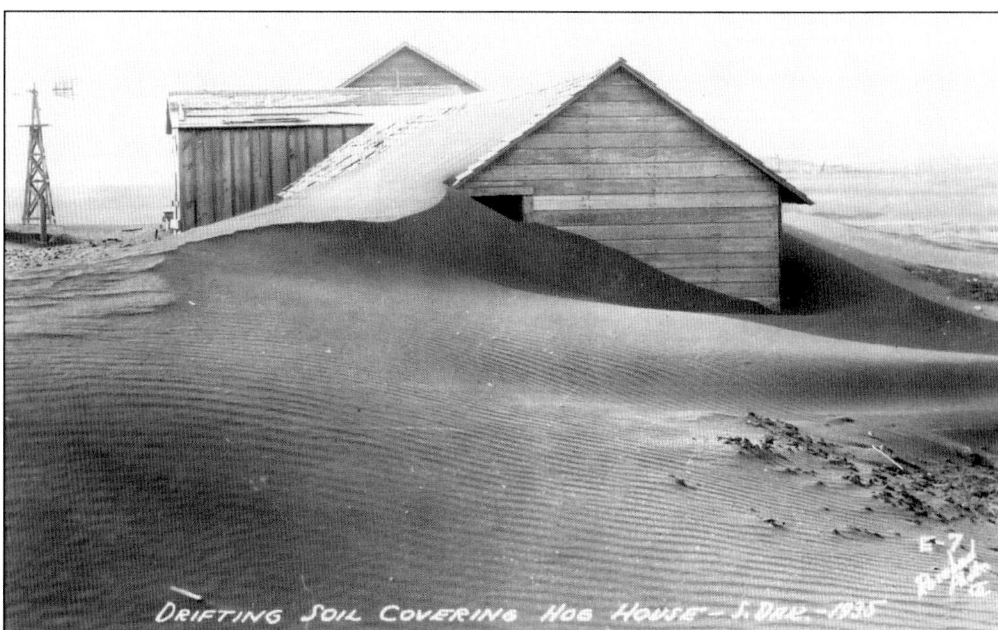

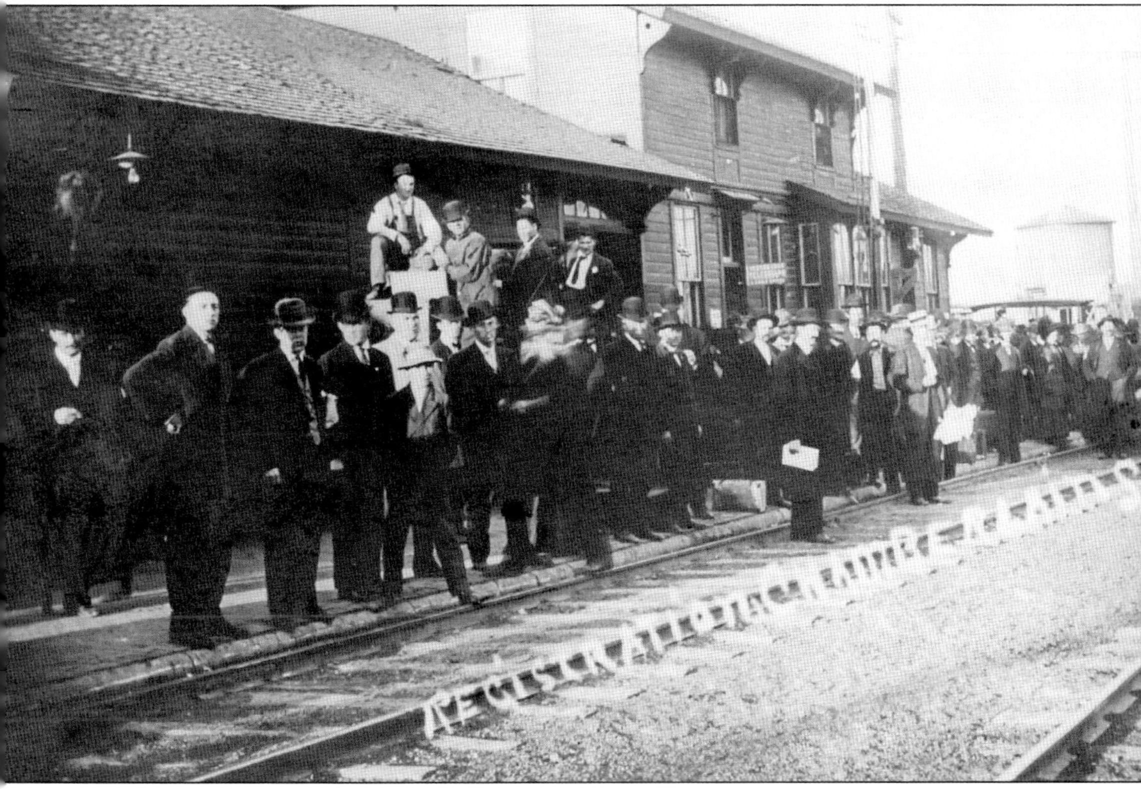

Chamberlain was one of the main registration points when Indian lands were opened up for settlement. The original Homestead Act of 1862 would allow a claim of 160 acres of land. In order to retain the land, the owner needed to build a shanty and live there for five years and plow at least 10 acres. In 1900, after which the registration photographs were taken, the law was amended so a person could get up to 320 acres of land, of which 80 acres had to be tilled by the third year. Here, men are crowded along the railroad tracks in town during registration, during which the days were chaotic. The train came and went and was loaded with so many people that they filled the streets until Chamberlain resembled a large city. At one point during a four-day period, 60,000 people had arrived, with more than 10,000 people at a time fighting to fill out the applications that would give them a chance at the land drawing and a new start out west.

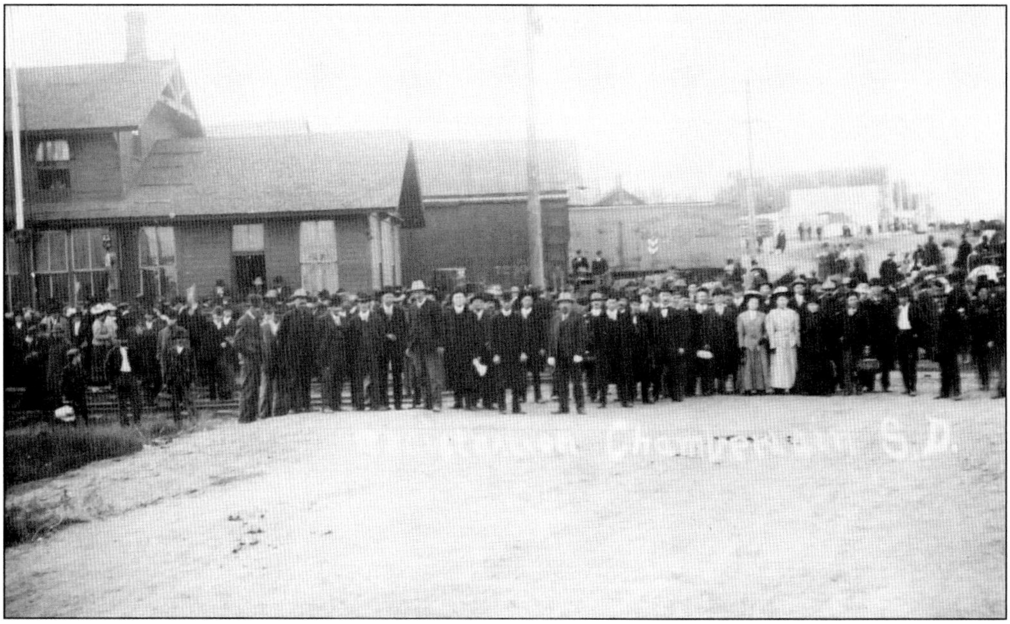

These two views show the great number of people gathered near the railroad depot at Chamberlain during registration. During this time, the land office clerks worked in shifts, and the office remained open 24 hours around the clock. This was a booming time for Chamberlain businesses, with the hotels filled to overflowing, as was any saloon or eating establishment. With the good also came the bad, as gamblers and crooks arrived in town to take advantage of the situation. Chamberlain would also benefit when the homesteaders claimed land in the area, bringing hardworking new blood and ideas into central South Dakota.

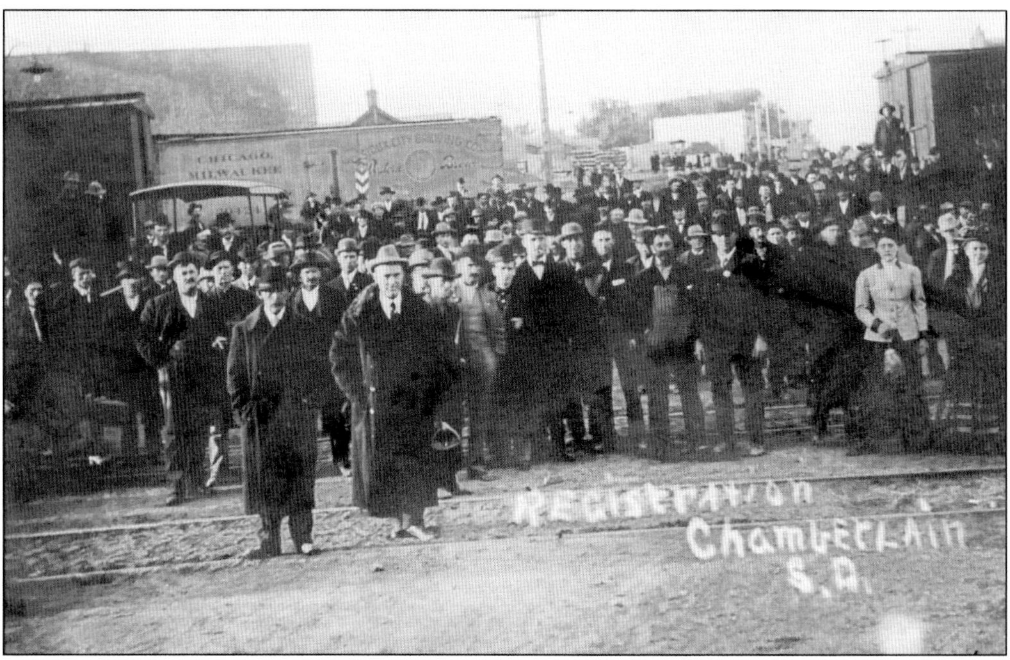

Seven

Native Americans

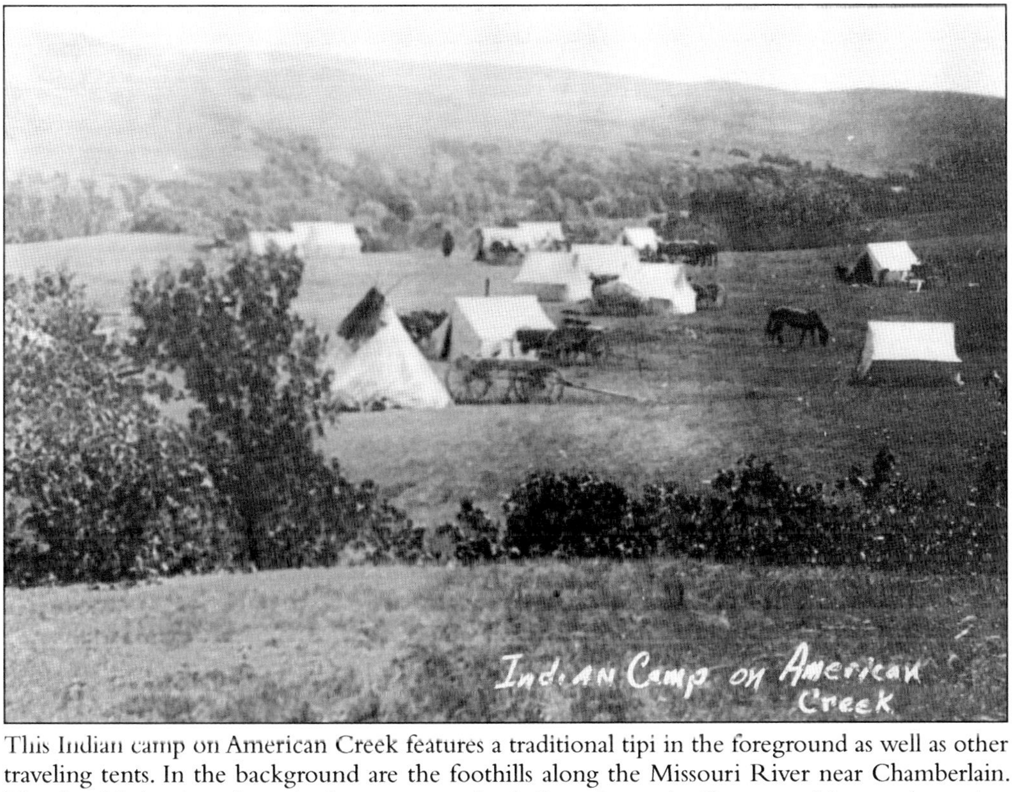

This Indian camp on American Creek features a traditional tipi in the foreground as well as other traveling tents. In the background are the foothills along the Missouri River near Chamberlain. The first Native Americans in the area were the Arikara. Later, the Sioux would enter the region and remain.

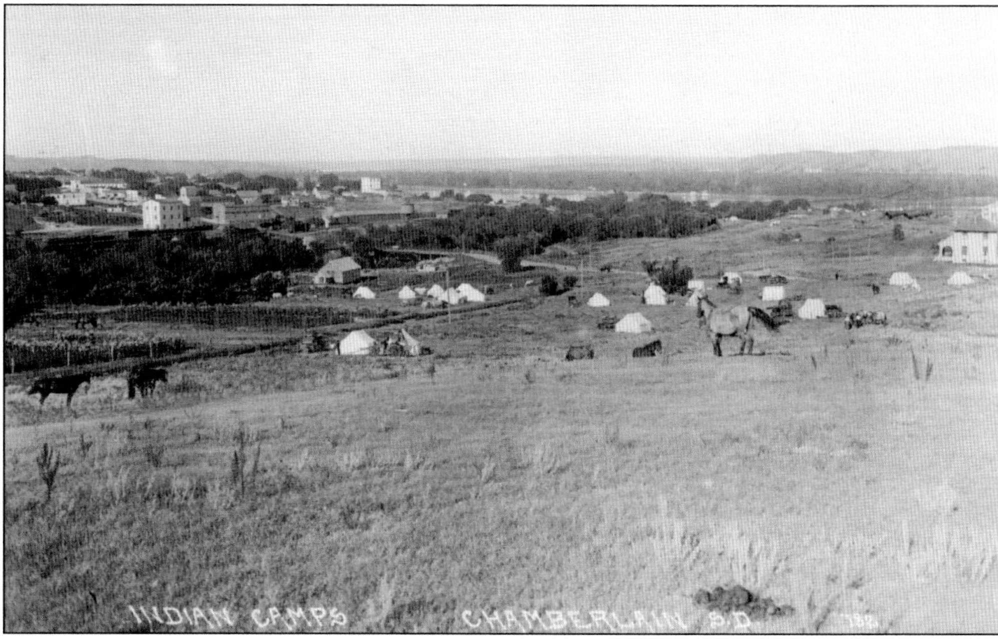

These Indian camps consisted mostly of canvas tents and were located north of Chamberlain close to American Creek. Horses graze in the foreground. In the background, the two largest buildings are the two flour mills, and on the far right is the office of the Portland Cement Company.

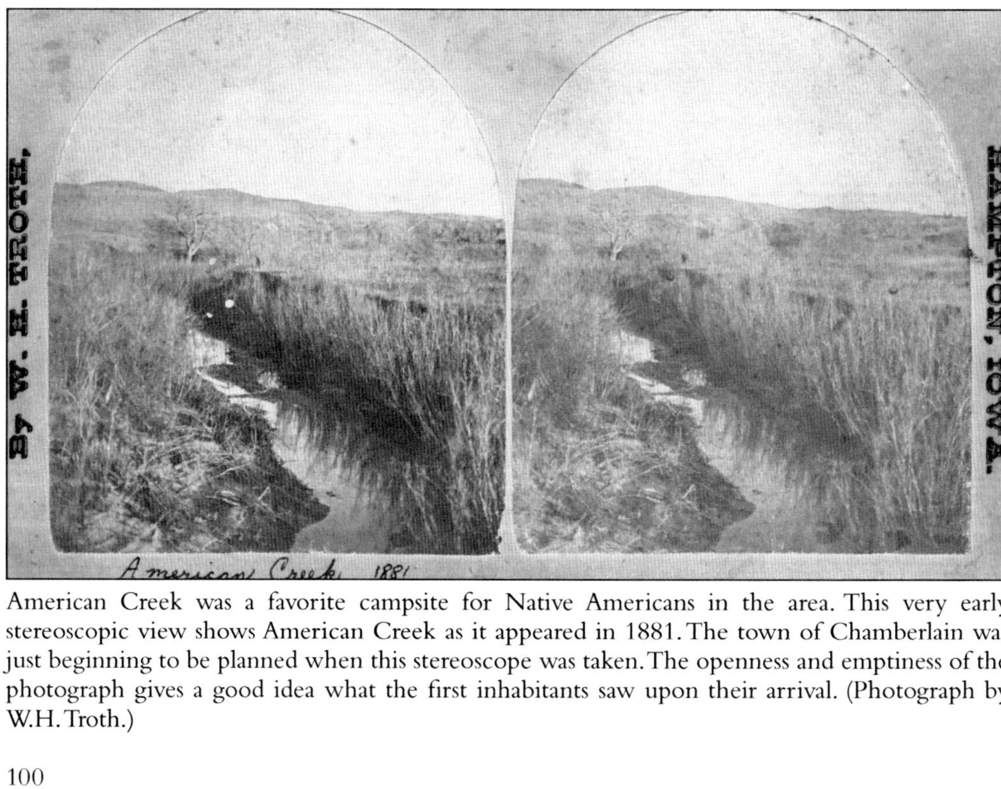

American Creek was a favorite campsite for Native Americans in the area. This very early stereoscopic view shows American Creek as it appeared in 1881. The town of Chamberlain was just beginning to be planned when this stereoscope was taken. The openness and emptiness of the photograph gives a good idea what the first inhabitants saw upon their arrival. (Photograph by W.H. Troth.)

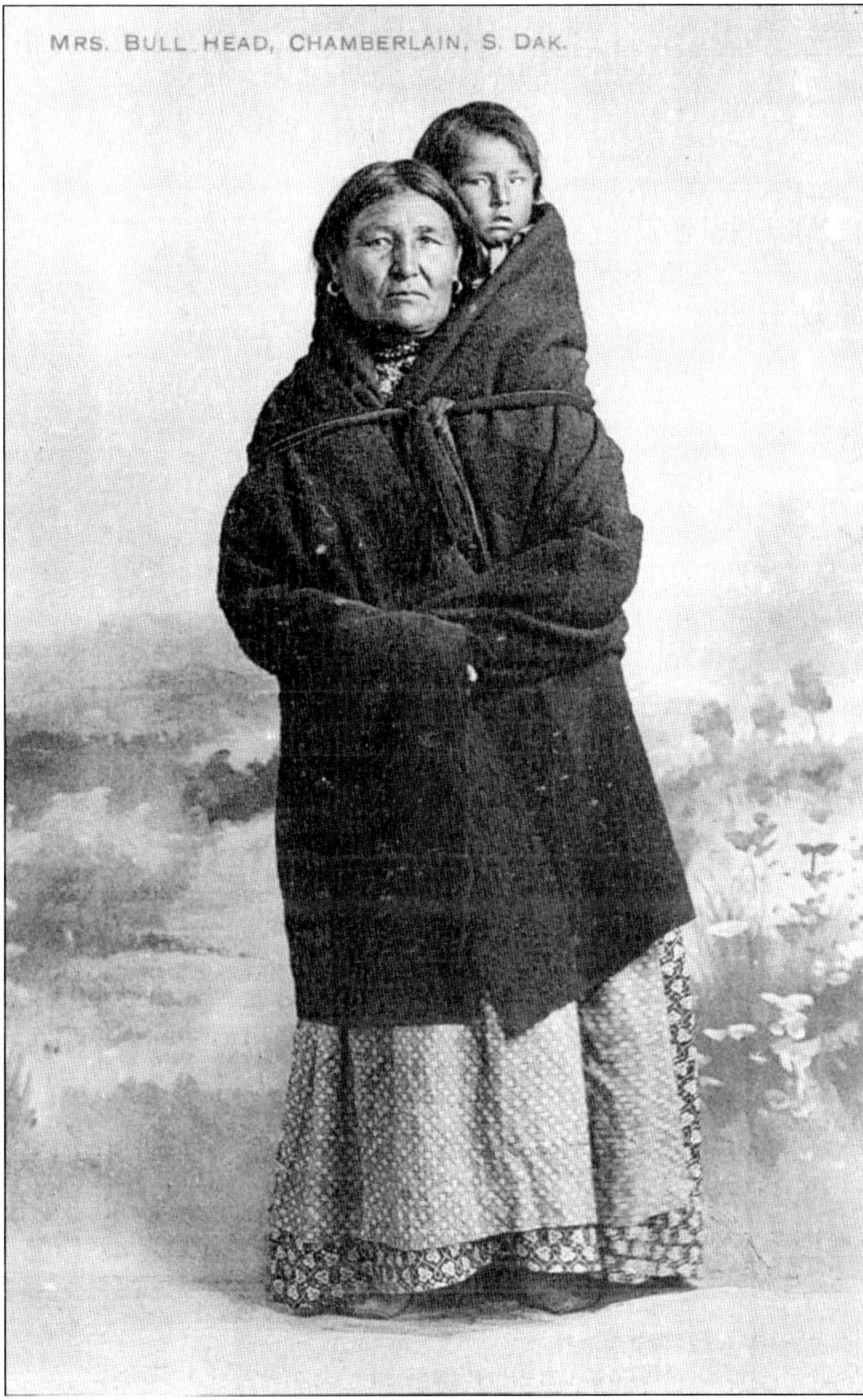

Mrs. Bull Head, a Sioux woman, is pictured wearing a typical calico dress of the time period. A child wrapped up in her cloak is seen beside her head. The background indicates this photograph was taken at a photographer's studio.

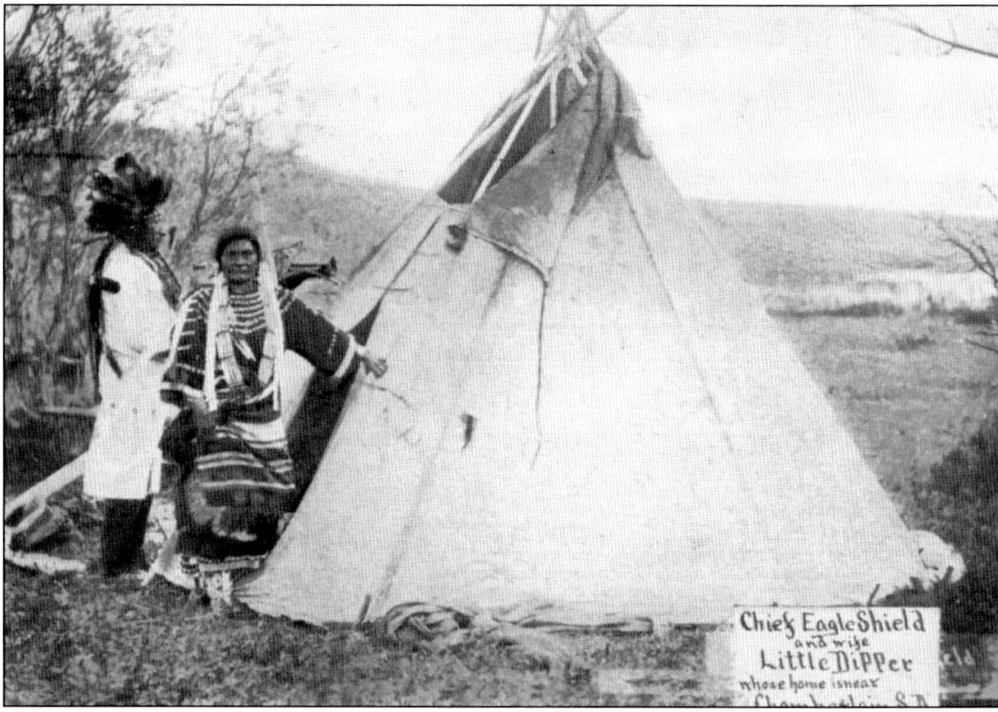

Chief Eagle Shield and his wife, Little Dipper, stand beside their traditional tipi. They lived near Chamberlain. (Courtesy Barry Betts collection.)

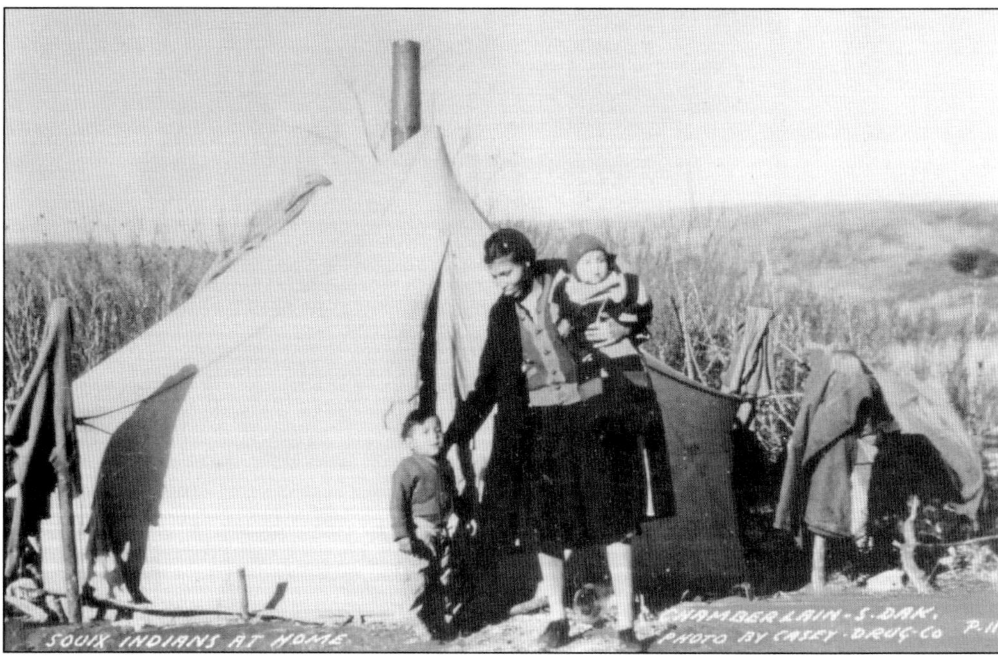

This card is entitled, "Sioux Indians at Home by Chamberlain, SD." A mother and two children stand in front of a canvas tipi with a stovepipe protruding from the top. It looks to be around American Creek or somewhere near the foothills along the Missouri River. There are some coats hanging outside to the right.

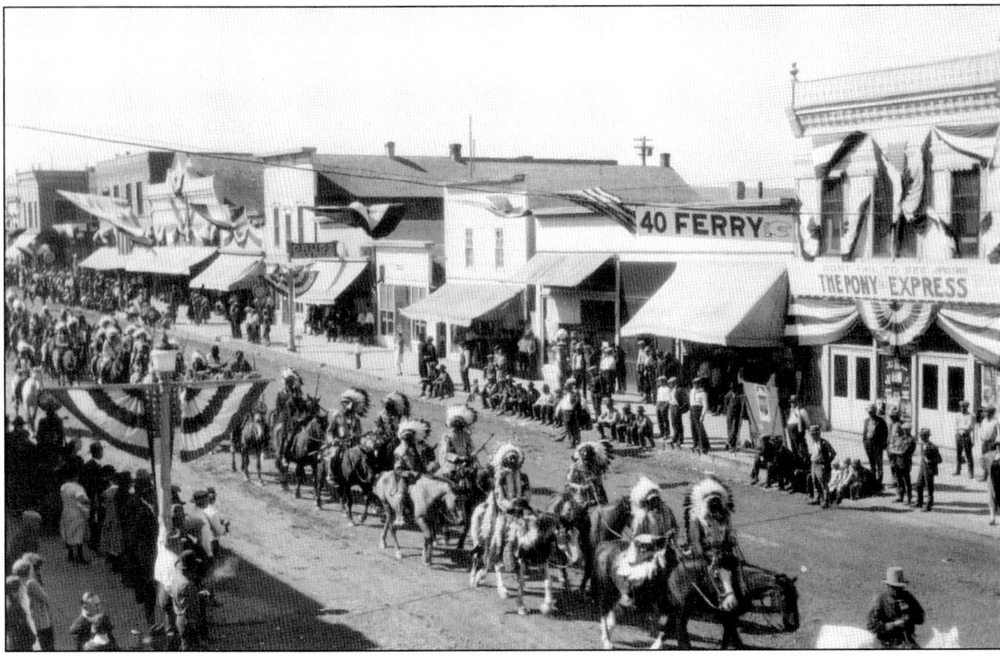

The 1925 Chamberlain Bridge Celebration brought people from all over the state and beyond. Here, a large delegation of Native Americans riding on their horses side by side is taking part in the parade. It was said that this line was longer than two city blocks. They were dressed in full regalia, including moccasins, beaded leg strips, and headdresses. They would be the first to cross the new bridge. What a spectacular sight it must have been to witness.

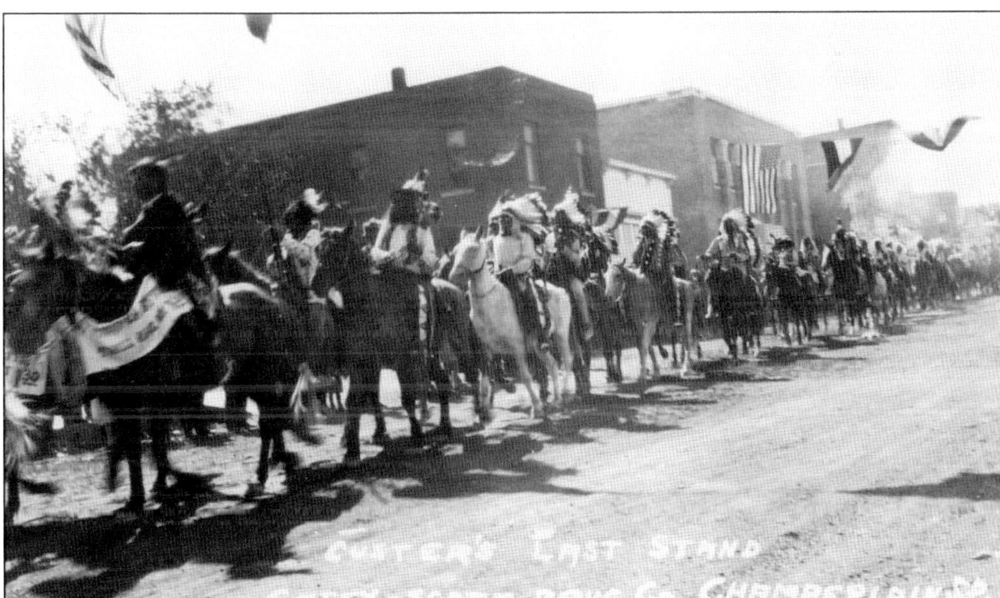

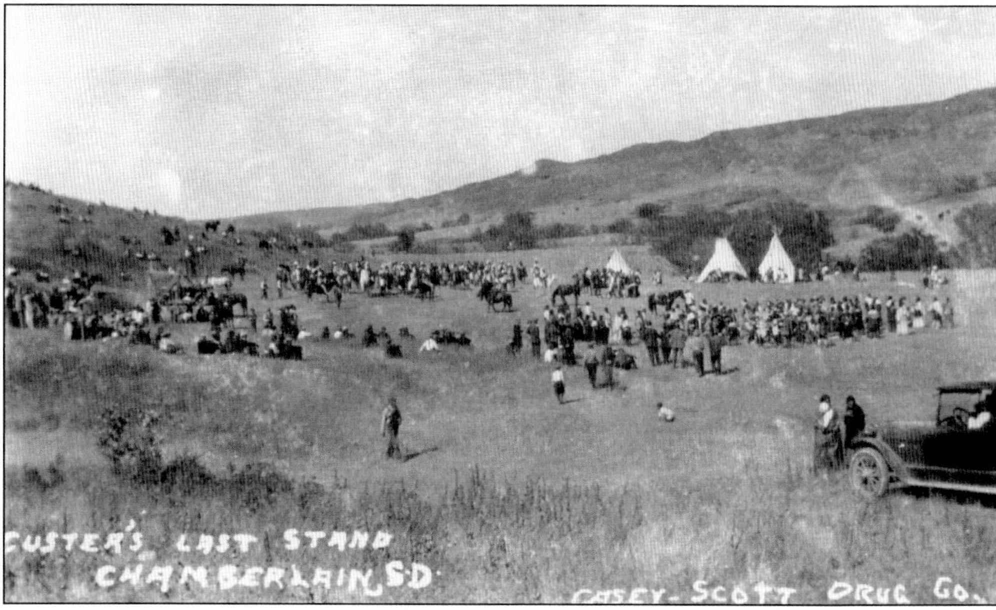

During the 1925 Chamberlain Bridge Celebration, a large reenactment was performed of Custer's Last Stand. Approximately 5,000 Native Americans participated as well as 250 soldiers from Fort Meade. The tipis and other items used were kept as authentic as possible to what would have been in use at the time of the original battle. This makes the automobile seem very out of place in the photograph above. Large crowds gathered for the reenactments held on American Island. All in all, approximately 35,000 viewed the performances.

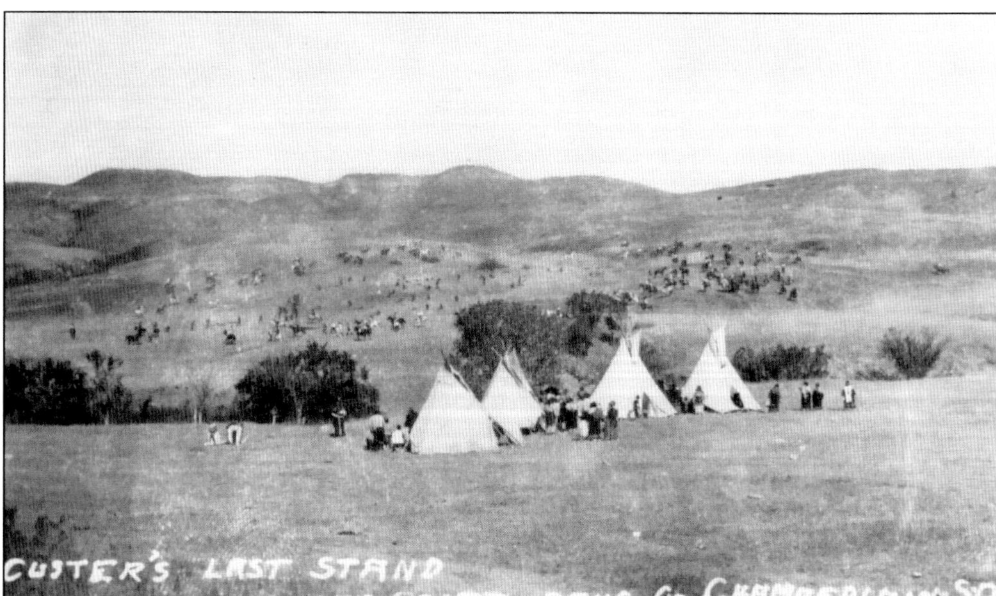

At first glance, this photograph looks like it could have been taken long ago rather than in 1925. This close-up of participants in the Custer's Last Stand reenactment shows some of the great details of Native American clothing, weapons, and horses. The foothills along the Missouri River can be seen in the background. (Courtesy Barry Betts collection.)

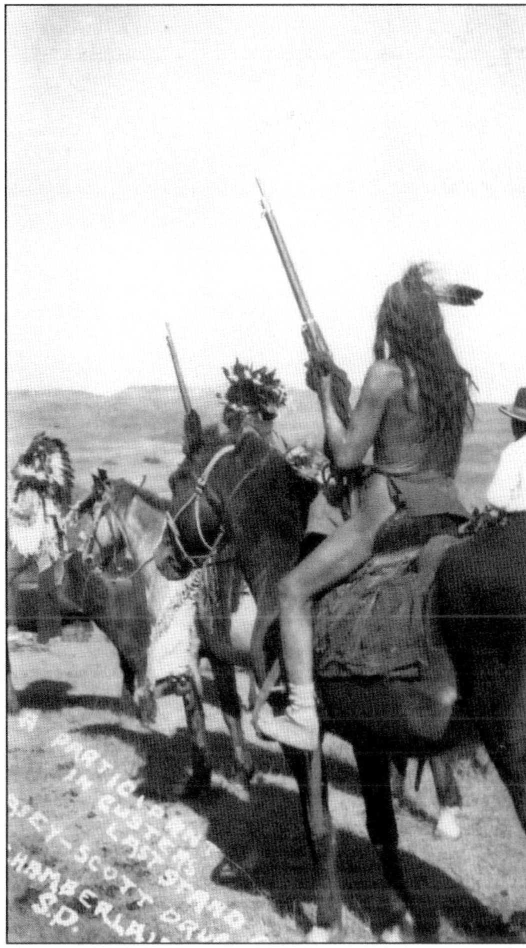

A number of Native American women are pictured here participating in the Custer's Last Stand reenactment during the Chamberlain Bridge Celebration of 1925. Various types of dresses with different styles of decoration are being worn. The men can also be seen in the background, closer to the tipis and the rolling hills along the Missouri River.

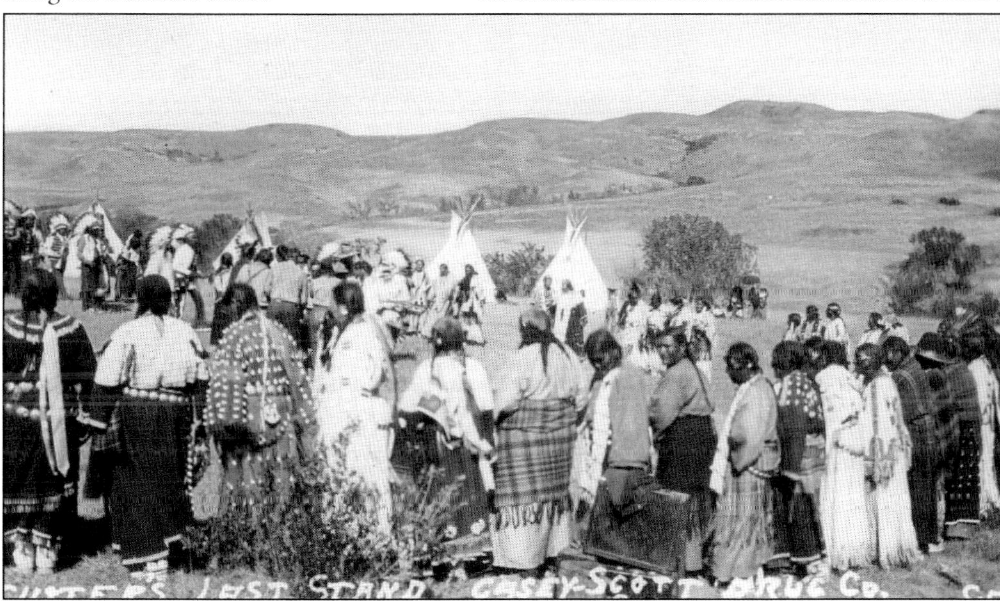

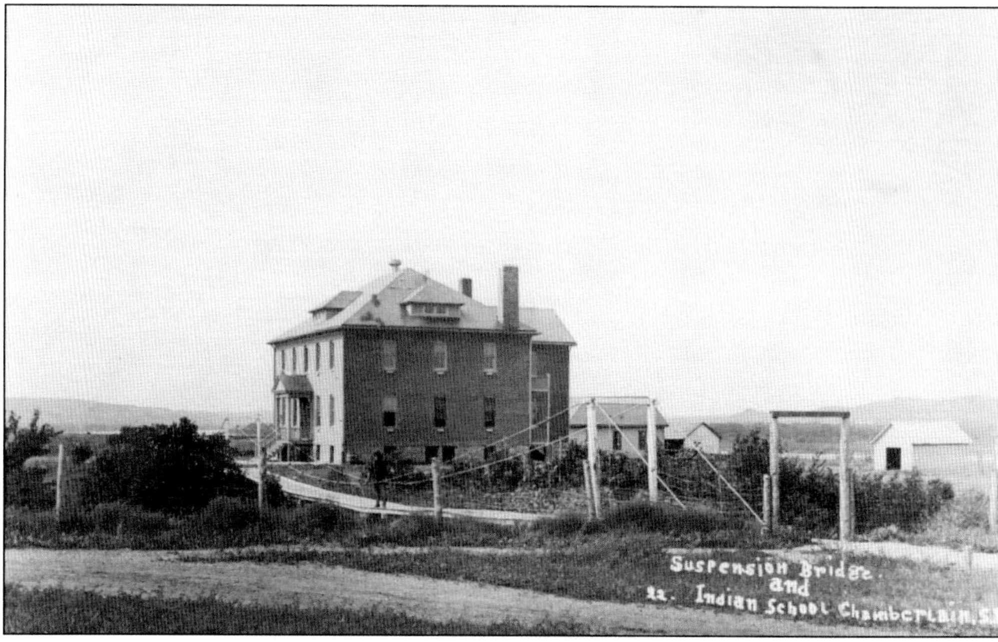

The view above is an early photograph of the US government's Indian School at Chamberlain. The school opened on May 5, 1898, and cost the government over $40,000 to build. The students worked half days and attended school the other half. There was a suspension bridge over a small creek next to the school. Below is a 1908 view that shows more of the school's campus. Many more buildings were added as it was expanded to meet the needs at that time. This later became Columbus College, and in 1927, it became St. Joseph's Indian School, which is still in operation today. (Below, photograph by O.S. Leeland.)

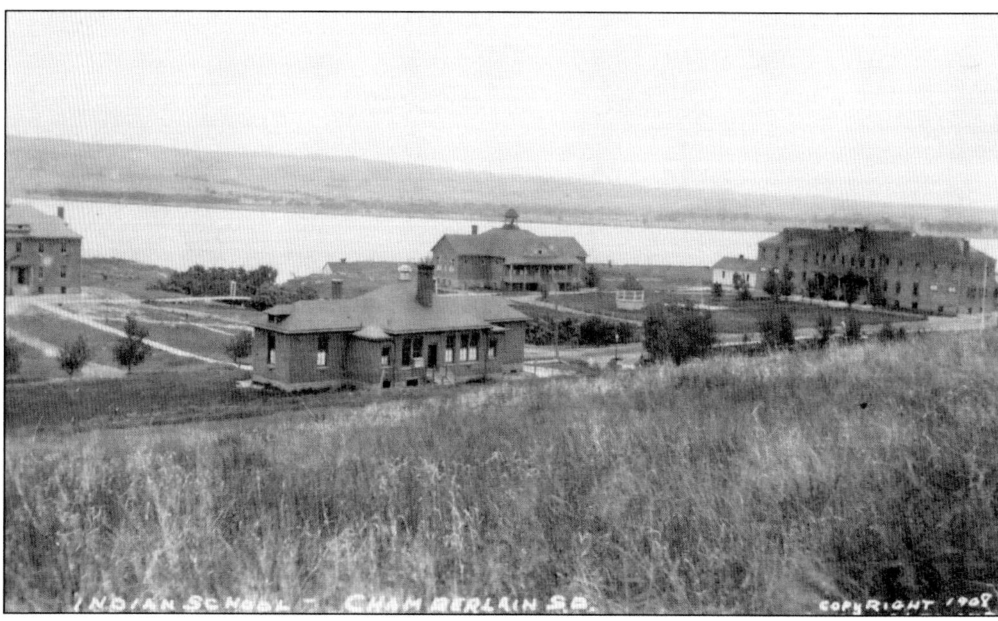

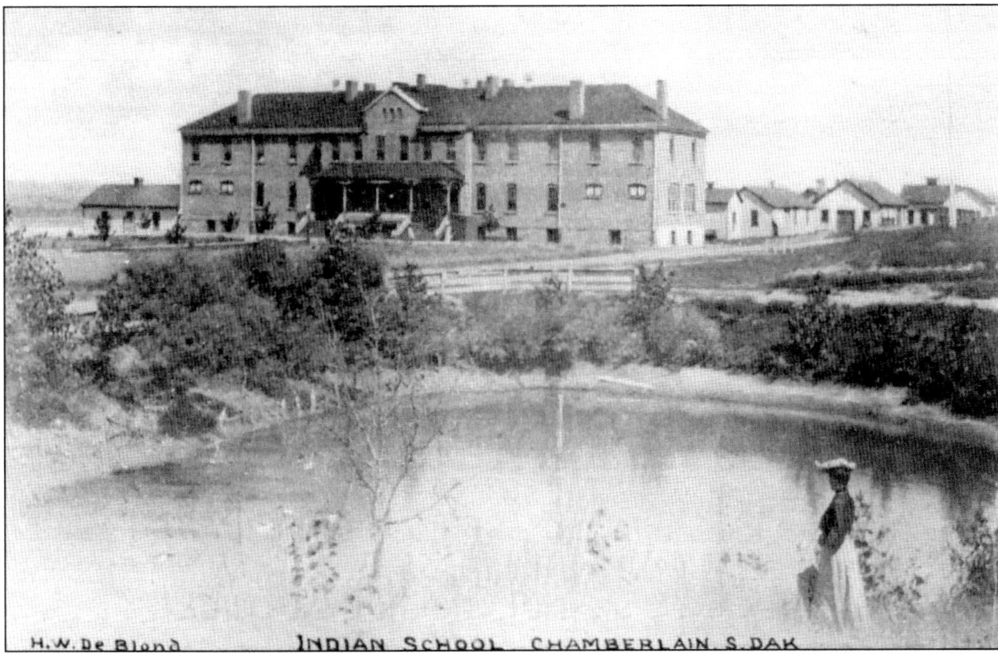

Printed in the bottom left of this card picturing the Indian school, H.W. LeBlond was the name of an early druggist in Chamberlain, He must have sold this card. His wife was an artist who was known for her watercolor paintings. Over the years, she also taught many residents of Chamberlain how to paint.

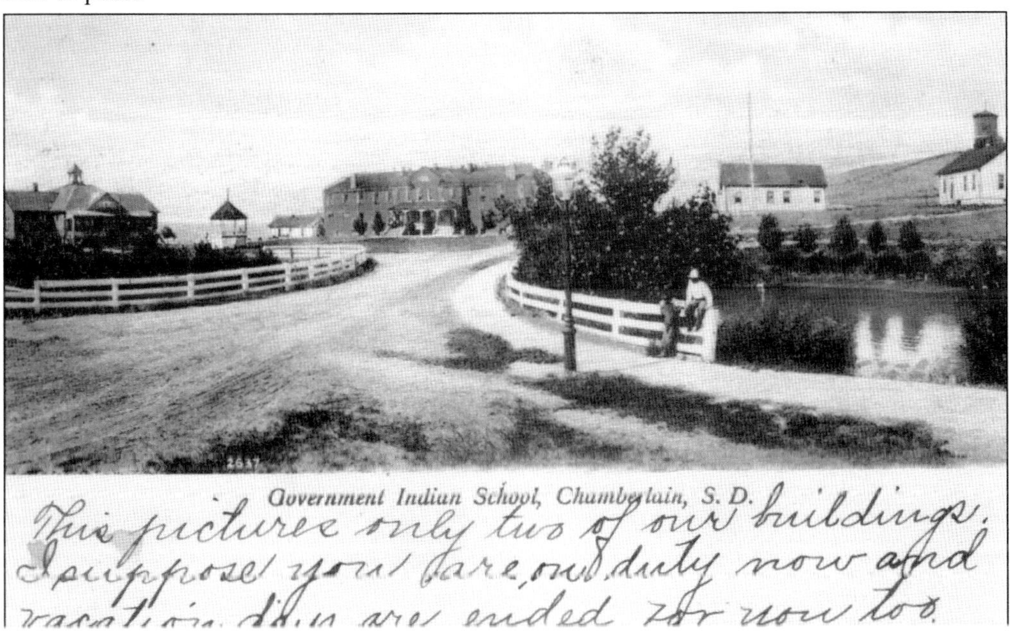

Postmarked in 1907, the message on this card appears to be written by a woman employed by the school. She writes on the back: "I have been here just a week, Oh! For a breath of the pine scented mountain air! Wouldn't it be grand? Kindest regards from Lulu M. Marm." In the photograph, two men are having a conversation at the fence along the path leading to the school. The grounds appear well kept.

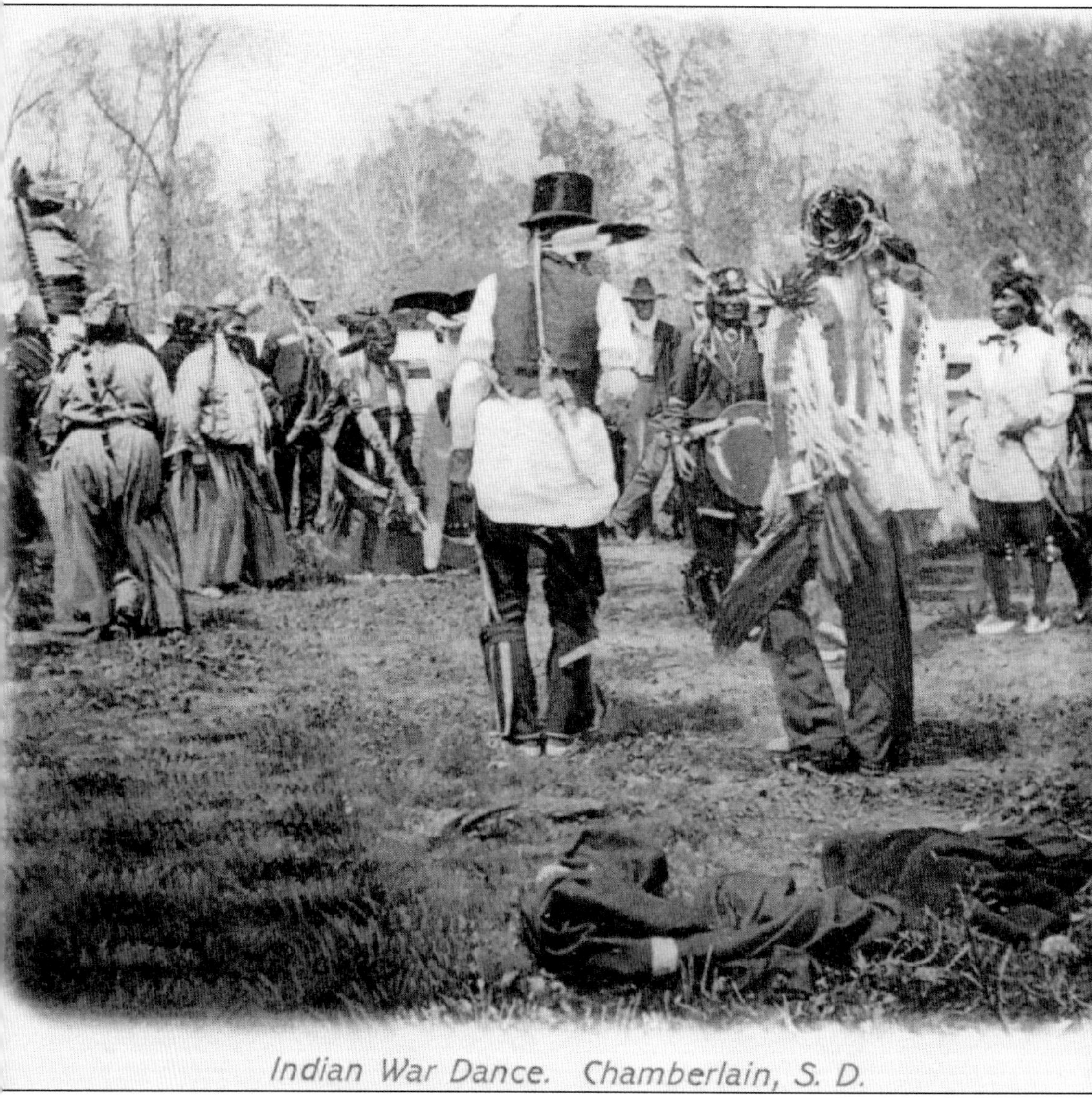

This postcard was printed in Germany. It is most likely not really of Native Americans at Chamberlain but a postcard that was used throughout the United States. The postcard company would print different town and state names below the same photograph. The Indian dress seen in this photograph is not typical of the Native Americans in the Chamberlain area.

Eight

Tourism and Curiosities

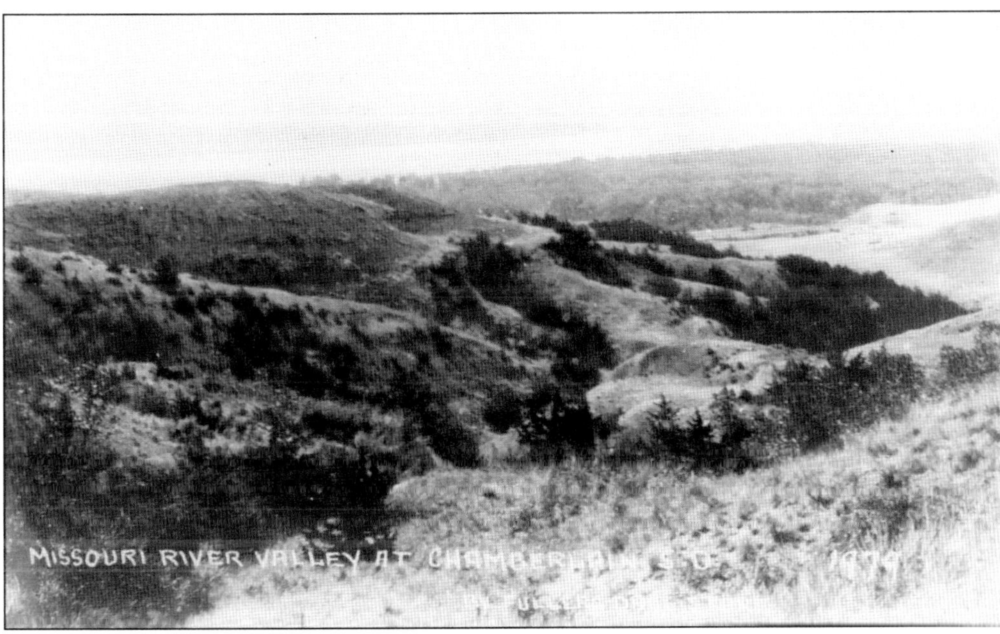

Travelers crossing the state of South Dakota first notice a real change in the terrain when they reach Chamberlain. Gone are the corn and bean fields at the descent into the Missouri River valley. West of the river, the grassy rolling plains begin. The abundance of cedar trees and wildlife near the river made it an excellent place for the town of Chamberlain to be established on the east bank and Oacoma on the west bank.

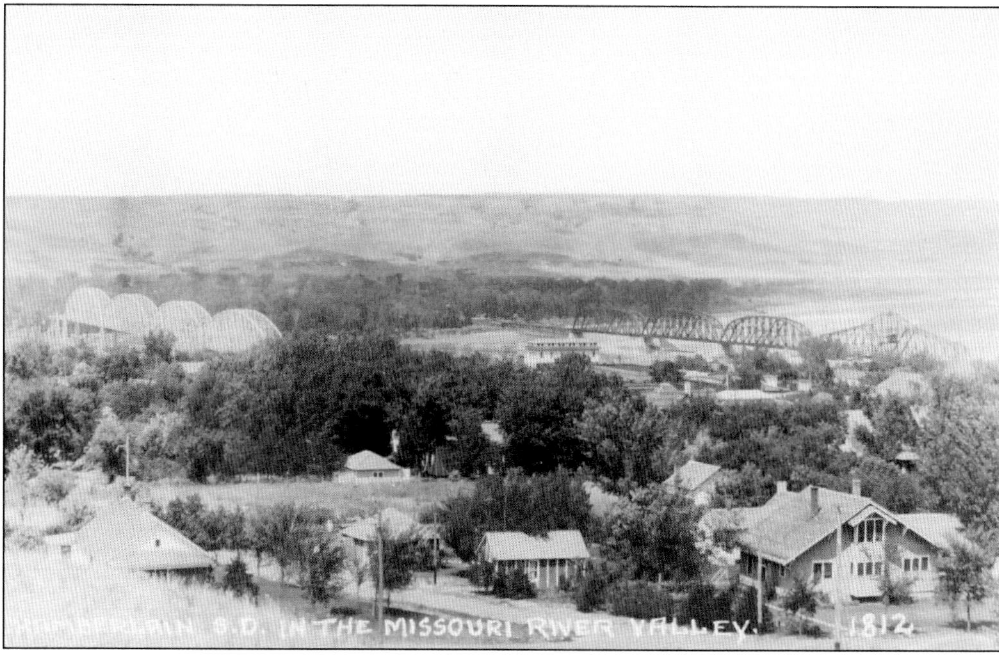

For someone who has never traveled through Chamberlain before, the vista of the Missouri River is breathtaking. These views from years ago are no less impressive than the actual sight of the same scene today. Several of the houses visible here are presently occupied, and more surround them. At one time, when this was the edge of town, a farmer kept sheep in the barn partially behind the trees in the picture below. He would herd them into the hills during the day and back to the barn at night to guard against coyotes that also lived in the hills. Nowadays, there are still cattle grazing just outside of the city limits.

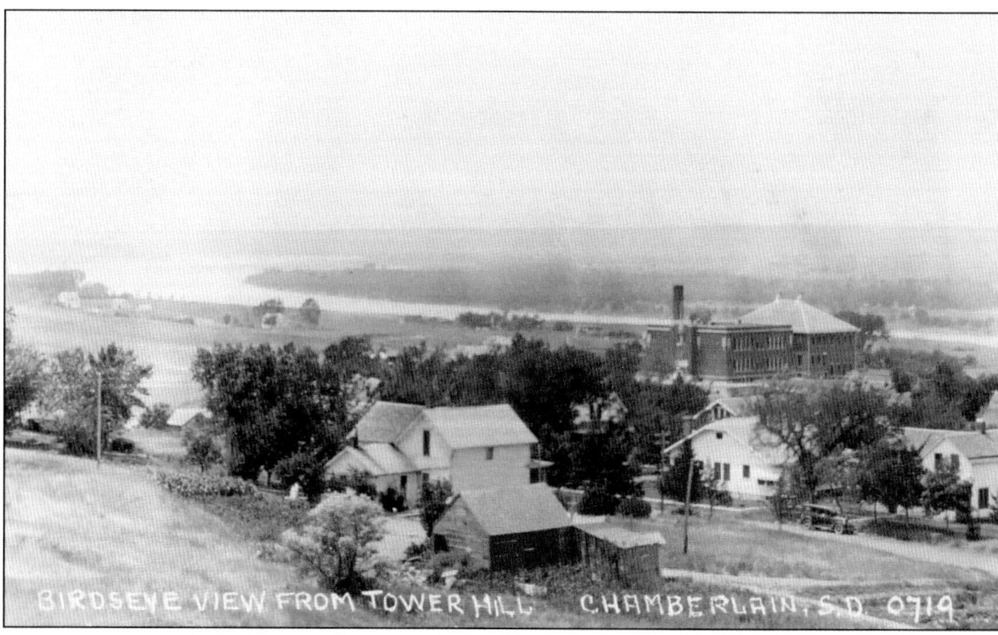

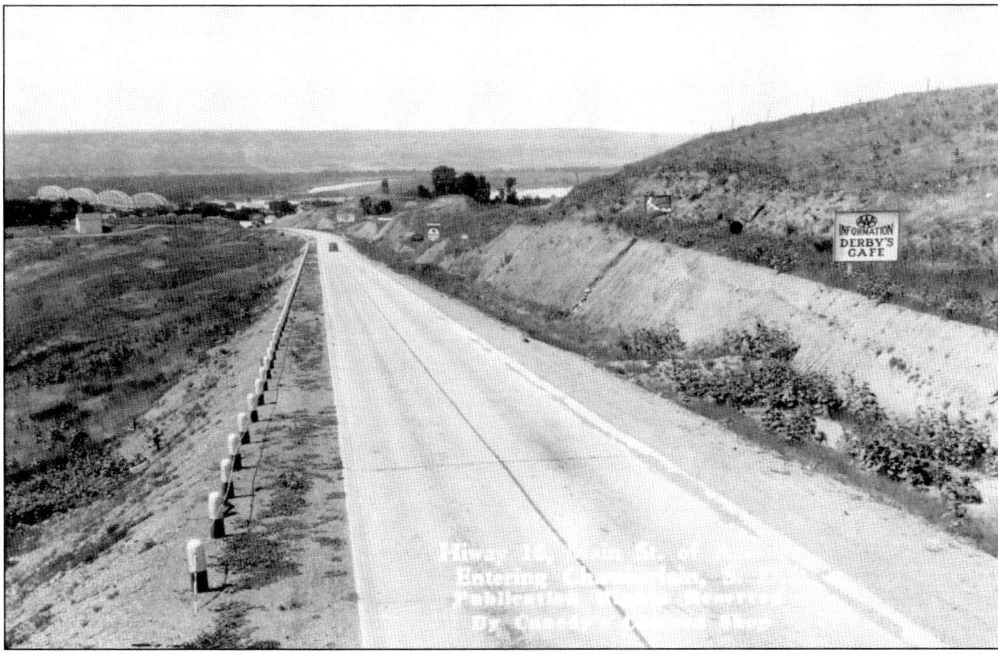

Before Interstate 90, Highway 16 was regarded as the main gateway to the west. It was the first highway in South Dakota to be paved all the way from the east to the west border of the state. When the surfacing was completed, there was actually a celebration held in Chamberlain, where the governor dedicated "America's Main Street." The above card, mailed in 1948, contains the following message: "We stayed in this town last nite. We got up at 5 a.m. and drove thru cattle and wheat country and feel for the first time we are in the West. We saw a tall cowboy with a ten gallon hat and cowboy boots and we took his picture. Momma and Daddy."

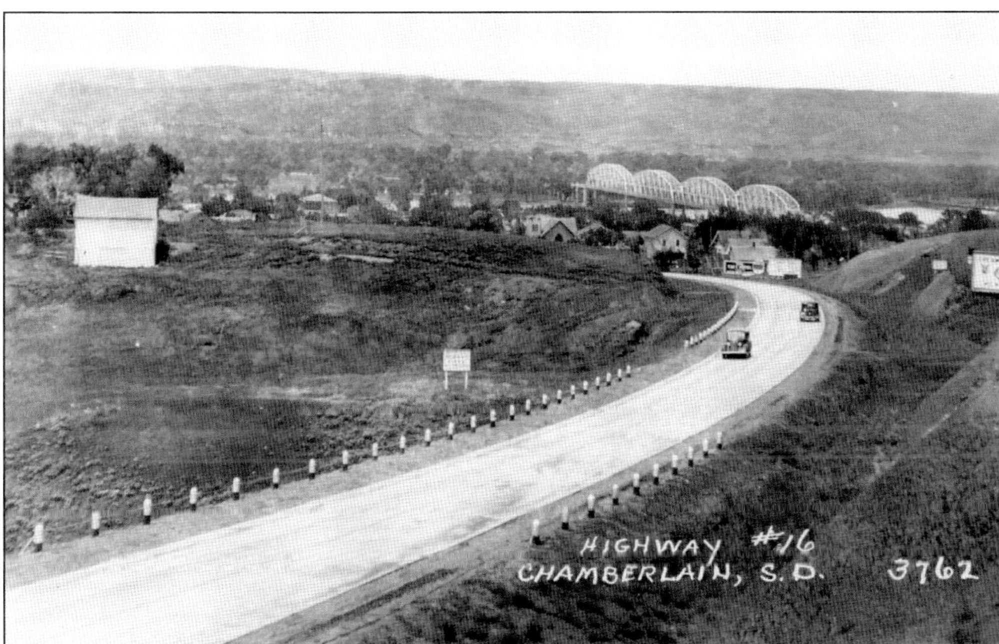

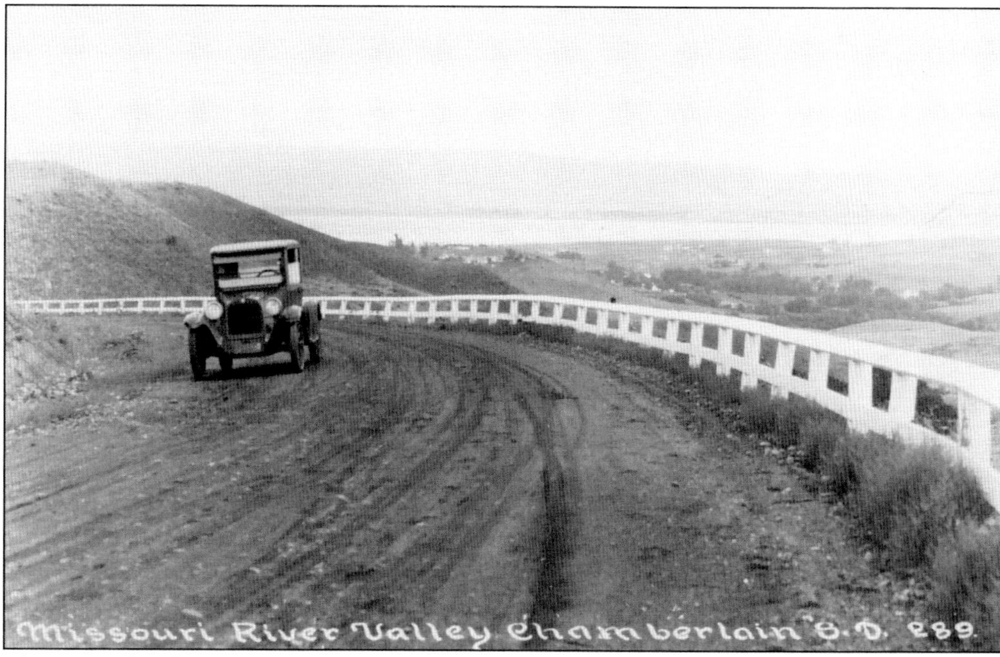

This car is heading up the hill on Highway 47 going north towards Fort Thompson. Many times, cars had to back up and take another run up the hill in order to make it over the steep grade. Vehicles have also had problems going down hills into town. There have been accidents where drivers ended up in the river, and some have even been killed. Even today, the hills can be treacherous, especially in bad weather.

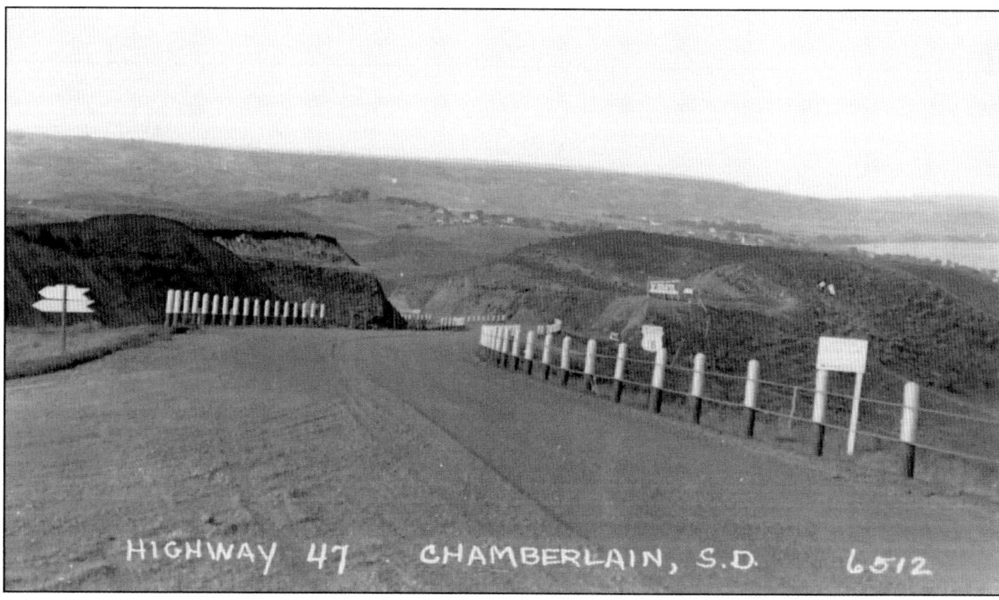

This view of Highway 47 going north of Chamberlain shows the addition of cement guardrail posts and heavy cable instead of wooden fence posts. On the side is a Highway 16 detour sign. The message on the back of the card is dated July 17, 1947. The sender, who lived in Hamill, South Dakota, at the time, writes, "(the) Missouri River here is 20 air miles east north east of ranch and 34 miles by auto."

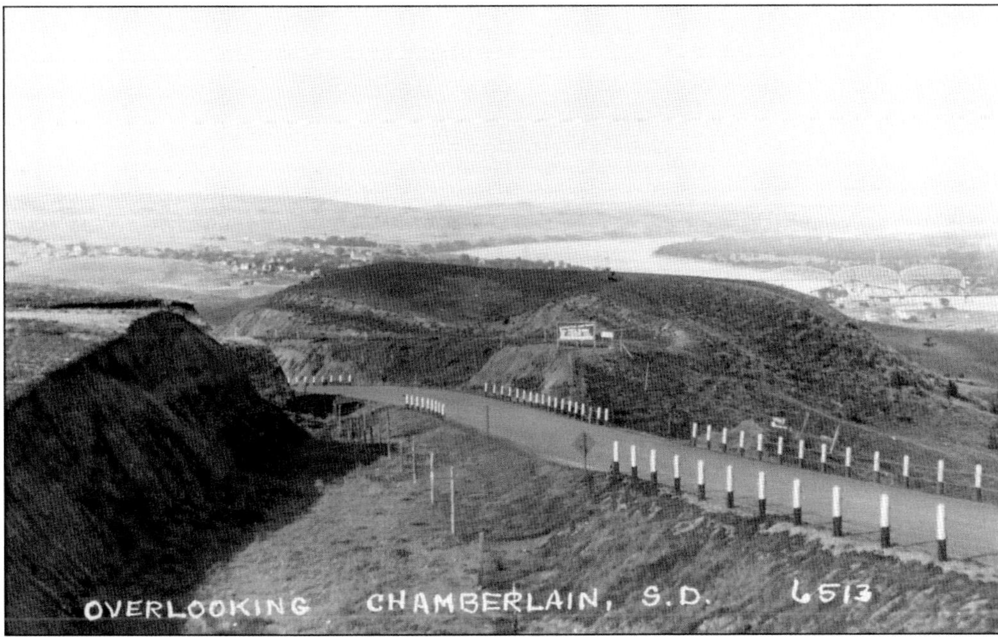

This view along Highway 47 north of Chamberlain shows how the hills were graded in order to build the road. Chamberlain, American Island, and the auto bridge can be seen in the background to the right. The sign in the distance advertises Nelson Motor Company.

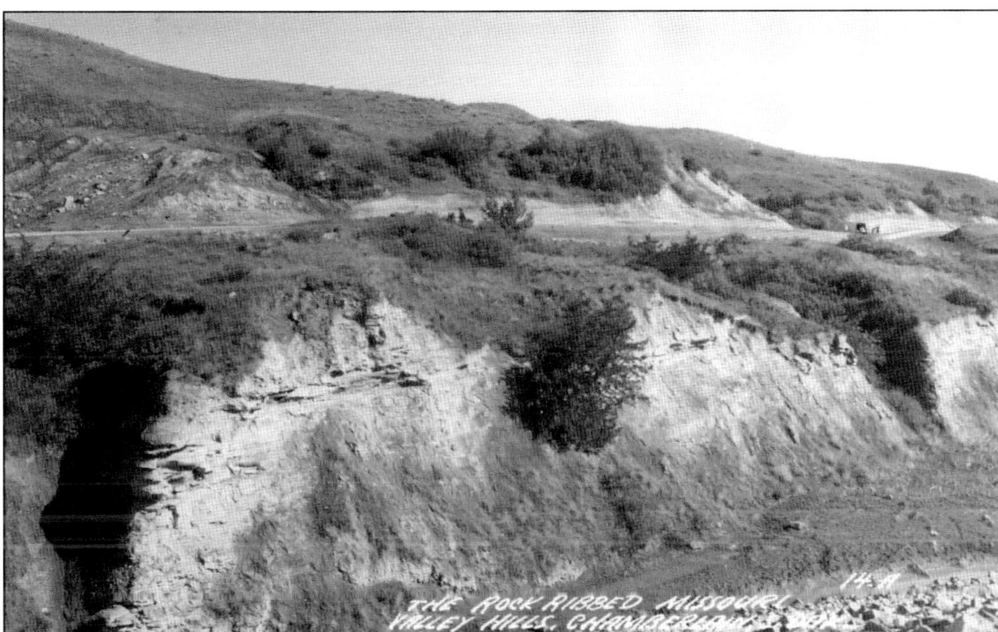

Part of the unique geography of the area is the "rock-ribbed" banks along the Missouri River. These are best observed when boating on the river. The road seen here is now called Mickelson Drive, after the late Gov. George Mickelson, who died in a plane crash while in office.

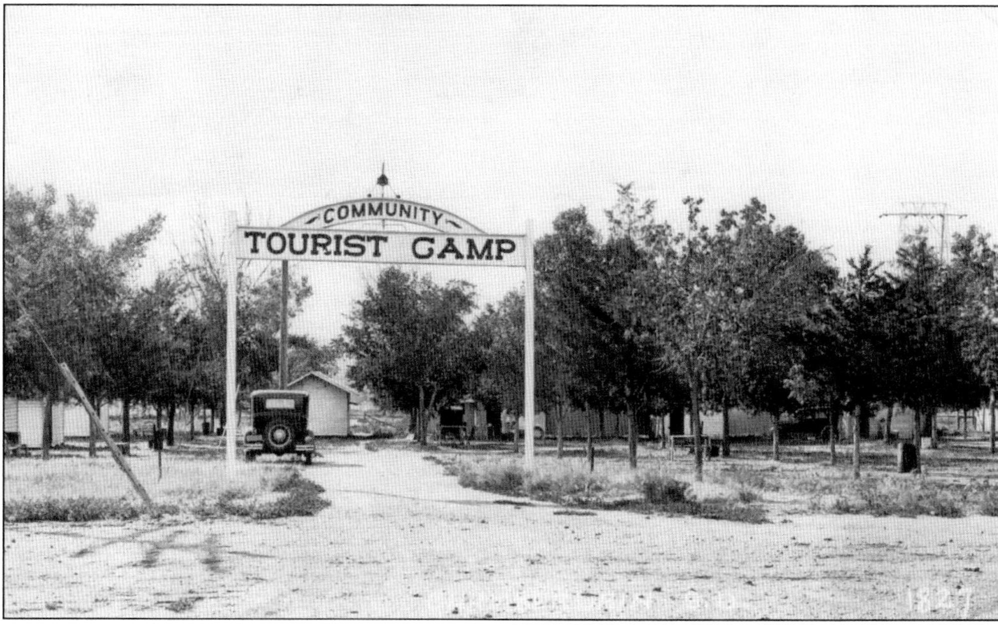

The Chamberlain area has always provided many options for lodging and camping. The Community Tourist Camp was located on American Island. It was a popular camp, with many shade trees and comfortable cabins. Mailed in 1935, this card shows an automobile parked just inside the camp and some of the cabins in the background.

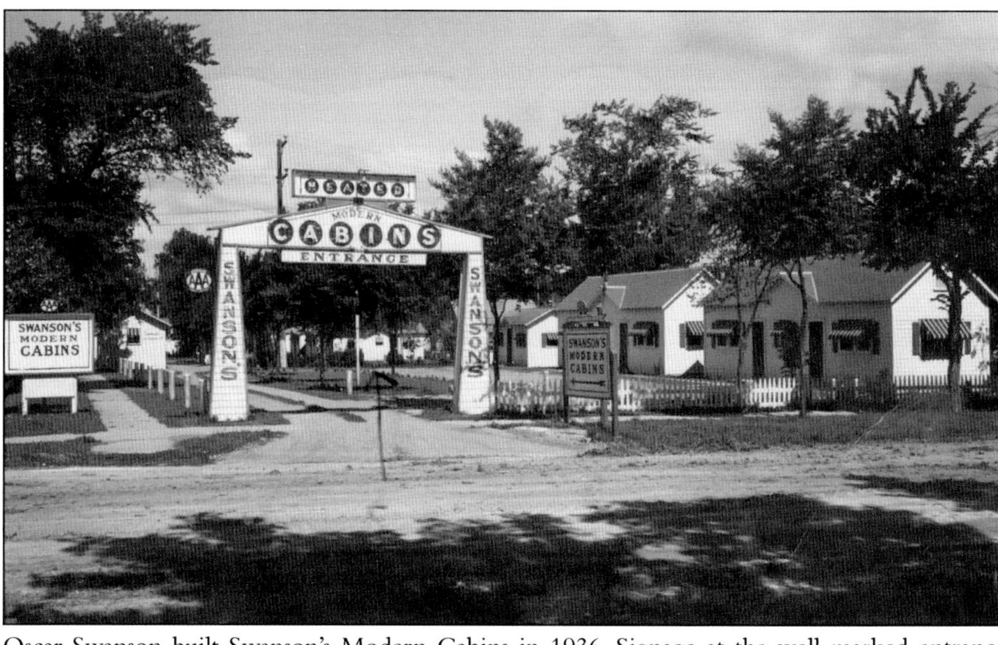

Oscar Swanson built Swanson's Modern Cabins in 1936. Signage at the well-marked entrance states that they are heated, and the neat, inviting look of the grounds made them a popular choice for tourists on their way to the Black Hills.

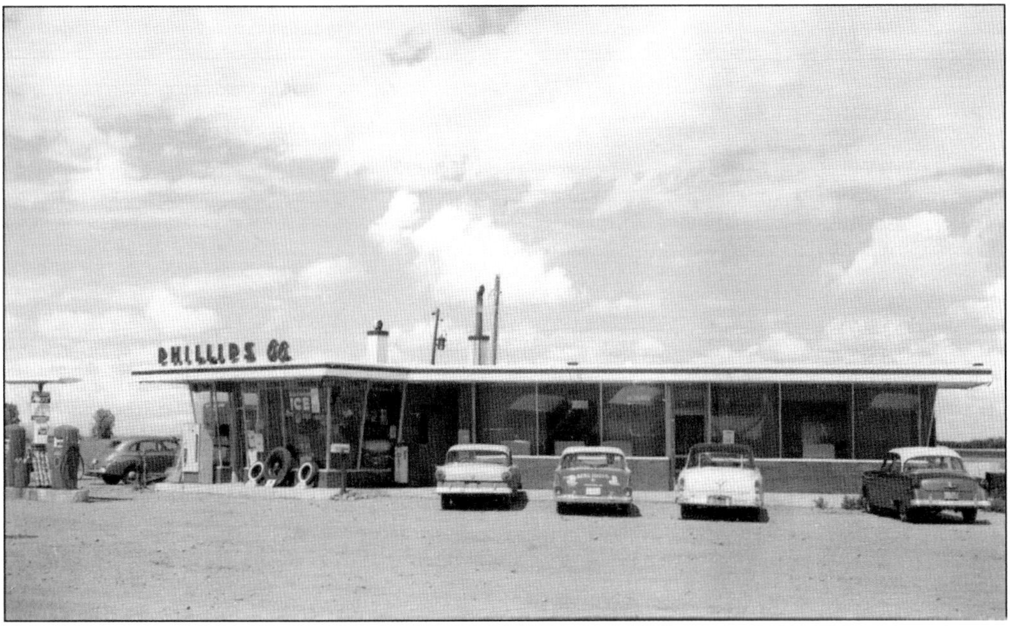

Built in the 1950s, the Truck Arena Phillips 66 Station and Café was located on Highway 16 approximately two miles east of Chamberlain. It featured 24-hour service, and on the back of this card advertises itself as "Where the Truckers Eat." Truckers also liked the location because it was located before starting downhill into the valley. (Photograph by Orrion Barger.)

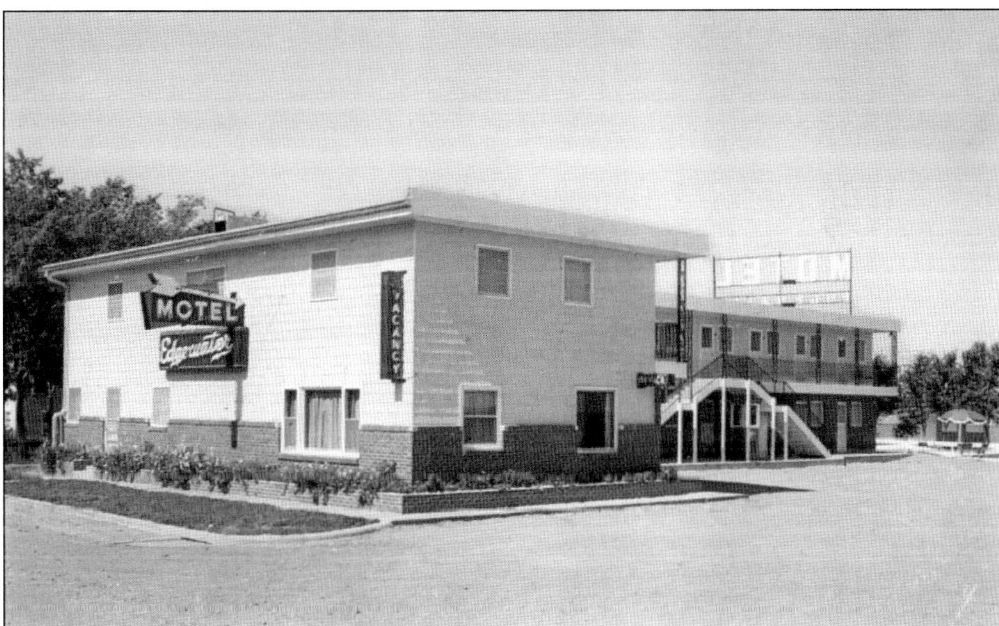

The Edgewater Motel opened in the 1950s only one block north of the Missouri River bridge. Initially, it consisted of 23 rooms and provided an apartment for the managers. It also advertised air-conditioned rooms and a beautiful view of the river. The first owner was Sandy Tyrell. It is now being used as part of the Bridge View Inn. (Photograph by Orrion Barger.)

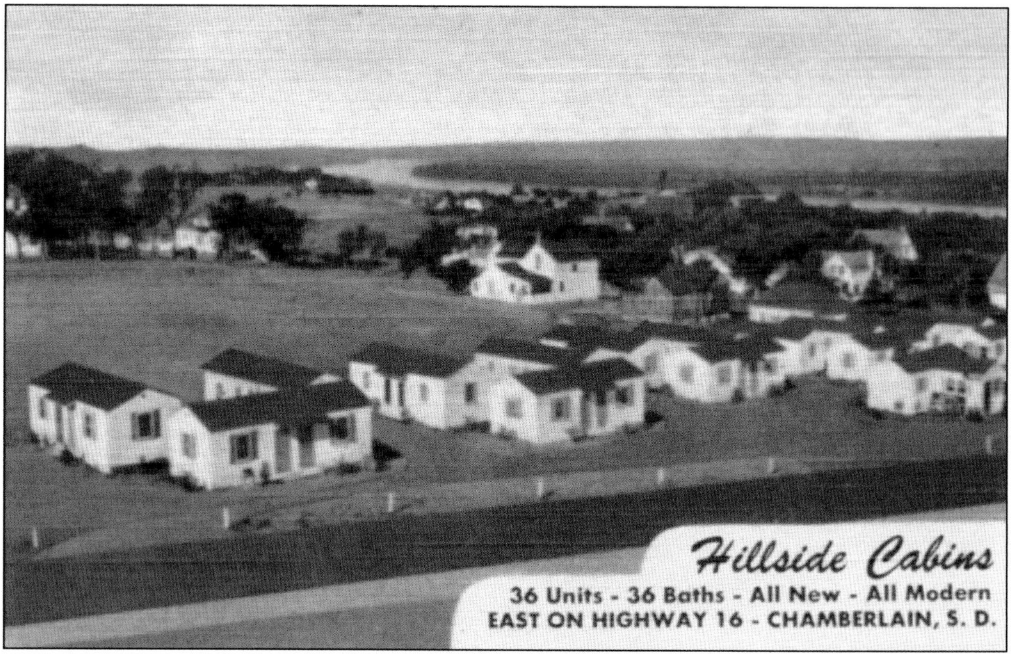

The Hillside Cabins consisted of 18 cabins with two rooms each. Cabins like these were popular in the 1930s and 1940s. This card advertises the fact that each unit has its own bath. On the back, it describes Chamberlain as "the biggest little city on the only completely hard surfaced road across South Dakota."

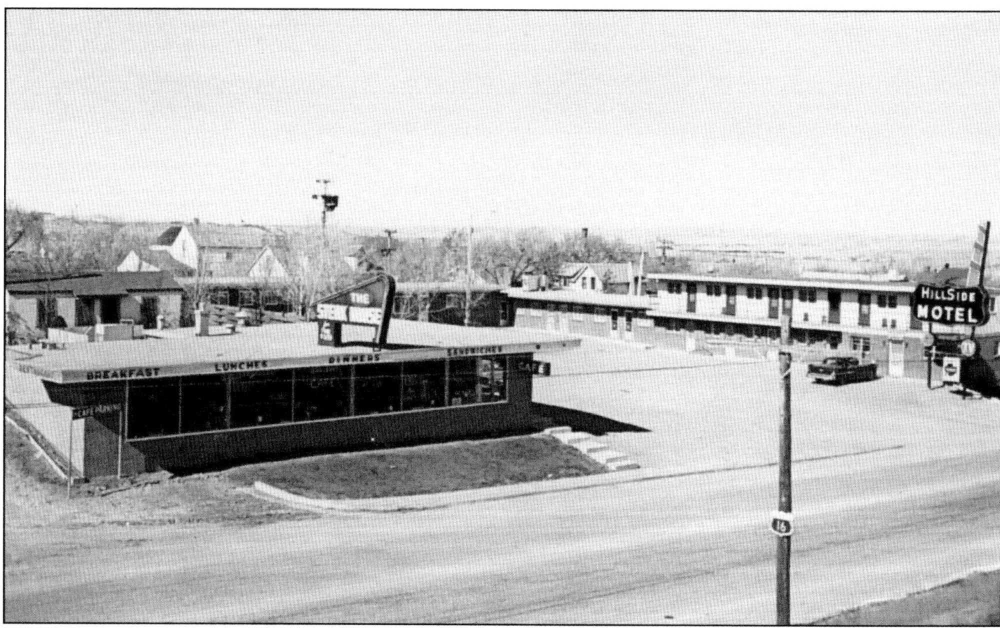

The Hillside Motel and the Steak House were located in nearly the same place as the Hillside Cabins. Behind the restaurant to the far left, one of the cabins is visible. A Highway 16 sign can be seen on the post in the foreground. The Hillside Motel is still in the same location and caters to sportsmen. The Steak House is now called Charley's Restaurant and continues to serve steaks and burgers.

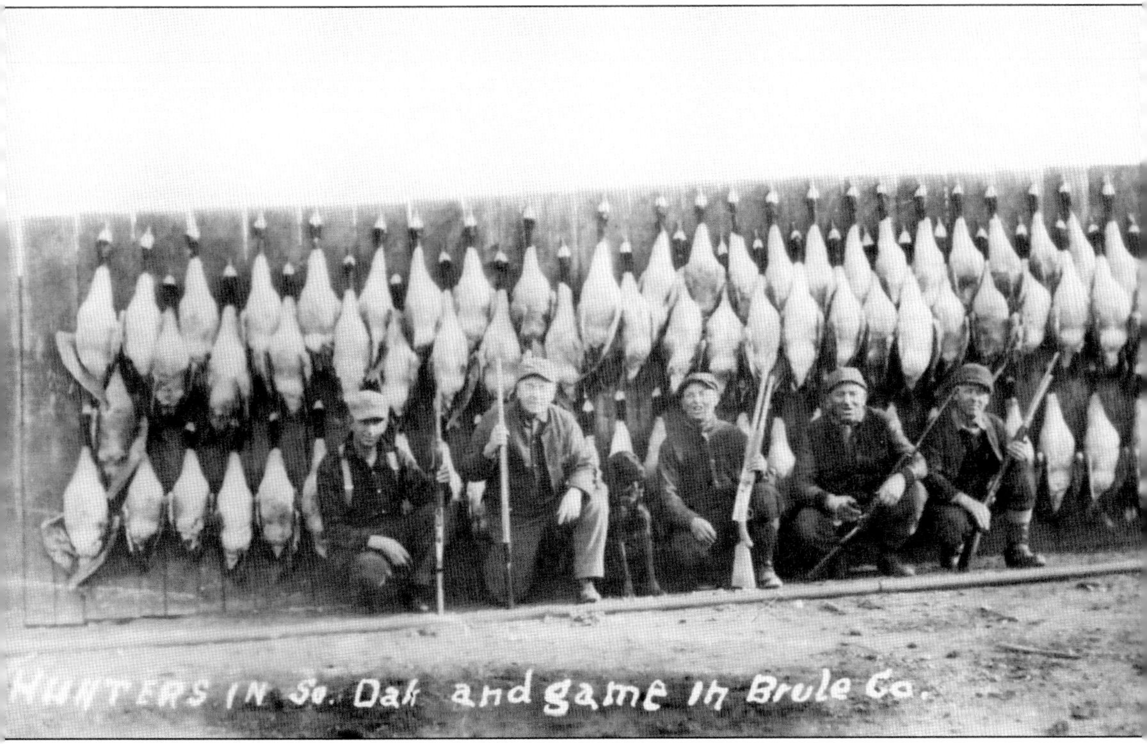

Throughout the years, Chamberlain and the surrounding area have been a favorite place to go hunting. These five men had a fabulous day and are proudly showing off the Canada geese they shot in Brule County. Years ago, before the dams were built on the Missouri River, Canada geese and mallard ducks would fly in and out by the thousands. The birds would rest on the sandbars in the river and fly out at intervals to the cornfields to eat. The ring-necked pheasant is now the big hunting trophy in the Chamberlain area, and hunters come from all over the United States to stalk the wily birds. Hunting has changed some with the advent of private hunting lodges. Not nearly as many hunters are seen "road hunting." Pheasant hunting season is still one of the biggest boosts to the local economy. Birds, jackrabbits, prairie dogs, deer, and coyote also draw avid hunters to the area.

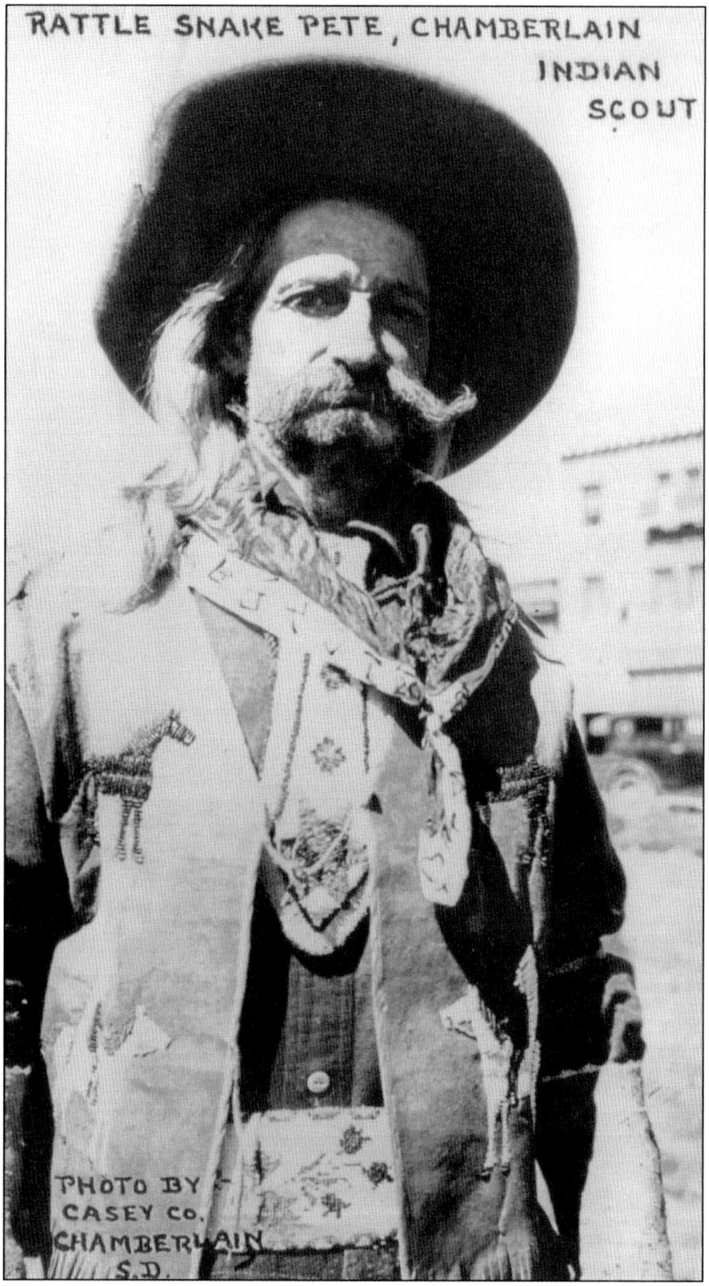

Rattlesnake Pete's given name was Gustave Robson. He was called Rattlesnake Pete because he was known to collect rattlesnakes in gunnysacks and he wore a rattlesnake skin hatband. He claimed to have associated with the likes of Buffalo Bill Cody, Pawnee Bill, and Calamity Jane. Although a short man—only about five feet tall—his manner was confident and self-assured. He traveled around South Dakota portraying himself as an Old West cowboy dressed in boots, an oversized hat, and a bandana. Long hair and a handlebar mustache were part of his signature. Barbering was Pete's other occupation. At one time or another, he had shops in Reliance and Oacoma, South Dakota, as well as various towns in other parts of the state. According to him, his shaves were the fastest of any barber—only 15 seconds. Rattlesnake Pete died in 1946 in Bon Homme County.

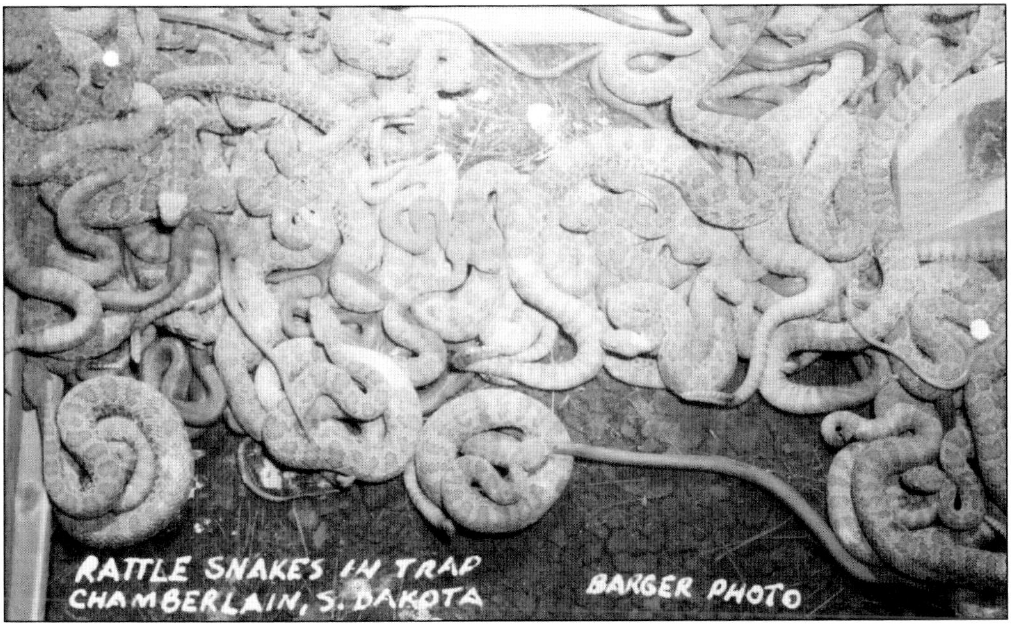

Rattlesnakes are common in the area along the Missouri River. There are numerous stories of large dens being unearthed during Chamberlain's early days, when buildings and wells were being constructed. One such den was found near the sanitarium in the 1930s, and it contained hundreds of snakes. One observer thought that he would have to find a pair of tin pants before he went back to that area in the future. (Photograph by Orrion Barger.)

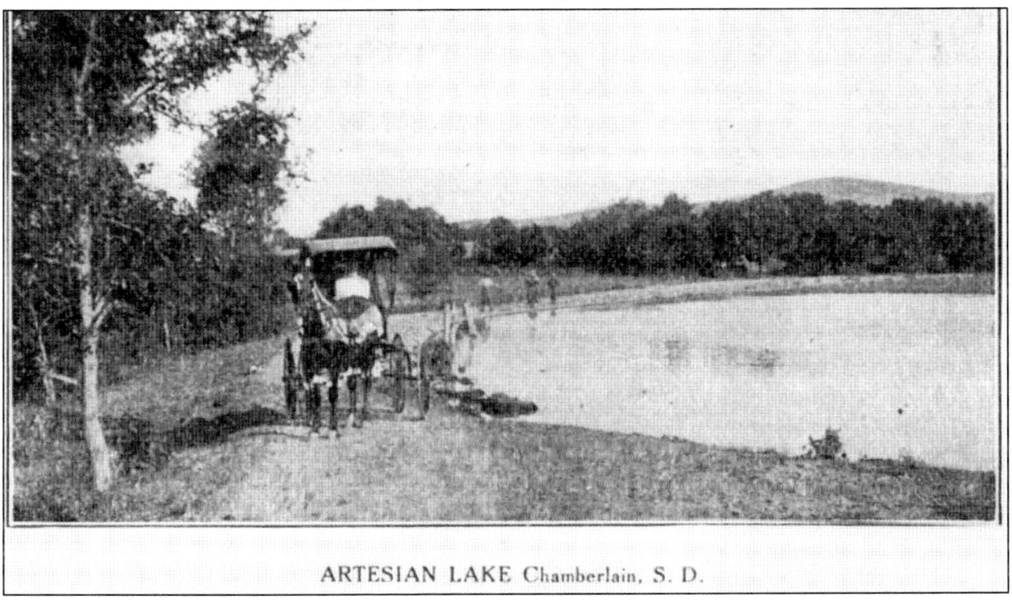

A single horse-drawn buggy is on a leisurely drive next to an artesian lake near Chamberlain. Artesian water flows up to the ground from a well drilled into an aquifer. The water is under so much pressure that it defies gravity and many times will shoot high into the air. Some artesian wells are shallow, and others must be drilled very deep. Years ago, most farms had artesian wells dug to provide drinking water for people and livestock. Some artesian wells would run wild and produce lakes, like the one seen in this photograph.

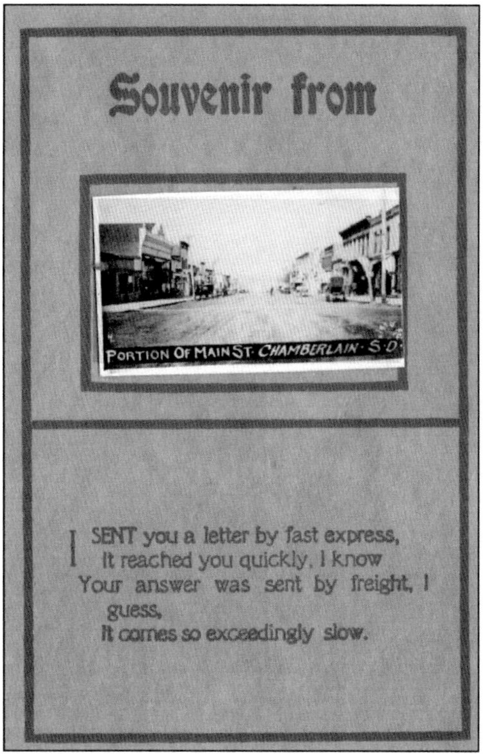

Postcards like these were mass-produced by postcard companies that just needed to change the center photograph to fit the town they were selling to. The cards would also have cute poems or funny lyrics. Both of these cards show portions of Main Street Chamberlain on them. These cards were postmarked 1913 and 1914. Both horse-drawn vehicles and automobiles can be seen. These were nice souvenirs to keep or to send to a friend with a message.

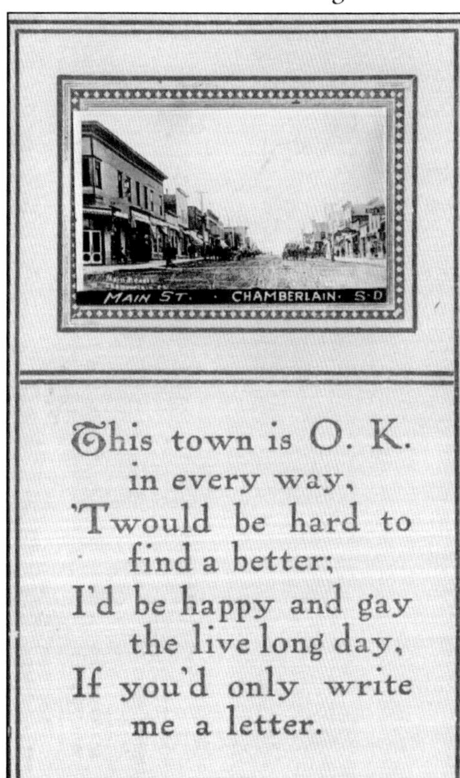

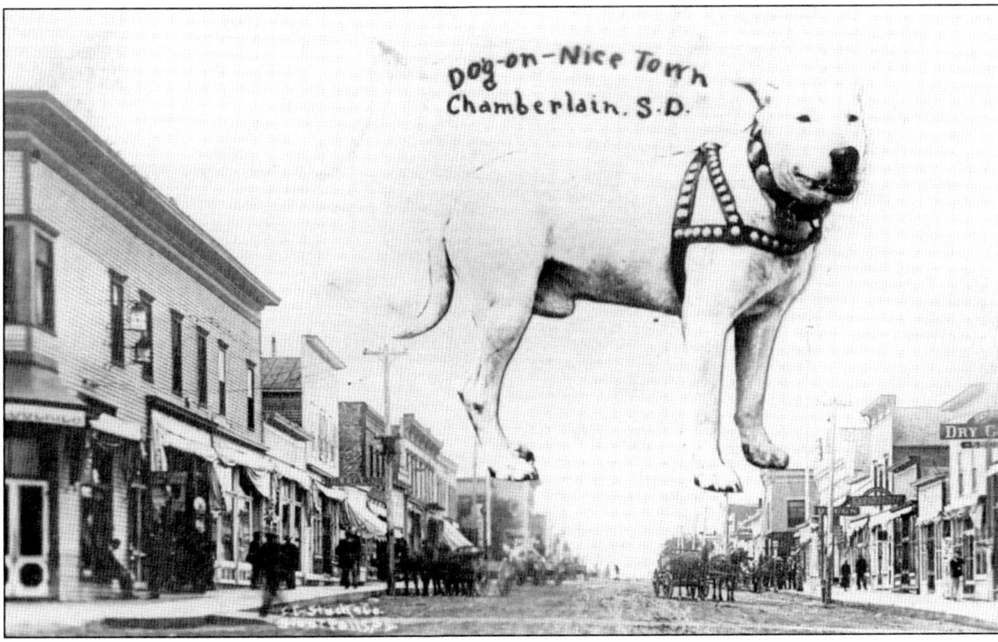

This "fantasy" Main Street scene of Chamberlain has a large dog standing on top of some of the Main Street buildings. It is captioned, "Dog-on Nice Town." Dated 1910, the message on back states, "we didn't get across the river till late last night, the boat don't run [*sic*] only when they feel like it."

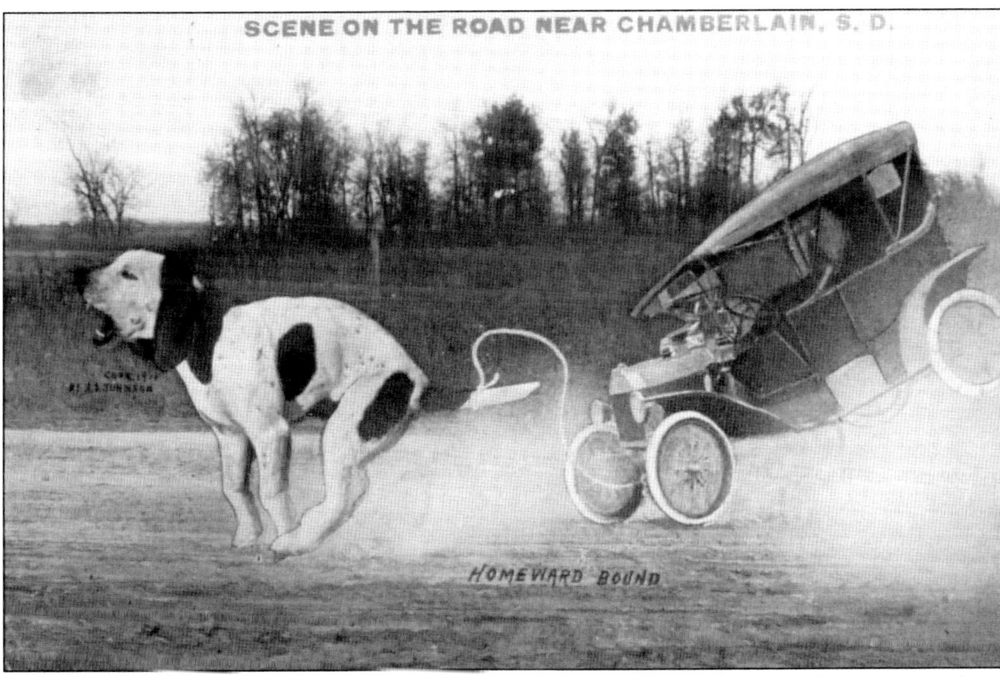

Entitled "Homeward Bound," this fantasy card, dated 1916, shows a dog pulling a car with his tail. The dog is going so fast that the car is pulled up on its front wheels. On the back, part of the message reads, "Dear Friend—Here is hoping you are about homeward bound by the time you get this."

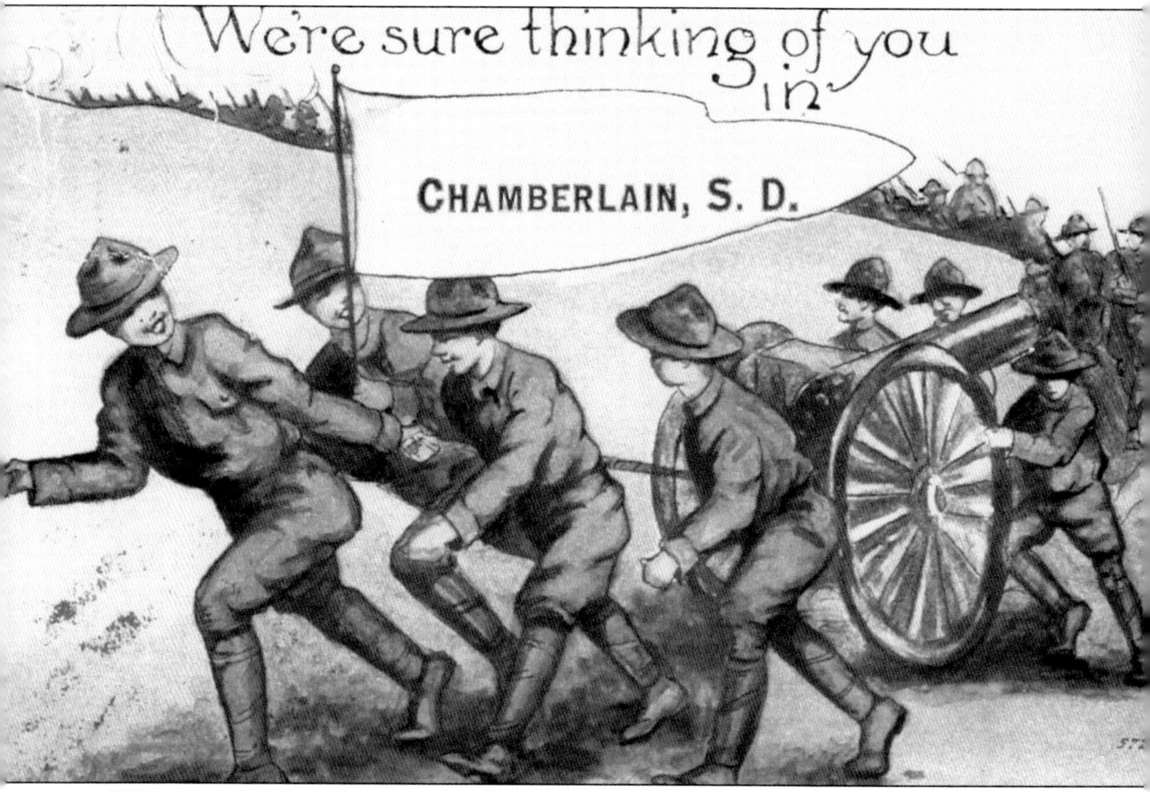

"We're sure thinking of you in Chamberlain, S.D.," reads this card that shows soldiers in World War I uniforms. Chamberlain did its part during the two world wars. In World War I, men volunteered or were drafted. Many farmers were deferred because they were needed to harvest the crops. Wheat was in short supply, so the government urged people to use barley, potato, soybean, and peanuts for flour. When World War I ended, the news was telegraphed in Chamberlain at 2:00 a.m.; by 9:00 a.m., the streets were filled with celebrations. During World War II, Chamberlain area residents again helped the cause. Twenty-foot-by-twenty-foot victory gardens were plowed near the water plant, and blood drives were very successful. Farm labor was in short supply, so business owners closed their shops and helped on the farms. Gasoline, coffee, and many other items were rationed. The end of the war was again met with great celebration and hope for the future.

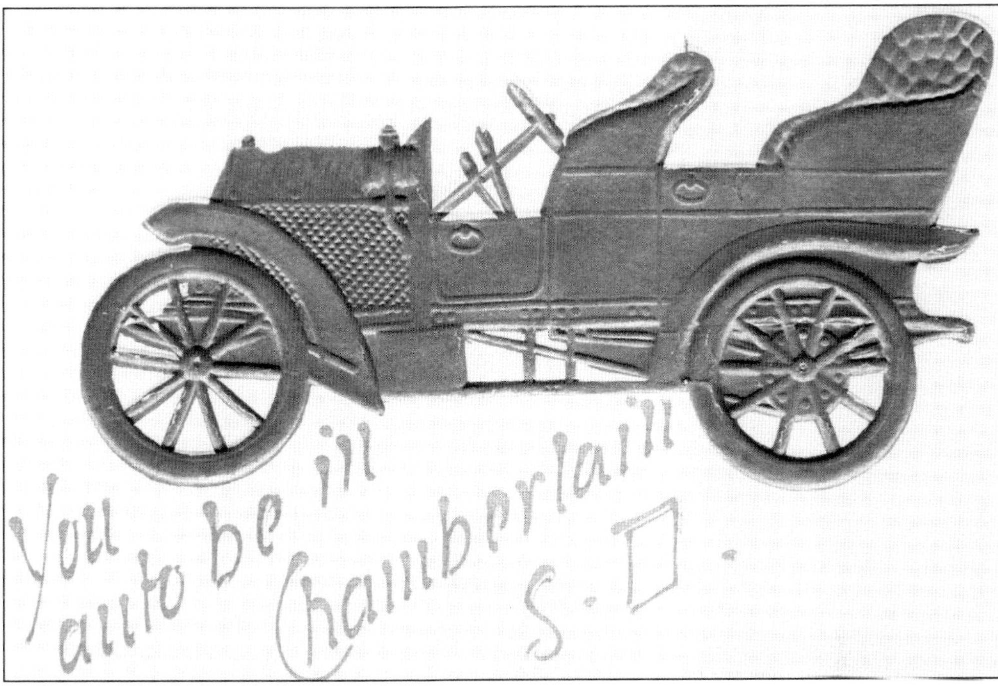

An embossed silhouette of an old-fashioned touring car is featured on this card. A fun play on words, "You auto be in Chamberlain, S.D.," is handwritten below the car. The card was mailed in 1909.

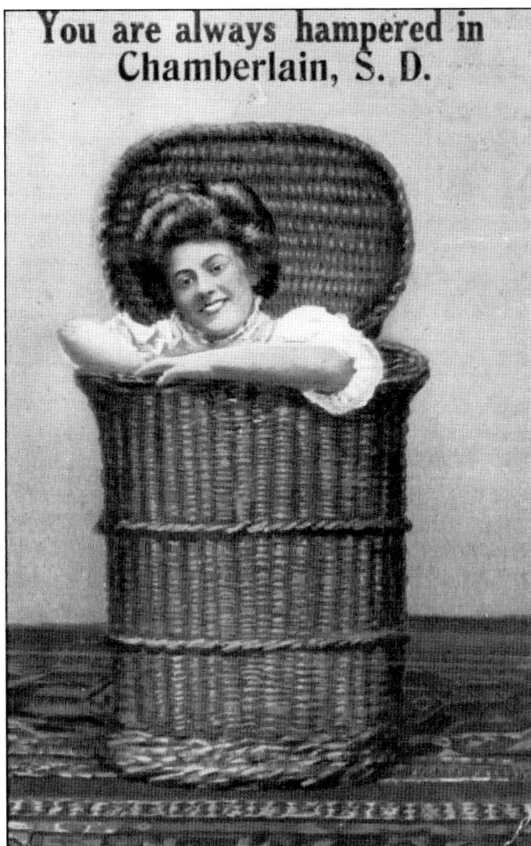

Back in the early 1900s, it must have been a good thing to be hampered somewhere. The lady in the large wicker basket looks happy. Nowadays, a person probably would not want to say that he or she was "hampered" in Chamberlain.

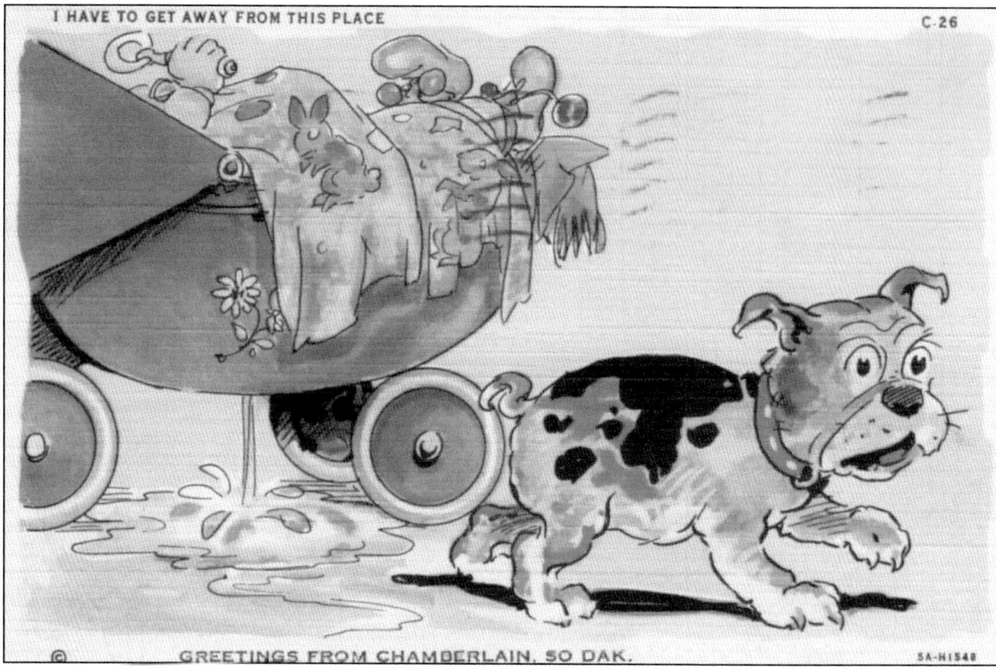

Sometimes, when on a vacation, a traveler just wants to send a humorous card. These are from two different comic series from the 1930s. The dog card was postmarked in 1937. These generic cards could be printed with any town name at the bottom. Places that catered to tourists, such as motels, gas stations, and attractions, might have a small spinning rack full of these cards near the cash register. It would be fun to see all the other cards in these series.

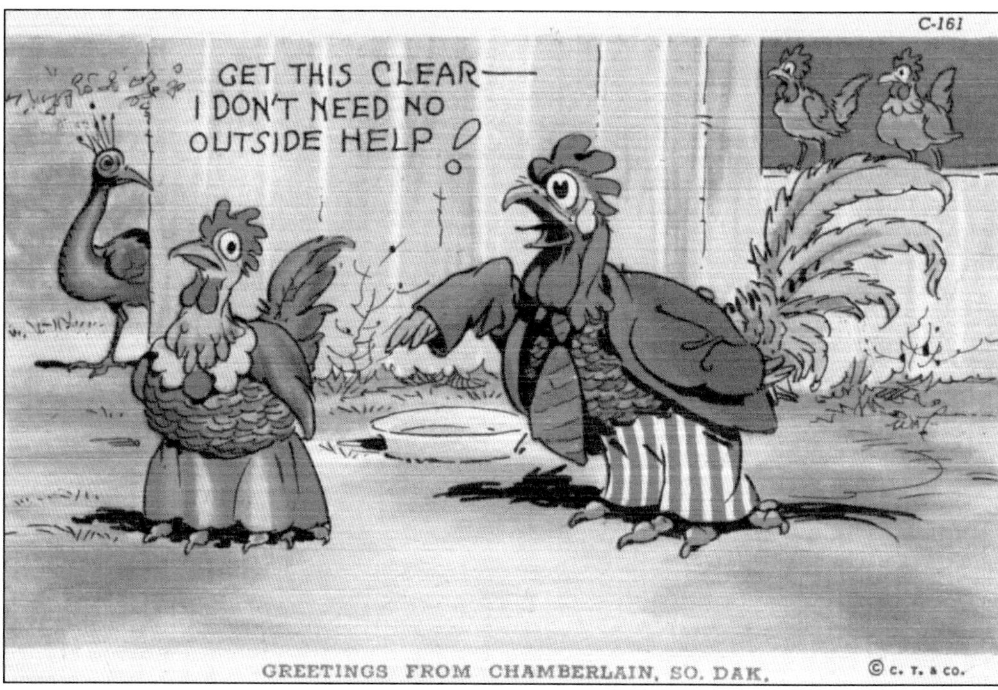

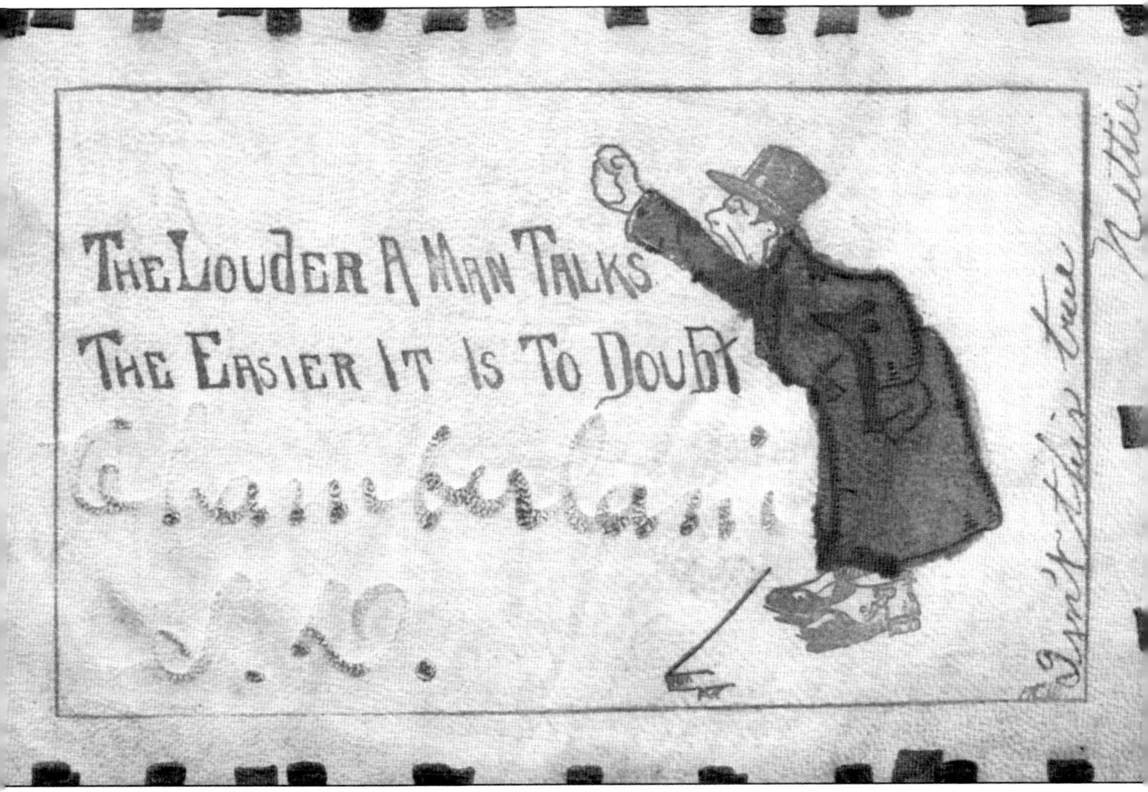

This postcard is probably one of the most unusual: it is made of leather. There were quite a few leather postcards made in the early 1900s. Most were printed with humorous sayings and the name of a town. Apparently, the sender of this card, Nettie, believed this sentiment to be true. Most leather cards did not have much, if any, room for a message on the back, and a good pen needed to be used because the backside was rough while the front side was smooth.

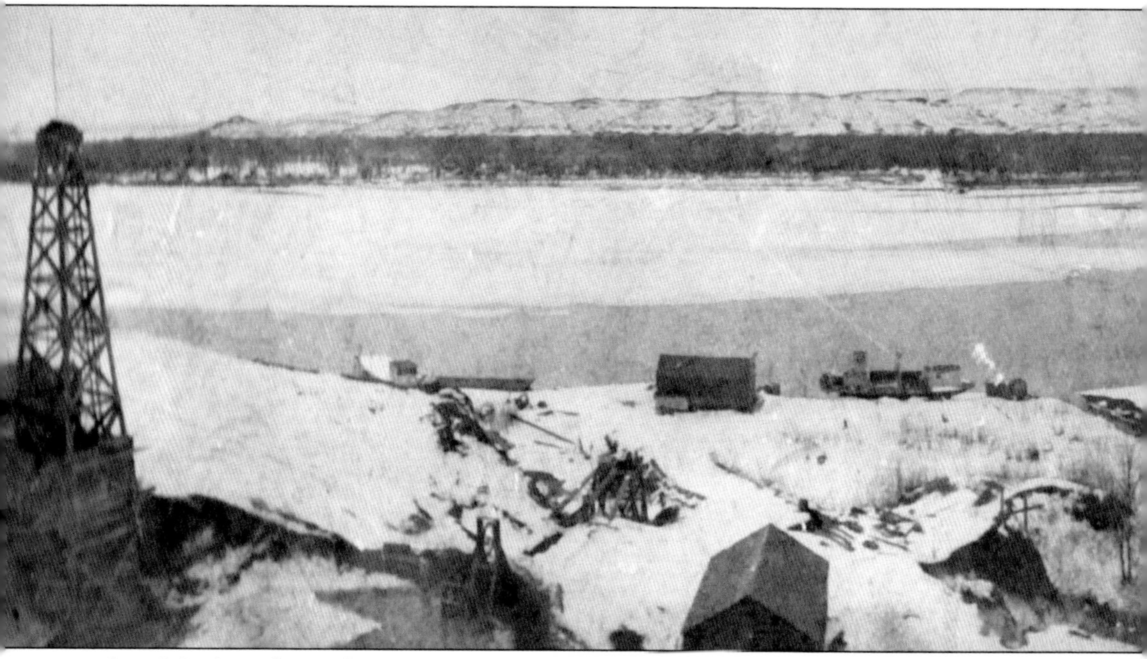

Saved for last, this early panoramic view of the Missouri River at Chamberlain is the rarest image in the Olson collection. The lighthouse at the far left made it safer for boats to navigate the oftentimes unpredictable river. It also made the dock and railroad bridge more visible. At least three lights can be seen at the top of the lighthouse. Paddle-wheel boats are docked at the

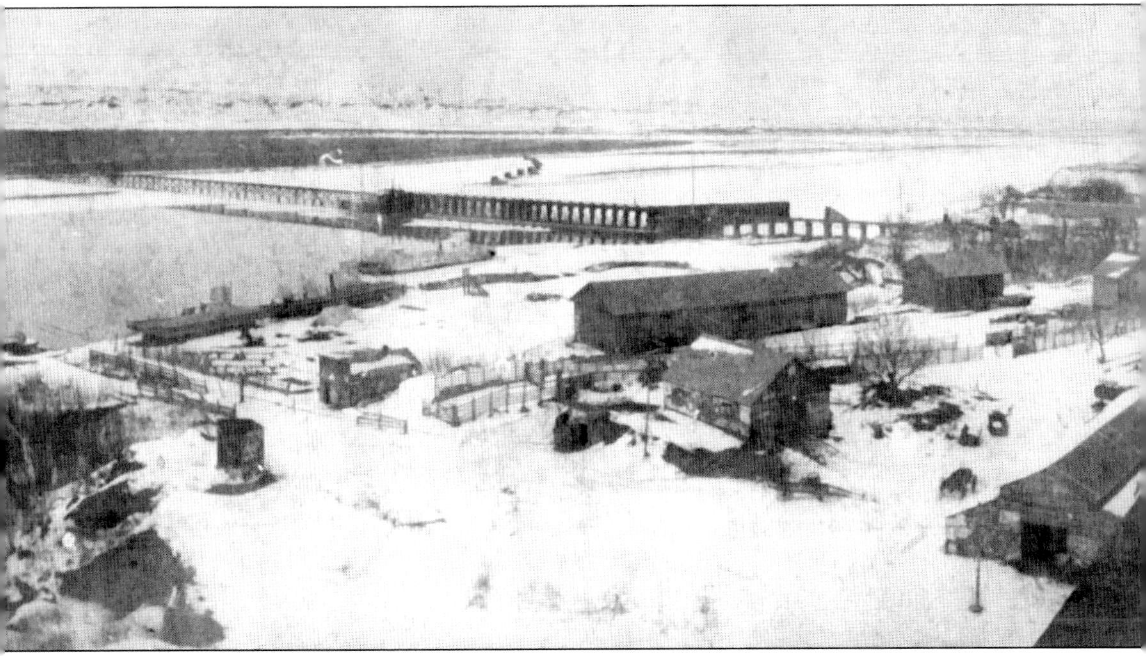

shoreline, and nearby livestock corrals stand waiting to hold animals before they are shipped by rail or water. The panoramic format here truly gives a sense of the wide-open river valley, with its rolling hills and a tree-covered American Island to the west.

Consistent with our mission to preserve history on a local level, this book was printed in South Carolina on American-made paper and manufactured entirely in the United States. Products carrying the accredited Forest Stewardship Council (FSC) label are printed on 100 percent FSC-certified paper.

MADE IN THE USA